I'M STILL STANDING

"Mel shares her moving and often heart-rending story with such raw courage that you can't help but root for her to find the true love and happiness she so deserves. Her story will inspire thousands of readers around the world and show them that it is possible to get through anything that life throws at you. She shows how one should never give up – and to keep your head high. Ultimately, you become a better person and the harsh lessons of life become gifts. This book will change many lives – and all the challenges Mel has faced, endured and ultimately conquered will have been so worthwhile."
Arvind Devalia, Success Coach, International Speaker, Blogger and best-selling author of 'Get the Life you Love'

'An inspiring story for anyone who's faced challenges in life, no matter how large or small."
Barbara Bentley, author of A Dance with the Devil: A True Story of Marriage to a Psychopath

"A famous Winston Churchill quote comes to mind when I think of Mel – "History will kind to me for I intend to write it...." Having worked with Mel a few times, I know she has the courage to write her own future history. She has been on a real roller coaster ride of life. One we will all be able to relate to and gain strength from.
A book to have by your bed for sure. I'm Still Standing....
the title says it all."
Billy Schwer - Former world boxing champion Founder and creator of Mental Boxing, author of Mental Boxing the 'Science of Success'

"Your story is truly amazing and inspirational, and if anyone out there needs a bit of inspiration and motivation, this is the book for you. I can so relate to what Mel has gone through in life, and I felt every word and emotion reading her story. It made me realise that we need to take life by the horns and live it and enjoy it."
Papa Spyk, author of 'A Naughty Thing Called Life'

"In Mel Carnegie's I'm Still Standing, the reader is presented with a woman's story of a life of achievement and success being systematically evaluated, devoured and dismantled by an encounter with her 'soulmate' in the guise of a classic psychopath. After the destruction of her sense of personal identity at the hands of her cunning, ruthless and manipulative ex-husband, Mel decided to fight back by unleashing the most meaningful revenge of all – to return back to the person she was meant to be. Inspiring and profoundly insightful."
Thomas Sheridan, author of 'Puzzling People: The Labyrinth Of The Psychopath'

"Mel's buoyant personality and humour shine through her writing, making this a compelling read. Her achievements are incredible and her story will, no doubt, inspire many women to become their own driving force and turn disaster and pain into success. Mel isn't just still standing, she is running, leaping and dancing from strength to strength!"
Gillian Jones, co-founder of Emotional Independence, co-managing director of Emerge UK and author of '50 Top Tips For Coaching: Coaching: A Complete Toolkit for Developing and Empowering People'

"There is something deeply satisfying about Mel's story and her telling of it. Happy as a child and happy now as a fully developed woman, she has endured more than her fair share of heartbreak and tragedy in all of the chapters of her life. Yet she lives with so much gusto that the sheer force of her spirit is contagious and addictive. So is her insistence on being fully connected and to go on living right through the amplitudes of pain and joy. What did she get in return for it? The best price I can think of – she found herself and she found happiness. Mel is a spirit well worth catching!"
Misha Votruba, film director 'I Am Fishead'

"Inspirational ... uplifting ... Mel Carnegie's "I'm Still Standing" is a testament to the human spirit. Her life was a series of traumatic upheavals, starting when she was a small child, yet she found a way to not only survive, but thrive. She tells her story with passion, with insight, and with the intention of conveying that if she could overcome all the tragedies and betrayals she faced, then anyone can overcome anything. If you think that your problems are too big, that you cannot go on, Mel's message is simple: Yes, you can, and you'll discover that you have more courage and grace than you ever knew."

Donna Andersen
Founder of Lovefraud.com and author of "Red Flags of Love Fraud – 10 signs you're dating a sociopath."

"Mel Carnegie's devastating and heartfelt story of discovery is not only courageous, it is insightful, invaluable and beautifully written. Read, find and stay on your own two feet!"

Eileen Munro, author of 'As I Lay Me Down to Sleep' and 'If I Should Die Before I Wake'

"This inspiring true story takes you through the highs and lows of this amazing brave woman. Mel has an open and easy written style that allows you to be there in the moment. This book is for those women wanting confidence and courage to get the life they want, whatever that might be."

Kirstin Furber, Senior Vice-President of Human Resources, BBC Worldwide

"Mel's story is one of survival against the odds. She has met more than her fair share of adversity but thrived through it all. Each time she was pushed under, she rose back up to the surface stronger and more aware. I am inspired by Mel's attitude, strength and determination. Her story will help any who read it - whatever challenges they face. We can all learn from her positivity and hard earned wisdom."

Mary Turner Thomson – best-selling author 'The Bigamist'

I'M STILL STANDING

Mel Carnegie

Matador
9 Priory Business Park,
Wistow Road, Kibworth Beauchamp,
Leicestershire. LE8 0RX
Tel: (+44) 116 279 2299
Fax: (+44) 116 279 2277
Email: books@troubador.co.uk
Web: www.troubador.co.uk/matador

ISBN: 9781780885551

www.melcarnegie.com

British Library Cataloguing in Publication Data.
A catalogue record for this book is available from the British Library.

Typeset by Troubador Publishing Ltd, Leicester, UK

Matador is an imprint of Troubador Publishing Ltd

For Dylan – my son, my reason, my inspiration.

Also to Abigail, my sister – thank you. We held ourselves together against the odds and made it through the storms.

Mum and Dad – thank you for giving me life and love, I hope I'm making you proud.

Tanya – thank you for teaching me the value of true friendship. Our bond continually inspires me to find more.

Contents

Preface   xv

1.	Of Birth And Death	1
2.	The Grim Reaper Strikes Again	7
3.	Being A Good Girl	19
4.	Moving Out And Moving On	31
5.	Unconditional Legal Aid And Desertion	42
6.	My Roaring Twenties	57
7.	I Am A Mother	71
8.	Meeting My Soulmate	88
9.	Of Love And Miracles	100
10.	Living The Dream And Waking To A Nightmare	107
11.	No Going Back	128
12.	Forgiveness And Paradise Found	139
13.	La Vie En Rose	155
14.	Pushed To The Limit	164
15.	Counselling, Confusion and Confessions	183
16.	Ultimate Torture – Ultimate Betrayal	200
17.	The Bitter End	214
18.	Life's Little Lettuces	223
19.	A Deal with Hannibal Lecter	229
20.	Sociopathy – A Whole New World	236

21.	Breaking The Silence	242
22.	Boy George, Handbags And Crutches	258
23.	Something Inside So Strong	271
24.	Life Is A Rollercoaster	283
25.	Bring Me My Soapbox	297
26.	Debt, Divorce And Discovery	302
27.	Happy Anniversary!	309
28.	I Know You're Out There	316
29.	The Mouse That Squeaked	324
30.	A Good Year	330

| Epilogue | 335 |
| A Final Message | 339 |

Author's Note

This book is a work of non-fiction based on the life, experiences and recollections of the author. In many cases, names of people, places, dates, sequences or the detail of events have been changed to protect the privacy of others. The author has stated to the publishers that, except in such respects not affecting the substantial accuracy of the work, the contents of this book are true.

Preface

I'm going to tell you a story. A true story. The story begins with a little girl who first saw her world collapse at the age of four. A little girl whose world continued to be rocked by seemingly insurmountable shocks – death, abandonment, abuse and ultimate betrayal. A girl who refused to let her spirit be broken no matter how many times she was hurt.

That girl grew up to become the woman I am today. Closer to 50 than 40, I have drawn on my experiences to give me a greater understanding of myself and of others. I am a mother, a sister, a friend and a professional businesswoman. I am also a survivor.

I know what it feels like to feel alone. I know what it feels like to be emotionally abused. I know what it's like to be abandoned by people I thought I could depend on. To be deliberately deceived by people I loved and whom I believed loved me back. To allow myself to be controlled and suffocated, on many occasions believing that 'they' were right all along . . . that I was worthless after all.

I know how all of those things feel because I've experienced them for myself. And I've come through every single challenge, each time stronger and even more determined to live my life to the full. The succession of emotional and psychological blows made me determined to find a better way. I could have shut off, laid down or simply bailed out; instead, I chose to fight. I fought to find meaning in my life and through doing so to teach myself how to survive and eventually how to thrive.

I am an ordinary woman who has faced a series of extraordinary circumstances to become the person I am today. Privacy laws dictate that I cannot divulge identifiable details about many of the people and situations that caused me so much pain. It's a law that exists to protect the innocent, even though many of the people I've come across have, in my opinion, been far from innocent in their actions. That law, paradoxically, has actually worked in my favour while writing this book because this is not about 'them'. In truth, it never has been; it's about me. This is *my* story.

1
Of Birth and Death

I was born in The Windmill, somewhere in Lincolnshire, on Friday, 18 December, 1964. My mother was told by the doctors to expect twin boys because of the movements they felt in her swelling tummy. She was also told that the birth wouldn't happen until the first or second week of January. They were wrong on both counts. I arrived a few weeks early – not twin boys, just me. Apparently waving with my right arm wrapped around my head and a big smile on my face.

The village we lived in was like something out of a picture postcard – light sandstone cottages, tree-lined lanes, a river running through, one pub, no shops and plenty of eccentric villagers. We were a happy family unit – Dad, Mum and I, and Daddy was the king of my world. I absolutely adored and worshipped him in the way, I suppose, that only a daughter can. To me he was my hero, my champion, my saviour, and I knew that however much love and adoration I gave him, he returned it ten-fold.

My real memories start from the age of about four, when my mum was heavily pregnant with my little sister. I guess she was more tired than usual, and so Daddy would often take me to work with him. 'The works', as he used to call it, was the family business that had been set up by my grandfather. It was a timber yard and steel foundry that specialised in making shoes for racehorses.

I loved going to work with my father, and I particularly loved it when we went inside the steelworks where the shoes were crafted. There was something about the heat of the furnaces, the glow of the coals, the smell of the molten metal and the sharp, clear swishing sound of metal against metal as the men heaved the long steel bars that were destined to adorn the feet of thoroughbred racehorses. That whole mix would send me in to another world – a world of dragons, kings, princesses and heroes.

I also adored the fact that the people who worked there would spoil me rotten – a bag of sweets here, a handful of glass marbles there . . . and if I was really lucky I got to ride in one of the company lorries. That, for me, was just the best feeling in the world! Climbing up over the enormous wheels, pulling myself in to the passenger seat, the heavy door shutting behind me, I would imagine that this chariot was taking us to the far-off lands I had dreamed up in the steelworks. Perched high above the other vehicles, I would pretend we were flying, my fantasies regularly fuelled by the tall tales of the drivers as we wound our way through the narrow country lanes.

During Mum's pregnancy, Dad had also taken it upon himself to be the 'clown' and 'entertainer', as Mum was understandably less energetic than usual. When I wasn't with him at work, he would frequently return home with special treats for me – small things, sometimes a paper airplane, other times bubble gum that he and I would sneak behind the sofa to eat, pretending to hide from Mum because she didn't approve of any kind of gum (all part of the game, of course!).

He'd regularly scoop me up above his head, laughing at my whooping excitement before placing me firmly on his shoulders. Mixed in with the play, I remember there were often more serious messages delivered in such a way that I understood completely. He had a knack of almost stopping time and holding people's attention, be it a crowded room or just me. There would be a silence and people would listen, and he'd use that same trick when we were playing. The giggling would suddenly stop, and I knew he was going to say something important. Instantly still, I'd hold on tightly and wait for the message.

'Pay attention, Boo [my nickname], and be sure to take in everything you can see around you,' he'd say, using one hand to hold tightly to my legs as I perched on his shoulders and he turned slowly around to facilitate a panoramic view. 'It's all out there waiting for you. The world is your oyster. Make sure you remember that!' A squeeze on the knee and minute or so of silence would follow before the games and laughter would continue once again.

He was a wise and gifted teacher, and with his help, I truly believed I could do anything. My daddy, after all, was the person who could create airplanes out of bits of wood and paper. Airplanes with real engines. Airplanes that would fly high above the trees. He was also the person who could create the most amazing oil paintings from his imagination. He had a friendly, easy smile that would start as a twinkle in his eye, before spreading right across his face and reaching out to warm anyone who was in his company. He was also the only person in the world who knew how to rub the back of my leg to cure my night cramps. I was so very proud of my daddy, and I absolutely adored him. I was convinced he could do anything, and I knew that with his guidance, I could learn to be the same.

The three of us were hugely excited about my sister's imminent arrival. We would sit for hours discussing names and what games we were going to share with her. We'd all cooed together over the new cot, and my dolls had even been allowed to try on a few of her tiny baby clothes. Yes, the beginning of 1969 was an exciting time, and it promised to deliver even more happiness with the pending birth of a new family member. But that promise proved to be grotesquely skewed.

One fateful evening, Monday, 3 March 1969, my daddy decided to return to his office to finish off some work. It was way after I'd gone up to bed, and I remember hearing the door shut behind him as he shouted out 'See you soon!' before the familiar roar of his car engine disappeared off down the lane. I snuggled deeper under my covers and settled down to a comfortable sleep. How could I have known that was the very last time I'd ever really know that feeling?

He died that evening, alone in his office. A mixture of the prescription drugs he was taking to shake off a cold, together with the glass of wine he'd had at home with Mum had apparently left him slightly drowsy. Since there was no illness or sickness in his body, after much debate – and to the abject horror of my family – the final coroner report gave the verdict as suicide. It was only years later it came to light that the new heater in his office, unbeknown to anyone, was leaking lethal carbon monoxide fumes in to the air. The following morning my Daddy's lifeless body was discovered slumped across his desk, pen still in hand. Very cold, very still, and very dead.

I wasn't told about his death until ten days later, after my sister was born. I can only now begin to imagine the torment my poor mother must have endured through this time. She was just 32 years old, facing life as a widow and about to give birth. All I remember was that I was to go and stay with my best friend in the village 'until after the baby arrives'. And I really don't remember much else until the day I came back home.

Trotting upstairs to mum's bedroom, I was at last introduced to my beautiful new little sister. I remember thinking I had never seen anything so small and perfect, as I marvelled at her tiny fingernails and her soft little mouth. She made funny noises and squirmed as I held her. I felt such a proud big sister. Her name was Abigail.

My nan, Mum's mum, had come to stay with us. We were all sitting on Mum's big yellow-quilted bed, three generations together, me with my chest puffed out because I'd been trusted to hold the newest arrival. I didn't notice anything unusual about the situation. I was just filled with excitement and love for my new sister. After a short while, Nan gently lifted Abigail from my arms and moved with her towards the door as Mum edged slowly towards me. She brought me close to her so we were lying together on the bed. Nan closed the door quietly behind her and Mum put her arm around me, tightening the cuddle and breathing deeply.

I remember it was a sunny day. The bedroom was filled with light. Dancing along the walls and across the bed were spindly shadows from the trees that were blowing softly in the wind. I remember the colour of the bedspread shone particularly bright that day – golden yellow with a patchwork of fluffy squares. Very modern for those days.

I remember Mum becoming very still, and I remember feeling her staring at me. I remember feeling confused and turning my face to meet her gaze. I remember her kind smile and the look of sadness and pain in her eyes. A look that immediately told me that something was very wrong. I don't remember exactly what she said, but I do remember the deafening silence immediately afterwards as in one fell swoop my whole world shattered and everything I had known shattered into tiny pieces around me.

I was four and a quarter, and from that moment on I knew that life would never be the same. My daddy had vanished. His funeral had already been and gone. I had a new sister to look after (that was how I saw my role at that point, because Daddy was no longer there to fulfil it) and I knew I had to learn to be strong for all of us.

Life became a haze of disorder and bewilderment – a monstrous mix of joy for our new baby and indescribable grief for our loss. Everything had changed, and there was nothing I could do about it.

Within a very short time I started to notice that the grown-ups had all changed as well. I became aware that everyone started to act strangely around me. The easy smiles and chit-chat were gone. Instead, heads would tilt, eyes would fill with tears and people would insist on forcing bags of sweets into my hands and giving me a squeeze or a pat on the shoulder. They didn't say anything to me, but I became used to the whispers that seemed to increase whenever I entered the room. I began to feel that I was somehow different – that there was something wrong with me. I also began to shut down.

Soon after Abigail's birth, we went down to the south coast for a few months to stay with Mum's parents. She clearly needed support – not only with her new baby but also in coming to terms with what had happened. I cannot begin to imagine the torture she must have gone through during those immediate few weeks and months. How she managed to keep going is beyond me. But keep going is exactly what she did, and the three of us became a tight family unit. Three girls with no husband/father – together we would be OK. We had to be. There was no other choice.

While we were all still staying with my grandparents, I remember developing scarletina, eczema, and all manner of other minor ailments for which I was given gallons of potions and mixtures. I remember playing in the park with my nan, I remember long walks along the seafront, I remember sitting on a huge model elephant on the pier . . . but I do not remember crying.

2

The Grim Reaper Strikes Again

We stayed in Lincolnshire until Abigail was five and I was nine. By that time, Mum had decided that she wanted to be nearer to her parents and so we all moved down to Eastbourne. ?

Town-life was a total change for us all. You see, everyone had known one another in our tiny Lincolnshire community. Growing up there was not dissimilar to many of the Famous Five stories I used to love so much. There was a whole gang of us – girls and boys Norfolk ranging from age three to ten – and we (usually) got on like a house on fire. Because everyone knew one another, we would roam freely around the village, popping into one another's houses, racing our bikes, making camps and inventing and indulging in the most fantastical adventures. They were good times and to this day some of my fondest memories are those attached to my early years in that village.

So when we moved to Eastbourne, things couldn't have been more different. It is a big town, and the plan was for us to live with Mum's parents. My grandfather (Gand) ran his own very successful company, and as a result they lived in a huge four-storey house that my mum referred to as 'a Victorian monstrosity'. Gand's office was in the basement, they lived on the ground floor, and we were to live

7

on the first floor. The second floor, known as 'the top flat' remained empty for visitors and storage.

There was a huge sweeping staircase that ran from top to bottom of the building, and there were no dividing doors to separate the floors. Everything was open, and very early on it became clear that there were a whole new set of rules we would have to follow to keep the peace. Abby and I were not allowed to play too loudly. If we wanted to go into the garden, we would have to go through Nan's living room to get there – unless we went out of the huge front door and around the side, which would then mean we'd have to ring on the bell to get back inside.

I quickly began to feel trapped. Used to wide open spaces and the freedom to roam, I soon became uncomfortable with all these new restrictions that were placed on us. Habits and rituals that had started off as quaint idiosyncrasies – niggles at the worst – gradually began to develop into something more oppressive and sinister. At least that was how I felt.

It also became clear that our space was not actually our space. Nan would regularly walk up the stairs and straight into our 'flat' to find Mum or help herself to a saucepan, a book, some music – anything she wanted to borrow. She'd also tell us to turn the television down or interrupt our skipping game to enquire whether we'd finished our homework. Mum used to say that it was Nan's way of keeping control, and I knew that she resented the interference as much as I did. Nan would also take it upon herself to criticise the way Mum was bringing us up. I would regularly witness the heated discussions – usually behind a closed door and always in whispers – that would finish with Nan scurrying downstairs tight-lipped and muttering to herself. There were many times when you could cut the atmosphere with a knife after such exchanges. It was uncomfortable to say the least!

On Sundays, we would be expected to have our lunch downstairs with Nan and Gand. It was always a long drawn-out affair, with far too much food and far too much emphasis placed on being correct (one of Gand's favourite and oft-repeated expressions was 'little girls should be seen and not heard'). I felt stifled and begrudged sharing my time with people who seemed to notice only the negatives. The whole situation clearly got to Mum as well. She was one of those people who kept a smile on her face regardless of the situation, but there were times when it was too much even for her. I remember one such occasion when she actually raised her voice in frustration. 'I'm a grown woman, for goodness' sake. All I want is my own front door and a bit of privacy!' she'd cried, before shooing Nan back downstairs.

I hated seeing Mum so upset. She was a beautiful, confident woman who'd grown strong and independent since the untimely death of her husband. I was hugely proud of her and loved her dearly, and it tore at my heart to see her pink-faced and flustered, blinking back her tears of frustration, clearly feeling powerless and confused by Nan's increasingly suffocating interference.

I remember one particular occasion where Nan had misunderstood something I had said and, rather than ask me about it, decided instead to purse her lips, get up from her seat and walk out of the room. She refused to speak to me after that point. I was both confused and hurt by Nan's dismissive behaviour, particularly since I'd actually been in the process of telling her how much I loved her! It took Mum over a week to convince Nan that she had misheard me – the exhaustion showing on Mum's face as she consistently reassured me that I'd done nothing wrong while spending many fruitless evenings reasoning with her own mother. In the end, Nan decided to believe Mum and begrudgingly agreed to speak to me once again, but after that I never quite felt relaxed in her company.

As time passed, 'I want my own front door' became a mantra – not just for Mum but for both of us girls as well. We'd all learned to tread carefully, and it was an oppressive existence. We now knew what happened if we stepped out of line, and Nan's cloying insistence that we all did things together eventually started to suffocate us. Despite the circumstances, Mum's approach had always been to look on the bright side, to find a positive no matter how exasperating the situation, so the three of us each learned to deal with the challenges in our own way. Mum would usually brush Nan's negative comments aside and give us both a hug. I would tend to be the one who took things to heart, venting my frustrations with the help of a tennis racquet and unripened fruit from the very large cooking apple tree that stood at the end of the garden. Abigail, on the other hand, developed her own unique way of dealing with things. She'd carry on as if nothing was happening and would then do or say something that would completely take us by surprise. She once had us all in fits of conspiratorial giggles by suggesting to some visitors, 'Let's all play snap and give Nan a headache!'

On the whole, Abby and I got on well together. We shared a huge bedroom and, sure, there would be the odd fallout (and an occasional 'end-of-the-world' sort of an argument), but most of my memories are of the daft games we used to play together. One such game was called 'Top-Flat Warfare'. We'd learned how to make water-bombs from single squares of paper, and would take ourselves up to the top of the house and out on to the flat roof. From there we had a bird's-eye view of our garden as well as those of the neighbouring properties. Pretending the gardens were a Battleship grid, we'd take turns to pick a target and throw our bombs. Of course we'd collapse in fits of giggles whenever we 'accidentally' blasted Nan in the process. 'Oops, sorry!' we'd shout from our perch, while at the same time planning our next assault and gauging the risk potential for another casualty.

Five years after we'd first arrived in Eastbourne, we finally moved to our own house. A move we'd anticipated with excitement and joy, all three of us thrilled to have our own space again! Built from typical Sussex flint stone, Manor Cottage was situated in a small country village, ten miles away from our grandparents' home. Over 500 years old, it was a Grade 2 listed building – quirky, interesting, full of character, beautiful and, most importantly, it was ours. It was the end of 1979, I was 14 years old and, to top it all, for the first time since Abigail had been born I had my very own bedroom!

Moving to Manor Cottage was the start of a whole new era for all of us. From a young age, Abigail had been a gifted musician. Annoyingly, it seemed that she could get a tune out of any instrument she picked up. At Manor Cottage she was able to practise her beloved piano as often and as loudly as she liked and was soon playing the most astonishing solos in school and public recitals. I was very proud of my little sister.

I, on the other hand, was just entering puberty and was also excruciatingly shy. My fair skin and freckles meant I would blush at the slightest provocation, which made me even more self-conscious. So when a weird set of coincidences led me to reconnect with a boy called John, who was an old friend I'd known years earlier at primary school in Lincolnshire, I was absolutely over the moon. Abby and I attended an all-girls school, and I had absolutely no understanding of boys. So when John's arrival on the scene also meant the appearance of a gang of male friends, I was even more delighted! All of a sudden I had the perfect opportunity to learn how to communicate with the opposite sex, which, as I'm sure you can imagine, opened up a whole new, exciting and innocent world of fun, flirting and frivolous entertainment.

Mum was also much happier in our new home. Her smile was now a natural, relaxed and permanent feature. She would sing around the house. She would cook the most delicious meals. She took pride in planting out the garden. She encouraged us to decorate our rooms in our own style, and at least once a week she would have her friends round for evenings of bridge or other such card games.

Her happiness and appreciation of the absurd was contagious, and the three of us would often be in fits of giggles laughing at some ridiculous programme or sharing tales from school. She could always find the funny side of things and refused to let anything become a problem.

I have a lasting memory of one particularly stormy night when so much rain had fallen that the river had burst its banks and flooded our house. Met by a stream of water running through from one end of the house to the other, Mum must have made a quick assessment of the situation, realising that we were in no immediate danger and there was nothing we could do until the rain stopped and the water subsided. Seeing our worried expressions, she gave a cheeky grin, winked and invited us to 'Come along and let's get our wellies on! Let's find some newspapers and make boats – we can have races through the house. Well, we'd best make the best of the opportunity while we can, eh, girls? It's not going to happen again!'

Yes, the three of us were flourishing, as individuals and in our relationship with one another. We were happy, and life really was as close to perfect as I believed it could be.

Then, towards the end of 1980 and not long before my 16th birthday, I developed a nasty bout of pneumonia. The weeks I spent recuperating at home meant that I missed out on a considerable chunk of schooling for my all-important O level exams the following summer. I remember still feeling pretty weak and sickly over Christmas, but by the beginning of the New Year I had recovered sufficiently to return to school. My form teacher recommended that it might be prudent to obtain a doctor's certificate to confirm that I had missed a significant portion of the previous term through illness, her explanation being that my school could submit the certificate to the examining board together with my papers. She reasoned that although my grades were always above average, with my English O level just a week or so away it would be foolish to ignore the chance to explain my situation should my marks suddenly come back lower than expected. It seemed like a good idea, and so we all trotted along to our family doctor to ask for his cooperation.

Monday, 12 January 1981 was a typically dark and foggy winter evening. All three of us were in the surgery together as Dr Jones wrote out, stamped and signed my certificate. We were just about to leave when Mum asked him if he wouldn't mind just taking a look at something for her. 'I'm sure it's nothing serious!' she added, motioning towards her chest and turning on her usual mega-watt smile. Dr Jones smiled back (it was impossible not to, such was the strength of Mum's beaming grin) and motioned for her to lie on the couch while Abigail and I settled back into the blue plastic chairs by his desk. 'Well now, Mrs Carnegie, it's always better to be safe than sorry!' he said, still smiling. 'Now then, let's have a look, shall we?'

The smile vanished from his face the very moment he touched my mother. I noticed a frown and a small shake of the head, and I sensed the sudden silent heaviness in the room. It was a vaguely familiar feeling, but at that time I didn't know what it meant. I just knew it wasn't good.

The doctor took his hands off Mum for a moment and seemed to be tussling with his thoughts. Taking a deep breath and pulling himself upright, he turned to Abby and me and asked us to go outside to the waiting room. The smile was still on his face, but it had changed. I could tell he was struggling to maintain his composure, although he did his best to appear normal.

I had learned from an early age how to spot when grown-ups were trying to cover things up. After Daddy died, they'd think they could protect me – or themselves – if they ignored the truth or changed the subject. I'd become skilled at knowing when something was wrong. It was an automatic response. Up went my instinctive radar the very moment I sensed the change in atmosphere, making me more receptive to the unspoken messages that were racing around the room. Mum's smile had lost its radiance, and she was just staring blankly at the ceiling. She seemed tired and beaten, her willpower gone. There was also something in the way the doctor had spoken (lower voice, overtly kindly) and something in the way he looked at us (was it pity?) that made me fix him with a questioning stare. This whole episode, from the time the doctor touched Mum to the moment when Abigail and I stood up to go to the waiting room, can only have taken a couple of minutes. But to me it had all happened in slow motion. And that final unspoken locking of eyes – mine and Dr Jones' – had been enough to turn my blood to ice. Because this time I knew what it meant.

Emotions, thoughts and sensations all exploded at once and started coursing around my body at a rate of knots, crashing into one another and making it difficult for me to move. My legs were heavy and prickly and my knees shaking like jelly as Abigail and I got up and made our way out of the consulting room. There was a fish tank by the reception, so I tuned in to the sound of the filtration pump and moved forward on autopilot. Everything else was a blur, but the rhythmic bubbling from that tank, together with the faded light and the movement of the fish inside, acted as a lighthouse to me, guiding me through the fog to the relative safety of the row of blue plastic chairs reserved for patients and their families. It was at least a place where I could rest my jelly-legs and take stock of my increasingly swarming thoughts.

I knew the truth. I don't know how or why I knew, but I just did. I remember sitting there, doing my best to match my jagged breathing to the rhythmic bubbling of the fish tank, willing my mind to slow down and give me a chance to gather myself. I looked at Abigail sitting next to me. She was swinging her legs and twiddling with her hair as usual, clearly totally oblivious to what I had witnessed, and my heart broke in two. I knew that I couldn't keep the words inside me, and I knew I had to warn her of what was about to happen. I was, after all, the big sister, and I wanted her to know that although something bad was happening, we would be all right. So I turned to her and, as gently as I could, I told her what I knew to be true.

'Mummy's got cancer you know.'

That was all I said. Abigail's hair twiddling stopped along with her leg swinging, and she faced me with a look of confusion. A frown appeared as she cocked her head to one side. So I added another few words.

'It's OK, though. We're going to be all right. We'll be OK.'

She seemed to accept that, because her hair and leg actions resumed immediately, although I noticed they were slightly less enthusiastic. She didn't ask for details.

We waited in silence after that until we heard the door to the doctor's surgery opening. Mum looked a little pink in the face, but the Hollywood smile and cheery voice were turned back up to their full setting as she thanked Dr Jones and strode across to us, shoulders back, head high, giving a jolly 'Right, are we ready, girls?' before bounding out towards the car park. But it was no good. I wasn't going to be fooled. Because I knew.

In the car, I waited silently for Mum to explain what had happened. The minutes seemed like hours as I willed her to tell us something about what had gone on in the doctor's surgery. But nothing was forthcoming. Just the forced smile and a carefree 'What do you fancy for supper tonight, girls?' That question was never answered. Because instead I took it as my opportunity to say something.

I was in the passenger seat right next to Mum, so I turned to her and asked gently, 'Are you going to tell us then?'

She faced my questioning stare, her smile not quite as convincing as it had been a few seconds earlier. 'Tell you what, darling?' she replied, the mask cracking just a tiny bit further.

So I had to say it. I had to know for sure. 'You've got cancer, haven't you?'

And with those five small words the truth was out. Tears suddenly filled Mum's eyes. She bit her lip, blinked and gave the tiniest of nods. And I knew that life, once again, would never be the same.

The three of us spent that evening at our dining room table, talking, crying, hugging and trying to understand what it all meant. It turned out that she had found a lump in her breast a few months earlier but had ignored it, pushing her concerns to the back of her mind and allowing the cancer cells to silently multiply in her body.

By the time she had finally asked the doctor for his advice, he told her it had spread so far that she'd need to see a specialist as soon as possible. The appointment was already booked for the following week – the same day as my English O level exam.

I asked how the doctor had known so quickly, and Mum gently took my hand and guided it to her right breast. I pulled back in horror almost immediately because it felt cold, grey and absolutely rock solid. Touching it again. I became more and more incredulous. Did it hurt? How long had it been like this? How she could have carried on this way? Why hadn't she done anything about it?

She had no answers, just tears and cuddles. 'I don't know, my darling girls. I don't know. I suppose I just couldn't.'

I can only begin to imagine how she must have been feeling at that time. The fear must have been overwhelming. I'm quite sure she didn't know where to turn. Her own mother was of little support and the only person she felt she could turn to that evening was her old friend from Lincolnshire. Maisy was one of those positive people who always seemed to find a helpful answer for everything. She had been exceptionally supportive to Mum after the death of my dad and had introduced Mum to the idea that she could help herself feel better by changing the thoughts in her head. Maisy was, I suppose, one of the pioneers of our modern-day self-help gurus. Focused, positive and absolutely certain about our own power to heal, Maisy was the only person Mum chose to call that night, and Maisy was the person who turned up the very next day.

Mum asked us to keep the news of her illness between us for the moment. During her friend's visit, she became insistent that nobody should know the truth. She reasoned that the less people knew, the less they would drain her energy by asking her all sorts of questions. I had absolutely no hesitation in agreeing to her wishes. It made perfect sense to me, and, in any case, I wanted to support Mum in every way I could.

On the day of my exam, I remember calling her at lunchtime from the school payphone (no such thing as mobiles in those days!)

16

and she told me that she had to have an operation. She said that if she agreed to the operation and if they could halt the cancer, then she'd have the chance to live for another few years. Without the operation she would be dead within three to six months. Mum and I had always had a frank and honest relationship, since the evening of 12 January it had become even more so.

It was hard news to take on board, but at least I knew the truth. I completed the second part of my exam that afternoon and the three of us spent the evening together talking around the dining room table once again. This time we discussed the prospects of what might happen if the worst came to the worst. Again, tough conversations to have, but it meant that we had the best grasp of the facts.

Mum went into hospital just over a week later, cheerily telling people she was going in for a hysterectomy. Nan came to stay and look after us, fully believing our concocted story. The conspiracy somehow gave us a bond that kept us close and Nan distant. During the first few days, I only told one person, my best friend John, what was really happening and felt wracked with guilt in the process. I believed I had let Mum down because she had bought into the idea that the less people knew about her illness, the more she could maintain her energy to fight it herself. But I just couldn't keep it all to myself – it was too much to bear.

With hindsight, of course, I realise that keeping silent was just about the worst thing that any of us could have done, but those were very early days in the field of therapy or positive thinking. The result was to put further pressure on all of us as we kept up the pretence that everything was OK, while struggling to cope with our emotional turmoil. And, as the three of us were no longer all under the same roof, it was even more difficult dealing with the growing fear of what was happening. But Abby and I stayed loyal to Mum's wishes. We didn't crumble and we stayed strong together.

As it turned out, the truth came out just a few days later. Mum's cancer had spread too far to be ignored.

The illness didn't last very long. Abby and I visited her no more than four times while she was in hospital. By Wednesday, 4 February, we were told she was too ill for us to see her. She died at 21.50 on Friday, 6 February, less than one month after we had first discovered she was ill.

3
Being A Good Girl

Neither Abigail nor I went to Mum's funeral. During our last few emotionally charged evenings around the dining room table, Mum had been adamant that she didn't want any kind of memorial service.

'Too much fuss and too much sadness,' she'd said, 'and such a waste of flowers. I hate to see cut flowers, they should be left to grow as nature intended!'

Mum had hated bouquets and bunches of flowers ever since Dad had died. Each year my paternal grandmother would send Mum a huge bouquet of flowers on the anniversary of my dad's death. And each year Mum would burst into tears and throw the bouquet in the bin.

'Why must she do this every year?' she'd sob through gritted teeth. 'She knows it upsets me – and it's such a waste! Why would I want to see beautiful flowers fade away and die in front of my eyes? That's not how I want to remember your father!'

And I'm assuming now that her hatred of funerals was linked to her own experience when she had to bury her husband just a few days before my little sister was born. I cannot begin to imagine the heart-wrenching pain and abject terror she must have faced at that time. She was just 32 years old, with one small daughter and a baby on the way. Her life had changed beyond recognition – all her hopes and dreams had come crashing down around her ears. But she'd had to stay strong for the sake of her children, and all in all I think she did an outstanding job.

Yes, we had the occasional rows – sometimes the odd furious battle – but we absolutely knew that we were loved and adored, and the lessons she taught us as we were growing up are lessons that have continued to guide me throughout my adult life. I was lucky with both my parents. In the few short years I had with them, I learned what it meant to feel safe and secure, and also to be given the freedom to find myself. They gave me the encouragement to push myself; to believe that the world was my oyster.

I remember the beginning of the new term in my new school. I was a shy child, and both Abby and I were scared about going in to a class full of people we'd never met before. 'It's OK, girls,' chirped Mum as we all drove up to the school gates. 'Remember that they are all exactly the same as you, every single one of them. No better, no worse – exactly the same, with the same hopes and fears. And if you still feel scared, well, then all you have to do is to imagine them naked and sitting on the toilet. That's what I do whenever I'm afraid. Give it a go, you'll be surprised!' Her cheeky smile and crafty wink had Abby and I giggling in no time, ready and able to face the day ahead with confidence.

So when she'd been so certain in asserting that she didn't want a funeral, I felt guilty that the family had gone ahead and organised one against her wishes. Of course, I now realise that this was the best and only sensible option available, but at the time, and from the viewpoint of a shy, hormonal teenage girl who had just been orphaned and wanted to set the right example to her little sister, I decided that I would follow Mum's wishes. So instead of going to my own mother's funeral, I went to school. I remember sitting there in lessons – present in body but nothing more – and wondering how the service was going. How many people were there? What was being said? What must Mum have been thinking if she was able to see what was going on?

Arguably, my actions were misguided, and looking back I can see that it was utter madness – first for me to request I go to school as normal, and second that I was allowed to do so – but I honestly thought I was doing the best thing and that Mum would have been proud of me for respecting her wishes and staying strong. Abigail didn't attend the funeral either. She spent the morning at our new home, our guardian's house, in the company of the family au-pair.

I was given no choice about coming along to the gathering after the funeral – thank goodness. It was the one and only chance I had to integrate with people. For the first time the craziness became reality. I could at last grasp the fact that my mother had died. No matter how brave I was, or how much of a stiff upper lip I kept, life would never be the same again.

There were, of course, questions as to why neither Abigail nor I were at the service.

'Mum wouldn't have wanted us to be there. She said she hated funerals and only wanted people to be happy. She said she wanted things to carry on as normal, so I went to school,' I retorted, to the obvious bewilderment of friends and relatives who couldn't understand my candid response and calm demeanour. My swan-like acting skills were developing with every new day – serene on the surface but paddling like fury underneath to keep myself in check.

After the funeral we were taken to stay with our new guardians, my mum's childhood friend Edward (Eddie) and his wife Gillian (Gilly) and their little boy, Jack. I had learned that fortune could turn on a sixpence and I knew not to take anything for granted.

My instinct told me that I would have to prove myself to my new guardians. I also knew that it was up to me to safeguard our home for my little sister. I was the older sister; there is a huge age and maturity gap between being 16 and 11, so I reasoned that I had a better understanding of the situation. I knew it would be up to me to learn how to fit in, help out and stay happy – and in doing so maintain a home for both of us. We had to be 'good girls' so that

21

they'd want to keep us. In short, I had to learn how to become invisible.

The first few days were surreal. Excruciatingly uncomfortable, Abby and I both felt like fish out of water. We painted on smiles and made polite chit-chat as we all did our best to get used to one another. Everyone's home and family has a culture of it's own. Whilst we had known of Eddie and Gilly for many years, we soon discovered that it was one thing to know them through parties and general gatherings, and a totally different thing to actually live with them. On a daily basis (sometimes minute-by-minute) my brain was processing new information about how the household worked and how we could fit in.

We went to school as normal, though there was really nothing 'normal' about it at all. I'd experienced the whispers and sideways looks from people after Dad died, so I thought I'd be prepared. But this time it was different. This time I was hardly a child and this time there were two of us. Mum had been well known and well liked at school – by parents, teachers and the pupils she taught in her weekly typing classes – so it felt as if we were the focus of everyone's attention. The whispers came from every angle. As did the questions.

'How is your sister coping?' was a regular one, from friends as well as teachers. I guess, in retrospect, it was an approach that allowed people to bring up a horribly difficult situation with me, without being too direct or indiscreet. But at the time it seemed to me that I was expected to be a grown-up and to look after my little sister. So whenever I was asked that question, I would pull myself up, take a deep breath and answer clearly and concisely – under the assumption that I was being judged for my capability to stay strong for my sister. I'm quite sure that the measured responses gave people the impression that I was in control. And because people thought I was coping, they continued to ask about my sister. The more they asked about my sister, the more self-control I developed as a result. It was a vicious cycle where I continued to play up to their expectations and buried my own feelings in the process – the ramifications of which I couldn't possibly comprehend at the time.

Everywhere I went I felt eyes boring in to me – there was no escape. Conversations would suddenly stop mid-flow as I approached, and less than subtle nudges would take over. The whispers would start as soon as I moved past.

'There she is – that's the one who's Mum died' 'That's the orphan!' 'She's got to look out for her sister as well now' 'Poor girl – what chance does she stand now?'

I felt like a leper. I could understand that people might find it difficult to talk to me – my loss and my sadness highlighted the frailty of human life, and I'm sure most people had no idea what to say. But inside I was screaming to be heard. I desperately wanted be treated as 'normal' again. I wanted the label 'orphan' to be taken away so that I could slip back into the safety of anonymity within the school. But of course that could never happen, because everything was different now and there was nothing I could do to remedy it.

I quickly learned to interpret, even anticipate, the approach people were likely to take with me. I perfected a strong walk, a determined chin up, shoulders back, and a constant smile in defence to any questions. I had become an unwilling 'celebrity', but not for anything that I had done. And I hated it. It was unbelievably uncomfortable knowing that everyone was talking about me. I had become public property, while on the inside I was feeling more desperately scared and isolated than I could ever remember. My life at that time was a daily torture that I choose to keep silent.

And there was no respite 'at home'. The drama continued with smiles for stage make-up and banter for scripted lines, but this was no ordinary auditorium and we were no ordinary actors. Here the stakes were much higher. We had to fit in.

Abigail and I quickly slipped into the role of the pantomime horse – working together to bring laughter to situations and providing entertainment for the family. It was our natural defence mechanism. We'd look at each other across the dinner table, make a silly face, or say a phrase that would stir private memories of life as it used to be, and we'd both burst into hysterical laughter. Laughter that just for a few moments would wrap itself around us in a warm bear hug. These were fleeting memories that reached inside our hearts and joined us together, allowing us to connect and give each other the silent reassurance, *It's OK, I understand – I feel it too.* Eddie and Gilly were understandably thrown by this behaviour, but for us it became a defiant act of united fortitude. The absurdity and inappropriateness of our howling laughter provided a mismatched backdrop to a surreal world that had become our new reality. It was in those moments that we were alive. Those moments that gave colour and emotion to a grey, mechanical setting that could easily have come from a science-fiction or horror film. Years later I saw the remake of *The Stepford Wives* starring Nicole Kidman. It reminded me of those times.

Abigail and I were desperate, but we couldn't scream and there was nowhere to turn. The pain was excruciating. The loss was unbearable. The changes that were thrown upon us were both terrifying and confusing. The routines were different. The house rules were alien. Nothing around us held any sense of familiarity, apart from our old piano, which we had brought with us and which had become our strongest ally. Abby and I would spend hours on it – perfecting duets when we were together, playing for ourselves when we were apart. The rest of our furniture and ornaments were all packed away. We were allowed to keep two of our cats; I don't know what happened to the others. But everything else around us was stuff that belonged to Eddie and Gilly. We were even given new dressing gowns almost as soon as we had arrived. I'm sure the gesture was intended to be a kind one, but the words that accompanied it made me feel that our old life, our mum, and all the things we loved so dearly were simply not good enough. As if losing everything was not enough, it seemed our memories were also to be wiped away as well. These were messages that were to be hammered home as the weeks and months progressed.

'Here you are, girls,' Gilly had beamed at the time. 'I thought you'd like these. They're good quality – Marks & Spencer, and very much in fashion. You'll look so much better!'

As time went on, I learned to settle in to our new environment. I adored playing with our guardians' little boy, Jack, who was a boisterous and amusing three year old when we arrived. He was a great distraction for me, lifting the heaviness of my moods and bringing sunshine into the days. I also knew that it helped Gilly, who was pregnant with their second child. That meant, I hoped, that I was earning brownie points and proving that Abby and I were good girls. If I could make myself useful, it would make our home more secure.

That was how I found myself becoming babysitter, dog-walker, friend and confidante to Gilly, as well as helper for Abigail. She wasn't settling as well, becoming rebellious at school and surly at home. The teachers at school were patient and understanding for a while, and Gilly did her best to appreciate the circumstances, but it can't have been easy. She was only twenty-six years old (ten years older than me), already dealing with an energetic toddler, with another child on the way, and had suddenly been made responsible for two bereaved girls. It must have been an impossible situation by anyone's standards. Eddie was a good few years older than Gilly. He was one of those charismatic people who could be the life and soul of the party in public, but there always seemed to be something unnerving about him in private. I felt there was a cold hollow side to him – his steely stare, crisp voice and piercing blue eyes could send shivers down my spine. He had a way of putting things across that made me feel I was being judged. I always felt I had to come up with the right response and my instinct told me that I would be wise to learn the rules of his game and keep my distance.

He was unforgiving of Abigail's displays of rebellion, and I would find myself being the middle-man between Eddie's judgment and Abigail's pain. I remember one particular evening that still makes me shiver to this day. My sister had already gone to bed, and

Eddie, Gilly and I were sitting around the large kitchen table where we'd eat our family meals. We'd been discussing a telephone call Eddie had taken that afternoon from Abby's form teacher. She'd misbehaved in class and been accused of being disruptive – nothing too serious by all accounts and, with hindsight, the sort of behaviour that was simply a cry for help from a little girl who was clearly suffering and in a great deal of emotional turmoil. In addition to being mischievous at school, she'd also taken to dragging her duvet in to sleep on the floor next to Eddie and Gilly during the night – another clear sign of a child who needed care and understanding. But Eddie didn't see it that way. He took a deep breath, tutted and shook his head from side to side – a sign that by that time I had learned to recognise as the forerunner to something bad.

'Well, it's up to you, Melanie,' he'd sighed, flicking his newspaper closed and folding it carefully on the kitchen table in front of him, the use of my full name deliberately emphasising the severity of the situation. Clasping his hands together and resting them on the newspaper, he then fixed me with those ice-cold eyes. 'I'm doing my best here, and so is Gilly – you know we are. But Abigail is not making life easy for us you know. She's trouble at school, and at home her nocturnal habits are affecting our sex life and our marriage. This kind of behaviour can't continue . . . you'll have to make it clear to her…" The thinly veiled threat lay heavy in his silent pause, as he scanned my expressionless face for a response "You know I can always have a word with your grandmother. I'm sure she'd have something to say about all of this.' His lips parted to show his teeth, but the chilling gesture was anything but a smile. My radar was on high alert, but I refused to show fear. Instead I diffused the situation by turning on the Hollywood beam I'd learned from Mum and the friendly laughter I'd practised with Abigail.

'It's OK,' I smiled reassuringly. 'I'll have a word with her. I'm sure it's just because she's feeling lost. She often used to sleep in Mum's bed, so it's going to take some time to readjust. I'll tell her

26

she can come up to my room. And I'll also find out what's behind her antics at school. Everything can be sorted out.'

And that, pretty much, was the pattern of existence at Eddie and Gilly's house.

Don't get me wrong – there were some fun times and I do have many fond memories, and Gilly and I shared a strong bond together. But, dictated partly by our own circumstances and partly by Eddie's unpredictable behaviour, any good times were overshadowed by the ever-present threat of disapproval, disruption or worse. I learned how to walk on eggshells and to keep a brave face, no matter what the situation. It seemed to work. Outsiders stopped checking that we were OK, life settled into a routine, and over time I even fooled myself into believing that everything was going to work out just fine.

But I was wrong.

It was Sunday, 9 January 1983, just a couple of weeks after we'd celebrated my 18th birthday with a huge party at home and almost two years to the day since we'd first discovered Mum's illness. I was in my second year of A levels and life was pretty good, all things considered. That evening, Abigail and I had arrived home late from a weekend visit with our paternal grandparents in Lincolnshire. We'd been laughing together the entire journey, giggling at some of the things Grandpa had been saying and doing over the weekend. So we were both happy and in high spirits.

The house was in darkness when we got home, and everyone was already in bed. We whispered good night to each other and crept quietly to our bedrooms. Abigail's was on the first floor and mine was at the top of the house next to the attic. I tiptoed up the narrow stairs and along the short corridor, reaching through the door to turn on the light and go into my bedroom. But the sight that met my eyes stopped me in my tracks.

I remember holding my hand over my mouth, stifling my scream. I knew I mustn't make a noise but I couldn't believe what I was seeing. I tried to make sense of the scene swimming in front of my eyes, questions and emotions whirling around my brain, crashing into one another and multiplying with each new collision.

'No, it can't be! Surely this is some kind of mistake?'

I peered closer, blinking, checking that it was true (and willing myself to be wrong) as the scene once again came into focus. There was no mistake.

There, strewn across the floor and over my bed, were my mother's clothes and some of her belongings – a handbag, a purse, a couple of shoes – the last remaining treasured personal effects that were usually kept carefully folded up and tucked away in the attic space beside my room. No, there was no mistake. The reality sank in and from the dark recesses of my soul, the two familiar demons, Fear and Pain, slithered out of the shadows towards me, enveloping me in their choking clutch.

Steadying myself against the wall, I stumbled towards my bed and gently moved aside my mother's favourite winter dress, the one that she used to wear at every possible opportunity. It was pastel coloured, made from a heavy wool material with a large sweeping cowl neck that showed off her fine collarbone and jaw line to perfection. Sitting on the bed, I held the dress to my face, closing my eyes and greedily breathing in what minuscule traces of Mum's smell were left on the fabric. Silent tears slid down my face as I tried to make sense of what could possibly have happened in my bedroom.

I simply couldn't work out what my guardians had been doing – how could the people responsible for caring for my sister and I be so cruel and unkind? I knew that Eddie could become angry and that he was prone to violent or unpredictable outbursts when he was drunk (one weekend he had clambered up onto the top of the roof, holding on to the chimney and screaming obscenities) and I knew that he and Gilly had not been getting on particularly well over Christmas. Even so, I still couldn't rationalise what might have prompted such a scene.

Perhaps they'd had a fight? Perhaps it had been about us? Perhaps they'd wanted to get everything to do with us out of the house? Perhaps we'd overstayed our welcome and they just wanted to frighten us? The questions ran around my head, but no matter how hard I tried I couldn't make sense of what had happened. All I did know for sure was that something was very, very wrong, and that it was going to have a massive impact on us.

There was no point in frightening Abigail with what I'd found, and the rest of the house was sleeping. I knew there was nothing more I could do until the morning, so I tidied Mum's belongings together, folding them neatly and gently returning them to the attic where they belonged. I knew how to do this. I knew how to stay calm under threat. As I finished and slid into bed, I knew beyond question that my life was once again about to change forever.

The following morning I got up and went downstairs for breakfast as usual. I don't remember whether or not I told Abigail about the scene I'd found the night before, but I do remember that neither of our guardians were at the breakfast table. Jack pottered in, rubbing his eyes and yawning, his dressing gown tie trailing behind him. Glad of the distraction, I busied myself with getting him fed and watered – a normal routine during what was clearly going to be a far from normal morning.

Eddie came down with just a couple of minutes to spare before the time we usually left the house, and I immediately took the opportunity to ask where Gilly was and if she was all right. He brushed me off with a brusque 'She's too tired this morning' and shooed us to pick up our coats and get in the car.

Slamming the door as he got into the driver's seat, Eddie turned on the car stereo and twisted the dial so it was on full volume. Steve Miller's 'Abra-abra- cadabra, I wanna reach out and grab ya!' filled the car. Gripping the steering wheel and staring straight ahead, Eddie's face was fixed, his jaw muscles flexing as he ground his teeth together. The message was perfectly clear – 'Back off and don't even go there!' – but it didn't stop the questions from racing around inside my head. My heart was pumping and my mouth was dry, but I had to know. I couldn't help myself. So, taking a deep breath, I steeled myself to ask the same question I had asked in my mother's car as we were leaving the doctor's surgery. It took every ounce of courage, but in the end I heard my voice coming out calm and clear. 'Well, are you going to tell us then?'

My enquiry was met with silence and coldness. There was none of the love and concern that Mum had shown when I had asked her the same question. No, this time it was a sneer. Eddie tightened his grip on the steering wheel and kept his eyes on the road ahead.

'You're going to stay with your grandmother. You're to pack your bags tonight and you're leaving tomorrow or the next day. You're not coming back.'

And that was that.

4
Moving Out and Moving On

I never did find out what had happened in my bedroom that weekend. It seemed pointless searching for answers to questions that would not alter our new reality. The fact was that our time with Eddie and Gilly was over after just 22 months. I had failed. But this time the failure was worse because, although I had done my best, I'd been unable to keep a safe home for my little sister. As the eldest, I held myself responsible. Now we were both to be moved, in disgrace, to live back with Nan. Back to the situation we were in when Mum was alive, before we moved to our dream home – only this time it was so much worse. Because this time we'd have to live under Nan's regime. This time there was no Mum to look out for us. This time we were on our own, and Nan made it perfectly clear that she was disappointed in our behaviour. After all, it was clearly our fault that Eddie couldn't put up with us – we simply must have done something wrong! So we arrived as bad girls. Girls who'd been given every opportunity in a loving home, but who had been unable or unwilling to be grateful for what they had.

Trapped once more in the 'Victorian monstrosity' that Mum had loathed with a passion, Abigail and I were put in to the top flat.

We hated it there and had convinced ourselves it was haunted. The place was always cold, and the linoleum flooring in the kitchen, bathroom and along the corridor amplified every footstep. It just had an empty, oppressive kind of feel to it, and we were terrified to be up there on our own. I remember even as small children, at family gatherings for example, if I was sent up there to retrieve a jar of Nan's homemade jam from the kitchen cupboards, I'd literally tear back down the two spiral staircases as quickly as I could, muffling a scream as imaginary ghosts followed me. Nan, of course, was fully aware of our fear when she moved us up there, but was having none of it.

'Don't be so utterly ridiculous,' she tutted. 'You're not children any more and all of that was pure fantasy. I won't stand for it. This is your home now, so just be sensible about it.'

Nan was a short, round lady who sported a shade-changing blue-rinse and perm. She was proud of her appearance and even more proud of her standing in the area. Her late husband had been not only a successful businessman, but also a pillar of the local community, so together they had enjoyed a life filled with business functions and charity events. Nan always tried to maintain a practised Home Counties accent, particularly on the telephone, but it would regularly slip, much to everyone's amusement.

Following the death of her own mother, when she was just a child, Nan was sent to live with a family friend. She would often tell us stories about how she had felt desperately miserable and isolated there, so I thought that perhaps she might be able to empathise with what Abigail and I had been going through. But no. The fact that we'd clearly misbehaved at Eddie and Gilly's seemed to heap shame on the family and, rather than being given comfort, we were told off for letting her down.

Nan had always maintained that Mum had meant everything to her and that she loved her more than she could explain. She even had a kind of 'shrine' to Mum, where she displayed old photographs, letters and always a vase of fresh flowers. So I couldn't understand why she wasn't more forgiving and caring towards me and my sister? If she'd loved Mum so dearly, surely she'd at least show Mum respect by caring for her daughters now that she'd gone? I remember asking Nan about that one day, after she'd once again told us off for doing something wrong (arriving late to the dinner table or refusing a second portion of cold cabbage – something trivial as usual). I said that surely Nan could understand some of the pain and fear that we had experienced after Mum's death? That surely, as children of her beloved daughter, we couldn't be all bad? That surely we should be allowed to grieve and heal in our own time? Her response was peculiar in the extreme.

'Melanie,' she sighed theatrically, rolling her eyes and shaking her head, hands firmly rooted on her hips, 'You just don't understand. Yes, you may have lost a mother. But what about me? I have lost a daughter, and that's so much worse. You have absolutely no idea how much it tortures me.' And with that she sniffed and scurried back into the kitchen, grasping a worktop for balance and wiping her eyes with her apron. To this day I remain astonished that a grown woman could have been so self-obsessed and blind to the pain of her own granddaughters, but at the time I just took it as another confirmation that it was not safe for us to share our feelings. We were not going to be believed or understood, so it was better to stay quiet and carry on as best we could.

But I couldn't carry on. Life under Nan's roof was intolerable. The rules had been strict with Eddie and Gilly, but with Nan it was even worse. We were discouraged from having friends round. We were expected to sit with her and enjoy her radio and television programmes; anything we wanted to watch was not allowed, as it would usually clash with something she refused to miss. How I grew to detest the theme tunes from *Emmerdale Farm* and *The Archers*! It was all made worse because, by now, Nan had vacated the ground floor and moved to the first floor – the very same space where we had lived with Mum. Rooms that used to belong to us now had Nan's stamp on them, which in a way made it worse than living with our guardians, where the house held nothing familiar. Here, not only did we know the place (and harbour memories of Mum's unhappiness there) but a space that used to be 'ours' had been changed and revamped to house Nan's belongings. Perfectly natural, of course, but for us it only made matters worse.

We now had to fit in with Nan's schedules, and it was torture. We had to join her for her regular Saturday lunch outing with her cousin and sister – typically a stodgy three-course meal at a local restaurant that catered for older customers. Whilst I was actually very fond of both the aunts (Daisy and Maud) both Abby and I felt squashed and smothered spending too much time in the company of three old ladies. After the meal, as if we had room for anything else, we'd then be expected to spend the next couple of hours at one of their homes eating high tea! This was typically a sickly synthetic Mr Kipling cake – pink Battenberg, iced frangipane or gooey ginger sponge. Not only did we have to join in with their conversation, we also had to make sure we finished the cake.

'Come along, you're growing girls!' Nan would insist, sliding yet another slice of sweet, calorie-laden goo onto our plates.

'Yes, yes, come on now, you've got to keep your energy up!' her sister would cackle, as all three of them dissolved into laughter about something of which Abigail and I had no comprehension. I was studying *Macbeth* at school at the time, and I couldn't help but be reminded of the three witches – a story I shared with Abigail, much to her amusement, later that day when we were finally alone.

I was 18 at the time – in the final year of my A levels. Abigail was 13, coming up for 14, and was about to start her O level studies. I still had no idea what had happened to go so terribly wrong at Eddie and Gilly's house. Eddie had offered us no explanation, and Nan had only told us that we'd been ungrateful. The office where Eddie worked was on our route to school, so we had to pass it every day. Never knowing whether we might bump into him, both Abigail and I felt very anxious every time we passed. It was a constant reminder of what could and should have been, of the bittersweet memories of a new life that I had tried and failed to achieve with them after Mum died.

I desperately missed the children, and I also missed Gilly. I thought we had shared a strong bond, and there was a huge hole in my life now that we couldn't see them any more. On top of that, I was beginning to burn with the injustice of it all. It was OK for me, because I was 18. But my little sister was only 13, and had been condemned to living out her teenage years under the restrictive out-of-touch regime of an embittered old lady. So I decided to ask for an audience with Eddie. I actually had to telephone his secretary to ask for an appointment – how absurd was that? After checking with Eddie, she booked me in for a 30-minute slot a couple of days later. By that time we'd been living with Nan for two or three weeks. We'd already collected our possessions from the house and it had been made clear that the move was permanent and that we were no longer welcome in the family. The memories of the day we picked up our belongings are burned deeply into my mind – it was yet another cruel and surreal chapter in the lives of two vulnerable girls.

We had been informed that our things would be packed up and ready for collection on the Sunday afternoon when nobody would be there. Abigail and I had arranged for one of my friends who had a car to come and meet us. After nervously ringing the doorbell of the house that until very recently had been our home, we were greeted at the door by a stranger. It was an older lady who had been employed to help with the children after we'd left. I dared myself to wonder whether perhaps they missed me after all.

She was a kindly lady and seemed to be as confused as we were about the situation. All our clothes and belongings had been emptied from our rooms and put in black plastic sacks. Our photographs had been removed, and in the dining room there were two new family members – a pair of mice they had named Melanie and Abigail, apparently to help the children get used to the fact we weren't there any more. It was at that point that I couldn't maintain my composure any longer. I bit my lip as silent tears ran down my face.

Refusing to make a sound, I looked into the face of the kindly stranger who was with us.

'Oh, my poor dear loves,' she said, her eyes welling with tears as she put her arms around both of us. 'I am so sorry for you. I don't understand what happened here, but whatever it was this is no way to treat people. Especially not children. I do wish I could make things better for you, I really do, my darlings.'

Those were the kindest words and gestures I'd received from an adult since this whole episode began. That same kindness reached into my heart and kick-started the sobs.

'I don't know either,' I stuttered, fighting back the tears and doing everything I could to regain my self-control. 'We did our best here, and I thought this was our home and our family. And I miss those children so much it hurts! But, for whatever reason, they don't want us any more. At least Abigail and I have each other.'

'You do, and you always will have,' the stranger nodded, clearly choked by what she was witnessing. 'And don't judge others by what has happened here. People do strange and cruel things that sometimes make no sense. You will be all right, mark my words. Stick together and you will be all right.'

Abigail and I took one last tour of the house together to check that we had everything before getting into my friend's Mini and driving away forever. We remained stony faced and silent, shutting down the pain and shoring up our walls.

So when I walked in that afternoon for my meeting with Eddie, it was relatively easy for me to maintain a dignified level of calm. Settling in the chair in front of his huge wooden desk, I reminded myself to keep a safe distance. *'Don't show your pain. Stay calm. Stay strong. You can do this.'*

Smoothing my jeans and pulling myself up as tall as I could, I waited for him to finish his telephone call. Eddie's was the only desk in the room, strategically placed in the big bay window. He shared the space with a few metal filing cabinets, some pieces of antique furniture and my mother's big dining room table, which was now strewn with paperwork, pens and a couple of coffee mugs. It was the very same table around which the three of us had shared so many emotionally charged conversations after we discovered her illness, where we'd bared our souls, shed our tears, shared out love and held onto one another for support. And now here it was in a sterile office, being used by the same man who had discarded us. Taking strength from the memories that were associated with the table, and giving a silent 'thank you' to Mum, I sat rock solid until Eddie finally put the phone down.

'Sorry about that,' he smiled, the Jabberwocky's snicker-snack blade suddenly springing into my mind. 'You know how these things are – business comes first! Right, I can give you 25 minutes – so what do you want?'

And that was how the conversation continued. Business-like. Emotionless. Facts rather than feelings. And all very, very controlled. He wouldn't tell me what had happened but just said that it had been too much pressure for Gilly having us there and that their marriage had suffered as a result. I asked whether there was anything specific that we'd done wrong, but he brushed the question aside, repeating that it was too much for Gilly. When I asked what was to happen to us, his response was typically matter-of-fact.

'You're 18,' he said, 'so you can make your own way now. Abigail is still a minor, so, if she wants, she can come back until she reaches 18. Or she can stay here with your nan. It's up to her.'

I asked whether I could see the children

'We'll see how that goes,' was his response. 'It's too much to expect of Gilly at the moment, and I don't want to confuse the boys.'

Finally, realising that I was not going to get the answers my heart ached for, I asked about the table.

'That's Mum's dining table,' I stated in a matter-of-fact way, nodding towards the pile of messy paperwork. 'It means a lot to me. It belongs to me and Abigail, and I'd like it back.'

'Well, what do you suggest you do with it?' sneered Eddie. 'I'm quite sure Dee wouldn't mind me using it. But of course, as and when you have your own home, then you must have it. Of course! Now, time's up and I must get on. Here, take this. It's all your important documents; you might need them.' And he handed me a brown envelope that contained my birth certificate, some old school reports and my premium-bond certificate. 'As Abigail's guardian, I shall be holding onto hers for the time being,' he added, before getting out of his chair and dismissing me from his office.

So that was that. Job done. Message clear. For whatever reason, we were no longer welcome even as visitors. I knew there was no way that Abigail would ever want to live there again. She had never settled and would certainly not go back without me. Equally, I knew she hated living with Nan as much as I did. I had to do something, and it was around that time that I first started thinking about becoming Abigail's legal guardian.

From everything we had experienced since Mum had died, Abby and I knew it was not safe for me to ask for help or expect support from any of the family. It was an unspoken agreement, but we just knew, and the only people we could trust were each other. Abigail was still only 13, and I knew that I was the adult. So I took to sharing most of my angst with friends at school and also with Betty, the lovely kitchen lady who had adored Mum when she worked at the school and who would now serve me piping-hot milky coffees and give me lots of cuddles and words of wisdom. My friends were kind and understanding, but I knew that for many of them what I was experiencing was too much to comprehend. I spent a lot of time sharing stories and comparing emotional wounds with a classmate and friend called Joan, who was herself reeling from being caught in the middle of her parents' difficult divorce. That helped, because we could be the two 'outcasts' together, but most of the time I would let out my pain through my art. It just so happened that Jane and I were both studying the subject for A Level and were widely regarded as the best artists in the school, so we'd share our thoughts and express our feelings through moody, dark and sometimes plain off-the-wall artistic creations.

It was Andy Granger who came to my rescue. He was another old family friend who had known Mum since childhood. He, Eddie and Mum used to hang around together when they were small, and Andy had remained a close friend to Eddie. He'd heard about our predicament and, while he didn't openly criticise Eddie's actions, the things he didn't say told me he was confused and upset by what had happened. It was half term, a good few weeks since we'd moved to live with Nan, and Andy said he was coming to collect me as he'd had an idea and wanted to show me something.

'Dee would be horrified to know what has happened to you both. I loved her very dearly, as you know,' he said once we were in the car, shaking his head and doing his best to keep his voice steady, 'and I just can't stand by and see you suffer. It's not right.'

We pulled away from Nan's house and down the long wide road that led straight to the sea. It was the beginning of spring, a crisp cold day bathed in beautiful sunshine. The sea glimmered as we drove closer, and I had the strangest feeling that everything was going to be all right. Andy was a local guy who had done good. What he may have lacked in academic muscle he sure made up with in terms of common sense and good old-fashioned hard work. He had bought and renovated a few properties in Eastbourne, which he rented out to long-term tenants. One of his flats had unexpectedly become available, and as we drove along the seafront he explained that he was willing to let me move into it if I was interested.

If I was interested? What? If I was interested? Flippin' heck, was he joking? A place of my own? Away from Nan? Where Abigail could come and stay? Where we could be free? Of course I was jolly well interested!

The flat was on the first floor of a terraced building in a tiny street that sat just a few hundred yards from the seafront and also within spitting distance of our school. Preston Road was just at the edge of restaurant- and bar-land, and as we got out of the car I was hit by two distinctive smells – the sea and restaurant kitchens. My senses were also flooded by the hustling and bustling sounds of the bars and restaurants that filled the adjoining street. It was intoxicating, and I couldn't wait to get in and have a look.

The door opened into a tiny square hallway (if you can call it a hallway at less than a metre squared) and an equally small galley kitchen – barely functional with just a sink and a draining board, but I didn't care. It had a good-sized lounge at the front, with huge bay windows that looked out onto the street. There was a double bedroom at the back with a fire escape that ran down from the window to the restaurant-filled street below. Off the bedroom was a sunny bathroom, the south-facing obscured-glass bay windows flooding the room with light. I fell instantly in love with the place but had no idea how I was going to afford the rent or how I was going to make it work.

'I love it, Andy,' I whispered, brushing my hands once again over the front windowsill. 'This is the answer to my dreams, but how am I going to make it happen?'

Andy then calmly explained his idea in full. It was an adult conversation and, for the first time since Mum had died, I finally felt that somebody understood. And, more importantly, I felt that somebody cared.

The rent, he explained, was £15 per week (incredible now, as I look back on those times!) and the electricity was on a meter in the bedroom cupboard. On top of those main bills, there would be telephone charges if I chose to put in a line, and of course food and transport. Since I'd never had to do any of this before, Andy gently guided me through what he estimated my budget would need to be.

What was left of Mum's furniture and other belongings had been stored in various rooms in Nan's house. This, said Andy, would be my opportunity to reclaim as much as I needed in order to furnish my flat. Anything that was missing, I could probably find in any of Eastbourne's countless charity shops or car-boot sales. It would be fun!

We worked out that I'd need a weekly budget in the region of £45 and that in order to fund this, since I was still at school, we would ask my paternal grandfather for help. Grandpa was a wealthy man, and Andy reasoned that he should be only too pleased to come to the aid of his granddaughter. As it turned out, he wasn't pleased in the slightest, and it took a whole lot of persuasion from another relative to convince him to come up with the money. But in the end we did it, and I finally moved into my new flat in the middle of April 1983, just a few weeks before I was due to sit my all-important A level exams.

Abigail, of course, was with me all the way. Nan refused to let her come and live with me but was perfectly willing for her to come and spend as much time outside of school with me as she liked. It wasn't ideal, but having the flat as 'our space' proved to be a massive lift for both of us. It was freedom, and at last we could be ourselves, on our own terms. We would share countless evenings after school and whole weekends together. I would have my friends and she would bring hers. It was crowded at times, but after all the upheaval we finally felt that we had a base that nobody could take away from us. Life was finally on the up!

5

Unconditional Legal Aid and Desertion

The summer morning that my A level results arrived was a strangely life-affirming experience for me. Results day was a moment that I'd been chatting about with my school friends for what seemed like forever. It was what our entire education had been leading up to. Our performance would mean the difference between whether or not we'd be able to continue on to the next level of education. Despite the disruptions and chaos in my personal life, I'd somehow managed to keep on top of my studies and had also secured myself a provisional offer of a place at a prestigious fine art polytechnic.

The verdict was close, and I scurried out of the flat and downstairs to the hallway to sift through the post in search of the envelope that would seal my fate. I wasn't afraid, as I imagined perhaps most of my friends would be, sitting around their breakfast table with their parents and family all eagerly awaiting the news. No, I was curious, that's all, and also acutely aware that I was alone. There was going to be nobody with me to witness this momentous occasion. Nobody to congratulate me or commiserate. I took the brown envelope back up to the flat, closed the door and made myself a cup of coffee. Sitting on the bed, I carefully opened the envelope, taking a deep breath as I pulled out the white slip of paper that would determine my next steps.

The results were there in black and white, and my hand instinctively shot to cover my mouth as my eyes prickled with tears. I had passed. Everything. And with good grades as well. Good enough to confirm that I could continue my studies and become an artist. I was over the moon – and on my own. I burst in to tears.

As soon as I could speak, I picked up the phone and called my sister.

'I've passed! I've done it!' My path was set, and I was absolutely delighted, as, of course was Abby.

My sister was still a regular visitor to the flat, and I was relieved that she seemed to be a little more settled at Nan's house. Her bedroom had been moved down to the first floor, so she was at least on the same level with Nan. She also seemed to have increasingly more freedom. She was, to be fair, turning into a bit of a rebel (who could blame her?) and was also developing the wickedest sense of humour. She and I would spend riotous evenings, weekends and holidays in hysterics as she recounted some of her more extravagant escapades! My friends all thought she was marvellous, and together we became a bit of a comedy double act. That first summer by the sea was a therapeutic and wonderfully expansive time for both of us. We were happy and free, and I believed we had finally come though the worst together.

September arrived and while Abby went back to school, I headed off to polytechnic. Excited and scared, I started the term full of hopes and plans for the future. To be honest, though, I found that I struggled to bond with my fellow students. Many people had moved to the area just to take up their place at the polytechnic, and for most of them it was their first time away from home. I couldn't quite relate to their pretend moans about financial hardships and loneliness. I found it absurd and immature that they'd be unable to fend for themselves and would expect their parents to bail them out by sending money or taking them home every weekend to do their washing, cook for them, buy them new clothes and everything else that a normal family unit would do for their child.

For me, it just brought home how alone I was, what a different hand life had dealt me, and how much I had to stay strong. Whilst I was glad to be out of school, where everyone had known my story, I found it a huge shock that it was even harder to be somewhere where nobody knew. Somewhere I just couldn't fit in, although I couldn't explain why. At school I had become gregarious, funny, confident and well-liked. Here, in this place that was meant to be the fulfilment of my dreams, I found I shrank away and very soon became overwhelmed with the shyness I'd suffered as a little girl. I became despondent and suffered from regular bouts of tonsillitis. Home alone and sick, I felt more and more isolated and lost. There was nowhere to go for help, and I just couldn't pull myself out of the sinking feeling that I was becoming a failure.

Sadly, after contracting what turned out to be glandular fever at the beginning of the second term, I made the difficult decision to drop out. I felt relieved and terribly sad at the same time. I had desperately wanted to study art, but I just couldn't do it. While I felt emotionally low, the sickness, thank goodness, was manageable. Since I had nowhere to go for nursing and care, I spent much of the time holed up in my flat. Glandular fever, for some reason, manifested itself in an unusual and thankfully relatively painless way. For me, most of the time I felt as though I was tripping and would spend whole days as high as a kite! Yes, I had the usual exhaustion associated with the illness, and the occasional excruciatingly sore and swollen throat, but most of the time I was just wandering around in la-la land.

It was one of those occasions when Abby found me in Waitrose supermarket. My sister had been alerted by one of her friends who'd seen me while she was out buying her lunch. I was wandering around the supermarket dressed only in my dressing gown and fluffy slipper-socks. By the time Abigail found me, I had filled a trolley full of all manner of bizarre foods and household items, and was trying to hide behind one of the displays while curled up in a hysterical fit of the giggles! Goodness only knows what I thought I had been doing, and goodness only knows how Abigail managed to excuse my peculiar behaviour, but somehow she got me safely back home. It might not have been funny at the time, but it was a story we have both told on many occasions throughout the years! On another occasion, while it was still February, one of my friends happened to be walking his dog along the seafront and found me lying on a beach towel, wearing a yellow bikini and sunglasses. Apparently I told him it was such divine weather I decided I'd get an early suntan . . .

By the end of spring, I had recovered enough to start thinking about what I might do, and before the beginning of summer, I had landed myself a job, working in one of Eastbourne's most exclusive menswear shops. Less than a five-minute walk from my flat and frequented by some of the most hip and cool people in the town, I knew I'd landed on my feet and threw myself into the role.

It was around this time that Abigail started displaying some strange behaviour. Her rebellious streak had become stronger, she was frequently staying out late and often getting hopelessly drunk. She'd become more secretive around me and to top it all her weight was plummeting. As children, we'd always been what Mum would describe as 'plump' or 'well-built' and, despite Mum's best intentions, both of us had grown up with pretty unhealthy body issues, compounded by our experiences since she had died. Although Abby had tried to hide it from me over recent weeks, it became obvious that she was quite literally wasting away in front of my eyes.

It was a concerned late-night conversation between one of her friends and myself that finally brought the truth out in to the open. It turned out that she'd been starving herself – hiding food that Nan gave her and vomiting up anything that she hadn't able to hide and put in the bin. Apparently it had been going on for some time, but Abigail refused to acknowledge it or talk to anybody about it. I knew this was serious, and it explained why I felt she'd become more withdrawn. Feeling ill-equipped to confront my sister with this on my own, I decided that the best course of action would be to seek expert medical advice. I also reasoned that it would make sense to involve Nan as soon as possible, even though I felt excruciatingly guilty at the idea that I was about to break Abigail's confidence; after all, we would need to work together if we stood any chance of bringing Abigail back to full health.

So it was, that a couple of days later Nan and I were sitting in the surgery listening to our family doctor explain what he thought we should do for the best. Dr Watson had known us for years, and I trusted his opinion implicitly. He knew, of course, what had happened to us and was sympathetic and supportive, as well as being one of those doctors who were ahead of their time. He was no stranger to counselling, alternative therapies and holistic medicine, and I listened attentively as he shared his opinion and recommendation with us.

'Abigail has been through a series of huge upheavals,' he explained, keeping a smile on his face although I felt that he was also attempting to convey a deeper message to Nan, 'and we must understand that she is a victim here. People who have experienced trauma – particularly a series of traumas and at such a young and impressionable age – will search for anything over which they can maintain control. They do it in an effort to bring stability to a situation that is overwhelming and frightening. It's logical, really if you think about it.'

I nodded, pleased to be receiving an explanation, and even more pleased that Nan was with me to hear, from a professional, that her young granddaughter had been suffering as a result of what had happened. Perhaps now, I thought, we can start to build a healthier relationship. Perhaps now we might have a better chance to care for Abigail in the way that she deserves.

Nan sat there, looking shocked and tearful. She rummaged in her handbag to find one of her perfumed lace handkerchiefs and dabbed at her nose. 'Yes, Doctor, whatever you say,' she sniffed, wiping her eyes before putting the damp material back into her handbag.

Dr Watson continued, 'For Abigail, it seems, as is the case with many of today's youngsters, she has decided that she can limit and control her food intake. That's OK in a healthy environment, but because of underlying issues of low self-esteem, which I suspect have been gathering strength since your mother died?' His eyes met mine, and I nodded my agreement. 'It's much more likely that the situation is very serious. If she's already lost a good deal of weight and is continuing to cover her tracks, then it's my professional opinion that Abigail is already in the grip of a serious eating disorder.'

Nan and I stayed chatting with the doctor until we had a proper understanding of what was happening and what we should do next. I can't describe the relief I felt, reassured that I had done the right thing and grateful that we had been given a clear set of guidelines to follow. *We can do this*, I thought, and I squeezed Nan's shoulders as we left the surgery together.

The instructions were clear and simple. We were not to say anything to Abigail, and we were not to tell anybody else about what we had discovered – at least for the time being. In fact, in the immediate future, nothing at all was to change. The important thing right now was for Nan and I to learn as much as we possibly could about eating disorders and become much more actively vigilant about Abigail's eating and vomiting habits. The more we could understand, the better equipped we would be to deal with the next stage, which would be to get a counsellor involved in the process. Dr Watson had said he'd research his database and recommend the best person or people who he thought could help, bearing in mind Abigail's particularly unusual set of circumstances.

I stayed at Nan's for a cup of tea but left before Abigail got in from school. We decided it would be better if I wasn't there, so as not to raise her suspicions. Once I was back home, I thought more about what Dr Watson had said, and my heart bled anew for the pain that both my sister and I had suffered over the past few years. I also allowed the sense of relief to grow – at last, here was somebody, a professional, who understood and who had made his point loud and clear. At last we were being heard. At last we would get some helpful and positive progress.

But I was wrong.

My faith, once again, had been misplaced. Rather than sticking to the plan, Nan had disobeyed Dr Watson's strict instructions and instead immediately gone bleating to Eddie. Bewailing the fact that she had been deceived and betrayed by Abigail's actions, she said that she couldn't cope and asked Eddie to help. It would appear that he immediately got on the case.

As soon as Abigail arrived home, she was summoned to the sitting room for a meeting with Eddie – enough to frighten anyone, let alone someone who was already bruised and battered from years of emotional trauma. The way I understand it, Eddie then spent the next half hour or so berating Abigail for her despicable behaviour. How could she lie to her grandmother? How could she be so disrespectful? Didn't she realise how much pain and suffering her selfish actions had caused?

He made it perfectly clear that her situation was untenable. Nan could no longer cope with her devious ways, and she had to get out and give Nan some space to recover. That was the reason, he continued, why he had been talking to an aunt (our father's cousin, Abigail's godmother) in America that very afternoon, and they had agreed she would go there in the next day or so and stay for at least a couple of weeks. No questions. No going back. No asking for forgiveness. Abigail had gone too far this time, and she had to take the consequences.

Looking back on this, and even as I now write the words, I am horrified that those people could be so ignorant of what is now widely recognised as a serious mental and physical issue. Even given that perhaps they didn't understand the true nature of Abigail's problem, it still doesn't excuse their unjust and cruel behaviour towards a child who was simply trying to deal with a set of overwhelming emotional traumas. I just don't get it.

Until the time she was put on the plane, Abigail was under strict house arrest. She was made to eat every meal in front of Nan and was not allowed to go to the toilet until at least an hour had passed. She was not allowed to see friends, nor was she allowed to make or take any phone calls. I heard about what had happened through Nan. She called me the next day to tell me what was planned for my little sister. Her version of events was, of course, much more self-serving, but she couldn't get away from the fact that she'd done the complete opposite of Dr Watson's explicit instructions. I felt absolutely terrible and powerless at the same time. I had betrayed my little sister. I had shared secrets that one of her closest friends had confided in me. I'd done it with the best of intentions, but the result was a nightmare.

I was allowed to speak with my sister on the telephone for only a few minutes, while Nan remained in the room. Abigail was cold. Hard. Emotionless. Exactly the same way I would be if I had just been through what she'd experienced. My heart broke once again for her. My eyes filling with tears, I fought hard to keep my voice steady and my words strong. 'It's OK,' I said. 'It will all work out for the best. You can chill out while you're in America with Auntie Penelope, and when you come back I'll be here. I'm with you all the time – remember that. And we'll talk while you're away.'

As it turned out, the trip to America wasn't all that Eddie had arranged. He had also called the school to let them know what had happened and to ask them whether they had any advice. Clearly my sister had become too much trouble for her grandmother, so could they accommodate her in the boarding dormitory? The school immediately said it was inappropriate for Abigail to become a boarder, since that still wouldn't give her a stable home. They asked for some time to consider options and then a short while later gave Eddie what he saw to be a perfect solution.

There was a lady teacher who was relatively new to the school; she taught economics and had a young family of her own. Her husband was also a teacher, and they were looking to take in long-term lodgers. The head teacher had brought up the idea of them taking Abigail and they had decided they would be perfectly willing and able to offer my sister a home. Job done. Abigail was off Nan's hands and out of Eddie's life as well. He would pay the family a regular sum of money to cover Abigail's keep, and everyone's conscience would be salved.

I was furious. Apoplectic in actual fact! How dare they? What on earth did they think they were doing? How could they be so heartless? Did they have no understanding of the damage they were causing?

I was 19 years old by this time, and I simply couldn't understand why my little sister couldn't come and live with me. We got on like a house on fire. We had been through the same traumas. We felt the same feelings. We supported each other. And we were going to stick together like glue. Surely, in God's name, it would be much better if she just came to me full-time?

But Eddie and Nan were having none of it. I called Nan to find out what on earth they had been thinking and why Abigail couldn't just come and live with me. 'What could possibly be wrong with . . .'

'It's all been arranged now, dear,' she retorted, cutting me short in a particularly haughty and dismissive tone. 'It's for the best. Eddie and I have made our decision, and there's nothing you can do about it. You can still see each other, of course, but you just couldn't provide a stable enough home for Abigail. She needs people who can control her and look after her properly.'

'That's rich!' I thought to myself, mentally closing the door on Nan, Eddie and their incomprehensibly callous ways of doing things. Determined to get my little sister off the merry-go-round of emotional abuse and unsuitable homes, I decided I was going to become Abigail's legal guardian by hook or by crook.

That was when I decided to seek out a solicitor, but I didn't know where to start. How do you choose? What do you look for? What questions do you ask? I picked up the Yellow Pages and then picked up the phone. It was going to be a case of trial and error. I was lucky. The second or third conversation gave me the connection and confidence I'd been seeking. The secretary put me straight through to her boss, and he calmly and patiently answered the myriad of questions I had in my head. I felt reassured. I had feared that I would be patronised – seen as either too young or too unstable to be able to provide any kind of home for a teenage girl who had been through such a raft of emotional trauma. But this man, James Getting, listened to me and explained the options that might be open to me. I booked an appointment to see him the very next day.

I liked James as soon as I met him. He had a kind face and an open smile. He was younger than I had imagined and very well turned out. He looked professional and also approachable.

During that first meeting, I discovered that I had a very good chance of becoming my sister's legal guardian. James explained that I had plenty of evidence to explain my reasoning behind taking legal action, and added that, as an adult, I had every right to apply to care for a sister who was still a minor. He hoped it wouldn't take too long – a few months at most – and he set in action the paperwork to apply for legal aid for the case.

The application was successful and, we secured unconditional legal aid. James rubbed his hands and welcomed me into his office when he got the news. 'This is exactly what we want, Melanie,' he smiled, grinning from ear to ear. 'We can go in as hard as we like – court and legal fees will be covered whatever action we need to take. This is the best possible outcome. Let's get started, shall we?'

I have to say I was absolutely terrified by the prospect of what might happen. I dreaded Eddie's response and was frightened about what he might do or say to my sister as a result. But I had to do it – I knew I had to do it! How could I possibly stand by and let my sister be pushed aside to live as a lodger with a teacher from school? I couldn't. I had to take a stand, and I had to stay strong.

It was something, of course, that I had to keep to myself. I could hardly tell Nan, and letting Eddie know was totally out of the question. I explained what was happening to Abigail, who gave me a small smile to let me know she was OK with it, and also confided in a couple of close friends.

James had explained that Eddie would need to be served with papers of intent and that when that happened I could likely expect some backlash.

'We'll do our best to handle the situation, but knowing what you've told me about these people, we'd better be prepared. You must remember that they can't hurt you any more, Melanie, and we have the whole weight of the law on our side. But they are likely to fight back – we know that.'

He was right. The backlash was immediate and delivered to cause the most possible pain. I received a telephone call from Nan.

'Melanie, you must stop this nonsense immediately.' Her voice was cold, calm and measured. 'Eddie has told me exactly what you're doing, and you simply cannot continue with this. There are many things you don't understand, and if you choose to continue with this ridiculous course of action then I will disown you. Do I make myself clear?'

'But I'm doing this for my sister!' I replied, shocked and confused by Nan's harsh summary of the situation. 'Don't you understand? I want to keep her safe. She's everything to me, as you know, and the only way is for me to become her legal guardian!'

'She's already got a legal guardian. Eddie and I are perfectly capable of deciding your sister's future. It's a shame you've been so ungrateful not to realise just how much we do for you! How difficult this whole situation has been for everyone concerned! I command you to stop this nonsense right now. I absolutely forbid you to continue.'

'I'm sorry, Nan. I just can't do that. I'm sorry if you think I'm ungrateful, but I'm doing what I think is best. I hope that one day you'll understand.'

'Well, if that's your decision, then so be it. You are now nothing to me. Do I make myself clear? Goodbye, Melanie, no wonder your mother despaired of you.'

And that was that. She hung up the phone, leaving me speechless and open-mouthed. And also more determined than ever that I was going to get my little sister out of Nan and Eddie's twisted clutches and protect her from their cruel power games.

I told James what had happened and instructed him to go for it, hell for leather. They were poisonous, and I was deeply concerned that Nan and Eddie would take out their fury on Abigail. We had to get her out of there!

It started off well, but the few months that James hoped the process would take proved to be a grossly over-optimistic estimation. Eventually it stretched out over the course of nearly seven years, turning into a legal minefield as Eddie tried every trick in the book to stop us succeeding. I had countless visits to London law chambers, swore affidavits, had meetings with Counsel, waited outside judges' hearings, and signed stacks and stacks of legal paperwork. It was soul-destroying and so very, very slow. Far from remaining a relatively straightforward project to secure guardianship, the legal system dictated that all extenuating circumstances were to be taken on board. The case widened as James asked for witness statements from the wider family.

My grandfather had been right behind me when I first started the court case. He was proud that I was standing up for myself. 'I never did like Eddie,' he whispered, conspiratorially swirling his favourite Cinzano and lemonade. 'Slippery fellow right from the start. And as for Nan – so terribly rude and uncouth! Where do I start?' He snorted and rolled his eyes. For some reason there had always been some kind of rivalry between the two sets of grandparents. I didn't understand it then and I don't understand it now. But it was certainly there!

'We'll show the lot of them, Melanie! We'll show them. You can't mess with the Carnegies, eh? Isn't that right?' he'd bellowed, downing his drink as he tottered into the dining room to freshen his glass.

I loved both my paternal grandparents very dearly. I shared my birthday with Granny, which gave us a particularly special bond. She died before the court case became too ugly, and when it did, Grandpa phoned me with a similar ultimatum to the one that Nan had delivered a couple of years earlier. It was coming up to Christmas and I took the call at work.

'Melanie, you must now stop this nonsense,' he said sternly. 'It's gone on far too long and now it's involving our side as well. It can only bring harm. It's no good and you must stop.'

I knew the case was out of control. We didn't seem to be getting anywhere, and now James was asking me for information about my father's finances, which, of course, I knew nothing about. I desperately wanted out of the situation, but at the same time, if I just backed out now, it would mean that Eddie had won. It would also mean that I'd lost my family for nothing (Nan had never spoken to me since that telephone call, and she'd forbidden anyone else to have any contact with me either), not to mention the fact that I believed I would be left with an enormous legal bill if I didn't see it through to the end.

Grandpa and I had never had a cross word before this. While he could be difficult and awkward with other people, he and I shared a strong bond and an equal appreciation for the absurd and ridiculous. We could laugh at anything, and we both thoroughly enjoyed each other's company. So his sudden change of heart – and the harsh tone of his voice – upset me and left me feeling confused and hurt.

'But I can't, Grandpa. You know I can't!' I replied, a lump forming in my throat. 'You've been behind me on this all the way. You understand the complications much more than I do. You know I can't pull out now. How can you ask me to do it?'

'There's no such word as can't,' he barked angrily. 'Now then, listen to me. I'm telling you now, Melanie. You must stop this or I will cut you out of my will. I will never see you again. Do you understand me?'

'I hear you, but I can't do it. You know I can't. I hope you'll understand.'

But he didn't understand. True to his word, he changed his will the very next day. He was ill at the time, although I didn't realise the severity, and he died just three months later. I never had the chance to say goodbye or to make peace with him. I was heartbroken.

I never understood what made him so cross. At the time I just thought he was having a funny turn and that we'd make it up again. I reasoned that there must be something that had been miscommunicated about the case and that James would be able to put him straight. I asked James to look after the situation and expressed my misgivings that we were achieving nothing but separation and heartache by continuing with the case. But he always had a way of reassuring me that we were near the end, that it would be practically impossible to give up now, and that I must stay focused and hold onto what was right. But in the end, by the time we finally got a resolution it was to be nearly seven years after I first started the action.

Looking back, was it all worth it? Absolutely not. I had failed in my sole intention of securing legal guardianship for Abigail, as she turned 18 a long time before the case had finished, and I had lost my family in the process. Abigail managed to keep them on-side herself because we never put her name on the official paperwork. While she was as involved as I was, we all agreed to keep her separate. It worked. Nan and her cronies still accepted Abigail into their lair, but my childhood photographs and any last memories of my existence had long since been purged. The case only drew to a conclusion because Eddie's solicitor died very suddenly from meningitis. Eddie took the opportunity to sue his solicitor's estate (this solicitor, by the way, had been a family friend for many years and left a grieving widow behind, who can't have been too chuffed by Eddie's actions!) on the grounds that he had been given ill-informed advice over the years he had been fighting the case. Can you believe it? The barefaced cheek of the man!

By that time, with both Abigail and I adults, the only measurable 'victory', if you can call it that, was a meagre financial settlement, and, I suppose, the fact that in the end we were proven right. It was a hollow victory, and it was through this process that I learned a huge amount about the legal system. I learned that if any matter is contested, and depending on the persistence of those contesting, the legal process can be gruelling and expensive. It's not a straightforward or as accommodating as it first appears. It didn't seem fair to me. I felt more and more isolated, but the lessons learned served me well for future dealings with the law. For that I am grateful.

Back at the beginning of the legal fight, Abigail had gone to stay with the teachers. She was moved there as soon as she came back from America. And you know what? It turned out to be the best thing that could have happened in the long run. The teachers, Mary and Will, were caring, understanding, generous, loving, balanced and stable. As well as making a home for Abigail, they also made a point of welcoming me into their family as well, and fully supported the idea that my sister and I should be together as much as possible. So it was that I would have her to stay with me most weekends and during periods of the school holidays. Mary even gave me a portion of the allowance that Eddie was paying to cover Abigail's keep. Mary and Will had two small children, Erica and Ben, and, while it was tricky at first, Abigail soon settled into family life with them all. She pushed boundaries and tested limits, like any teenager would, but overall she grew to become healthier and happier than I'd seen her in a long time.

To this day, Will and Mary are like family to both of us. They and their extended family have been more understanding and supportive of us than any of our relations. They say that blood is thicker than water? Well, with the exception of the bond between my sister and myself, I completely disagree.

6

My Roaring 20s

My 20s, to put it in a nutshell, was the decade where I learned how to get on with life on my own. Very early on I came to realise that the abnormalities of my childhood were something from which I could now distance myself. School, where everyone knew my story, seemed a long way behind me, and while I had struggled at art school, I found I could quite easily fit in to 'normal' society where I was working for a living. People didn't have to know what had happened, and most, like me, were already living on their own or in shared accommodation. I was no longer abnormal and simply blended in with the crowd.

After the mind-altering bout of glandular fever forced me to drop out of art school, I had been lucky enough to find work in an exclusive men's fashion shop. I stayed there for three years and to this day, I count those times as giving me some of the most valuable lessons in my life. It was there I learned how to serve customers, how to engage with people and how to guide them in their choices of clothing. I learned how to stock-take, how to window-dress and how to place clothes and accessories so that people would notice them. I learned that a change of music could dramatically change the mood in a shop. I also learned that the way in which I approached people could have a huge effect on how much they bought that day and how often they would return. I learned how to create customer loyalty, and I learned that, actually, I was pretty darned good at this stuff!

It was a Jewish immigrant family with two sons who employed me. Paul was the eldest. In his late 20s, he was always impeccably dressed and had an air of superiority, though not in a bad way. He'd worked hard to get where he was and, in my book at least, he had every reason to be proud.

The younger Mark, was a completely different kettle of fish. Only a couple of years older than me, he was a devoted student of Jewish laws and tradition. While Saturday was the best day for the shops, Mark would refuse to work because it was the Sabbath. No matter what his brother said, he wouldn't budge. I worked in the same shop as Mark and was intrigued. Our conversations often revolved around religion and spirituality. He was also very protective of me – too protective at times – and our relationship soon became something that promised much more than friendship. Having said that, it never went beyond the platonic stage because of his religion. I became increasingly frustrated by his declarations of love for me, coupled with his inability to do anything about it. Like an ancient Greek tragedy, ours was a love affair that was condemned from the start.

'I love you, Melanie,' he would say, tears streaming down his face, 'but you are a gentile and I am a Jew. It can never work.'

So that was the way it was. But my time spent with the family had a huge impact on me, and to this day I remain grateful for their support and guidance at a time in my life when I most needed it. Early on, I learned of the family's struggles when they first came to this country – penniless and without understanding a single word of English – and their story inspired me. Paul, the eldest, had worked tirelessly to create a business that would provide for all of them.

'I've never ever seen anyone work so hard,' Mark would tell me, pride shining from his eyes as he remembered the times he would go to bed and Paul would still be poring over books and plans when he rose again the next morning. 'He exhausted himself just to make a safe and secure future for his younger brother. Now that is what I call love and devotion, and that is why, even when I don't agree with him, I will never argue.'

I have to say that wasn't strictly true, as I'd heard many a cross word between them in the shop when they thought I was out of earshot in the stock room. Furious and loud, these arguments would usually end with Paul storming out of the shop and speeding off in his Mercedes, the wheels spinning furiously as he accelerated away.

But nonetheless, I admired their tenacity and was motivated by their determination and subsequent success. I also empathised with the 'differences' they had to overcome, and I became a loyal employee, giving my heart and soul to help them with their business. I felt honoured that they trusted me so much, and they became more like family to me. I would regularly eat with them at their home, and gradually I opened up to them and let them know my own story. One day I confessed to them that they meant more to me than my own family who had deserted me in my times of need.

'Melanie, I don't understand how people can be so cruel, and I can't say that I know what you've been through,' said Paul, handing me another dish of the most delicious food he had prepared for the family, 'but I can say that you are very important to us and you'll always be welcome in our home. You are the best sales person we've ever had, and the business is more successful thanks to your efforts. We depend on you, and you can depend on us.'

I remember one Christmas, when my sister and all my 'real' family were at Nan's house for the traditional festive celebrations. I spent the day working in the stockroom of the men's shop with Mark – a bittersweet and deliciously heady experience, due to our impossible love for each other. We brought food and played loud music (Pink Floyd was an absolute favourite), while we got on with work and chatted about our different life experiences. It seems odd now, looking back, but that was one of the happier Christmases I can remember. With Mark and Paul I didn't have to fit in, pretend, or be a 'good girl'; no, instead I was working hard for people I greatly admired, while swapping stories about how to grasp opportunities and make them count. I was accepted and cared for and that felt good.

Back home that evening, my two cousins turned up with Abigail. My sister had wanted to see me, but Nan would have none of it. Jane, the older of the two cousins, had her own car, so they told Nan they were going to drive to the seafront for a walk along the promenade. It was brave of them to disobey the matriarch. I was the black sheep of the family, and nobody was even allowed to mention my name! To this day, I still don't understand what kind of hold Nan had over the rest of the family, and why they danced so freely to her bitter tune, but at least I got to see my sister and thank my cousins for sticking their necks out for me. When they left, however, I was once again left alone with my thoughts and my tears.

Yes, there were many dark times when I would suddenly be overwhelmed with depression. These episodes could last a few hours or a few days. But I would not let myself give in to them. Knowing that there was nobody who would take care of me if I fell, I just kept going as best I could. Some nights I would cry myself to sleep, sobbing for the loss of my parents and my family, and crying for the hurt I had endured. I felt confused and betrayed by the actions of those who were meant to look after me and afraid of the gaping hole inside me that refused to heal, like a crevasse of swirling darkness that whispered my name and beckoned me closer to the edge. I would not let myself be sucked in by something that might overwhelm me and never let me out again, so instead I fought against it. I fought against the pain, and I held on tight with every raw sinew. I stayed away from the edge of those deep, dark emotions and was determined that I would become even stronger.

It was tough. Sometimes I would dig my nails hard into my skin, scratching my arms and legs until they bled. *Why has this happened to me?* I'd wail, alone in my bed, knowing that nobody was there to listen. *Why doesn't anyone believe me? I'm doing the best I can for my little sister. Why can't they see that!* I'd sob, as my body shook with stifled howls. I could not, I would not, let myself crumble. Heaven knows, if I did I might not survive, and then who would look out for Abigail?

Each morning I would shake myself down, tell myself it was a new day and go to the mirror to paint on my face of determination and courage. I vowed that I would never be vulnerable, that I would never let anyone see my pain, convincing myself that if I hid it away long enough it would go away of its own accord.

My strategy served me very well – or so I thought at the time. What I hadn't understood then, was that I was also displaying classic signs of somebody who has lived through trauma and emotional abuse. Instead of realising that perhaps I needed help, I learned to turn on the automatic smile and positive energy at any moment – just as I'd seen Mum do. Was her positivity also a mask? Well, I suppose I'll never know for sure. What I do know, though, was that her example gave me the best tools to deal with my situation and get on with life.

I'm normal, and I'm happy. How can I help? was the impression I chose to emit, and it worked.

Working in the shop during the day and also holding down a job in a nightclub for extra money, I quickly accrued friends from all different walks of life. I mastered the chameleon-like qualities of somebody who can flex to fit in wherever they choose. I also became sexually promiscuous, picking up men in the various nightclubs I would frequent. I was teetotal at the time, having witnessed the damaging effects of alcohol at the nightclub. While my contemporaries were still at university, here I was living independently, supporting myself, fighting for my sister and beholden to nobody. So because of that, I believed I had an element of control. I was confident in my appearance and thought that by picking up any man I chose I was showing my power. I also told myself that by going back to their place (never inviting them to mine) I was keeping my distance. I had a strong desire to kick-back against my ex-guardian and prove to him that I could be exactly the person I wanted. But my actions only succeeded in hurting myself. I put myself in danger (I'm so strong nothing can harm me), walked freely into the dark and unknown (all the bad stuff's happened, nothing can touch me now) and consistently lowered my self-esteem (perhaps 'they' were right after all? Perhaps I am only a worthless orphan?) – it was a subconscious pattern of self-harm that would take years to heal completely.

I worked at the boutique for two years and was very sad to leave, but I knew it was time to move on. I'd become confident in my talent for selling, and the next three or four years found me working in a variety of sales and business roles – not least of which was a long stint running a cleaning company. I'd stumbled across the job when the slightly shifty marketing company I was working for at the time decided to put me forward to help the cleaning company improve their sales and marketing approach. Still only 21, I felt completely out of my depth, but I knew I'd been sold in as someone who was 'a natural sales person', so I gave it all I could.

To my complete surprise, I found that I could actually identify ways in which the company could expand. The enterprise was the 'baby' of an older man called Bert, who'd long held a dream to run his own cleaning business. A retirement payout had given him the opportunity to start a company at a time in life when most people would retire. He and I were like a couple of misfits – the old bloke with oodles of expertise within the cleaning industry, and the young woman who knew how to win people over. But both of us were equally determined to make a success of the opportunity that was there. Our combined skills meant that within a very short time the business was winning new clients. I would make contact, send letters and follow up with phone calls, introducing Bert as the expert who would then quote, staff and oversee the projects. Our combined tenacity meant the company grew quickly and very soon Bert offered me a directorship.

It was a brilliant time and gave me something I could throw myself into wholeheartedly. It was there that I learned the rudiments of business – the difference between turnover and profit and loss, as well as how to manage cash flow. I learned how to put a business case forward to the bank, as well as how to deal with the Inland Revenue and Customs and Excise. I learned how to negotiate deals, raise invoices, chase payments and, most importantly, how to work with a team of people so that jobs were completed and our customers were satisfied. I absolutely loved it. There was never a dull moment, and I grew in confidence as my skills increased.

Sure, there was still the shadow of the court case hanging over me, and I was still keeping a close watch on Abigail. But I was learning to get on with life and was determined to make a success of myself. I might not have been able to make a go of university, but I was darned sure that I would make a go of my life! And anyway, I was getting the hang of this whole running-a-business malarkey and was even beginning to imagine myself as a future business leader.

Unfortunately, that particular foray into the world of commerce ended in disaster. We'd been working on a particularly large and prestigious project when, through no fault of our own, the client defaulted on our invoices. It was heartbreaking, and I will never forget the desperate sinking feeling when I realised that the company I'd worked so hard on was about to go bankrupt. But there was nothing we could do. The customer was a huge organisation that was playing political games. We, as the small business, were the pawns, and the business folded as a result. Whilst it was a horrible time, it afforded me valuable lessons that would serve me well in future years.

Immediately after the collapse of the cleaning company, I secured a sales position with the Yellow Pages field sales team. It was the beginning of 1991, I was 26 years old, and this was my first experience of working with a large company.

'You are the crème de la crème!' the smartly turned-out auburn-haired trainer told us on our first day. 'Many people want to join, but we pick only the best. Some of you will not make it to the end of the course. Others among you will only last a short time in the field. It's a tough job, but for those of you who make it, the world is your oyster!' I tingled as I remembered my mother and father using those exact same words.

As well as closing the business, I had just come out of a very brief and ill-advised marriage to a man I had known from my teenage years in Sussex with Mum. A friend of John (the boy who'd been my friend at primary school), Adam was a kind, gentle and decent person, and I had married him for all the wrong reasons. We'd met when I was 15 and he 16, not long after Mum, Abigail and I had first moved into our dream cottage. We'd all hang out together every weekend and as many evenings as we were allowed, walking, talking, playing music, watching *Monty Python* and *Fawlty Towers*, and beginning our first furtive experiments with cigarettes and alcohol. Those were magical times as we blossomed into young adults, and I still recall them with great fondness.

Adam and his family were what you might call the perfect middle-class family unit. Sunday roasts, family get-togethers and traditional values, mixed together with a liberal sprinkling of intelligent banter and an affectionate bond between them, meant that I absolutely loved spending time with them all. They lived in a beautiful sprawling home that had an old barn at the top of the garden. It was here that John, Adam, myself and numerous friends would gather for loud parties and illicit cigarettes, while sipping from the stashes of alcohol snaffled from various unsuspecting parents. It was also here that Adam and his younger brother would hold their band practice sessions – enthusiastic twangs and thrums vibrating around the village as they imagined themselves becoming the next Black Sabbath or Led Zeppelin. It was a dream that didn't stand the test of time as parties and adventures with the opposite sex gradually took over as a priority!

For Adam, it seemed I was his chosen girl, right from that early age. He expressed his love for me just a matter of weeks after we met, but I didn't see him that way. I was extremely fond of him, but it was nothing more than that. He would regularly turn up at our house for tearful heart-to-heart chats with my mother, telling her how much he loved me and wanted to be with me. Mum knew that I wasn't really interested in anything more than friendship with Adam, so she'd sit him down and give him supportive and realistic advice.

'Come on, Adam, pull yourself together. I know you love her, but she's not going to be impressed seeing you in tears now, is she? I'll tell you what, why don't you sit here and smoke a cigarette while I make you a coffee. I'm sure you'll feel better!'

After Mum's death, I lost contact with Adam for a good few years. We met up again at a friend's 21st birthday party and started chatting as if we'd never been apart. We very quickly became more than friends. Adam, it seemed, had always held a torch for me, and I honestly thought I was finally ready to explore the connection in the hope of finding happiness. I knew Adam loved me – he always had – and he'd also known me when I was a normal happy teenager, before all the bad stuff happened. So that gave me an added element of safety and acceptance. But the truth of the matter was that I was so deeply damaged by that stage, I don't think anything was real for me any more.

I so wanted to recreate my idea of the 'perfect family' and to feel settled and loved, but my own emotions were still too scarred to let that happen. While I know he loved me with all his heart, I was nowhere near free from my self-destructive patterns of behaviour. I was restless, ambitious and pushy, and had no time for anyone or anything that was going to hold me back or get in my way. That kind and tender man was one of the 'things' I felt was holding me back. I mistook his gentleness for weakness and his understanding for laziness. I looked outside at the faults of others, rather than daring to go within myself and explore my own emotions. I was a fighter and a survivor, and I would not tolerate what I saw as a flaw or limitation. How could I? If I did, then I might just crumble myself. But of course I didn't understand that at the time.

'I can't go on with this!' I'd shouted after yet another of his failed attempts to find employment. I was running the cleaning company at the time and felt it was left to me to be the responsible grown-up for both of us. 'Don't you see you're dragging me down? I'm not prepared to support you when you do nothing to help yourself! You say you love me, but I just don't believe you any more!'

I demanded a divorce just a few months after we married. It's a decision I bitterly regret, because my actions caused immense pain to two innocent people who could have stood a good chance together. But with no family of my own to guide me, I wouldn't listen to anybody else and simply didn't realise that I was being my own worst enemy. I couldn't see that not only was I cutting my nose off to spite my face but also slashing another invisible gaping wound in my already damaged psyche. More wounds, more scars that would take me many years to acknowledge and finally heal.

Burying any feelings of loss or trauma, I threw myself in to my work at Yellow Pages. It seemed to offer everything I had ever dreamed of – a respectable job with responsibility, a great salary, a company car and a wonderful team of lively (if slightly madcap) colleagues. The training programme was second to none, and all of us believed we were the very best in the sales game. Many nights I didn't leave the office until past midnight. After a long day of face-to-face sales calls, we had to draw up the advertisements as well as plan for the following day. It was hard work, but I absolutely thrived in that environment. It was boisterous, sarcastic, energetic and competitive, but at the same time we all looked out for one another and I learned the magical feeling of being part of a team.

'What are you planning for tomorrow then, Mel?' teased Mark, one of the reps who was usually near the bottom of the league table. 'I'll bet they only sign because you show them your underwear. That's your trick, isn't it?'

Pens and other objects would fly across the room as fast and as furiously as the continuous banter and innuendo, but I loved it there.

I found that my fellow sales colleagues all shared a similar drive to me. I felt accepted and for the first time, part of something that was bigger than myself. I made a number of strong friendships (some of which have stood the test of time) and I excelled at my job, quickly entering the top tier of achievers in the division. I absolutely loved it and adored the fact that people seemed to like me for who I was.

I also fell in love. It was a doomed affair from the start, since he was not only a colleague but also married with children. I am not proud of my behaviour and it was the first and last time I will ever get involved with a married man, but the connection I felt with Brett was like nothing I had ever felt before. I couldn't help but light up in his company. We shared the same ridiculous sense of humour, the same drive, and the same indescribably irresistible attraction for each other. Our feelings were heightened because it was an affair that had to be kept hidden from view.

He came across as being a bit awkward – geeky in his sense of style, weird in his music tastes and with a tendency to blush furiously at the drop of a hat, something about which I would tease him relentlessly, searching for any possibly opportunity to make his cheeks redden during our team meetings. Brett was also neck and neck with me on the leader board. We'd tease, cajole and generally behave like naughty school kids, creasing up with laughter whilst revelling in what seemed at the time like daring and outrageous behaviour.

'Aw, Mel, stop it, I like it!' he'd screech, mincing around the office doing his best Dick Emery impression in front of our colleagues.

'But, darlings, it's all done in the best pawwwsible taste!' I'd reply, Kenny Everett's Cupid Stunt pose causing me to fall off my chair in giggles.

Not only did our budding romance have to stay secret from his poor trusting wife (oh, how I wish I could turn back the clock!) but also from our bosses, as any kind of relationship within the team was frowned upon. Despite all of this, we would spend every possible moment together, and for the first time in my life I was in love – hook, line and sinker.

For the first time, I understood how it felt to be adored, what it meant to share my body with somebody who loved me, how just a few chosen words, a sideways glance or a ridiculous joke could cause me to melt with happiness. Laughter was a hugely important ingredient to our relationship, and I don't think I've ever laughed as much as I did when I was in his company – real, proper belly laughs and guffaws, as we tried to out-do each other with our renditions of phrases from *Monty Python*, *The Goons* or Steve Wright's afternoon radio shows. I loved him and he loved me – and, like most mistresses, I suppose, I convinced myself that his wife obviously didn't know how to look after him properly.

The laughter turned to tears when the affair finished. He had told his wife he was leaving, but (to her credit), she fought hard to keep him, and she won. I was absolutely devastated. I thought my world had collapsed, and the physical and emotional pain was so excruciating that I doubted my ability to survive. For three weeks, I stayed off work, giving my boss a convincing but made-up excuse that I had family issues to deal with. I couldn't bear to be in the same room with Brett, knowing what we'd shared and knowing that I'd lost him forever. But I had to pull through. I had to get strong. I had to come back and prove more than ever that I was worth my position at Yellow Pages. This was the core of my self-talk, and I was resolute that I would come back better and stronger than ever before. Frowning into the huge framed mirror that hung in my bedroom, I fixed my stare and pulled myself up tall. 'Hey! Nobody puts Melanie in the corner!' I growled, pointing at my reflection, doing my very best Patrick Swayze impression while *Dirty Dancing* played in the background. 'I'm coming back, and you'd better be ready!'

So, on my return, I gave everything I had to my job. With three week's worth of sales targets to make up, I was determined that not only would I achieve them, I'd deliver the best results they'd ever seen. I worked longer hours than ever before, I crammed in more meetings during the days than I thought possible, and I designed better advertisements than ever before. I was on fire, turning my pain into a gritty determination that propelled me forward to achieve the impossible. By the end of that particular sales drive, I had not only accomplished all my own targets but I'd smashed my way to the top of the league table, securing a top sales prize for my efforts. The reward and recognition helped me to regain my self-esteem, and it also helped me to bury my grief and still broken heart even deeper within me.

I stayed with Yellow Pages for another six months or so. I was promoted to the top tier of sales people and continued seeing Brett on an on–off basis. I just couldn't help myself. I knew it was unhealthy, and I also knew that if I kept working with him I would never be able to break free. He, of course, was unwilling to leave Yellow Pages, so I handed in my notice and walked away from the job I had loved so much. To add insult to injury, after I left Brett was promoted to my position.

After Yellow Pages, I found myself once again floundering in a position of uncertainty. The immediate plan had been that I would go and work abroad for a while, but when that didn't work out I found myself out of a job and out of ideas. Another of my less-than-healthy decisions had backfired on me. It was one more example of my ability to shake things up and press the self-destruct button just when things were going well.

Mel, when will you ever learn! I scolded myself after another fruitless day searching for employment. *You let your heart rule your head and, as usual, you got yourself in a mess. He wasn't even worth it! You idiot!*

As usual, though, I managed to get myself back on track. I kept telling myself that I'd been there before, that I'd overcome much worse, and that in the grand scale of things I could find a way through. Bit by bit, I strengthened my walls and prepared myself for the next episode – and it worked. *Come on Mel, you can do this! You've done it all before, and this time you're going to do even better!*

By this time I was becoming an expert in survival and overcoming difficulties. I was 27 years old and had already learned how to come through a series of bad situations, in the process becoming increasingly confident in my abilities to pick up and carry on. 'I don't know what it is about you, Mel,' teased one of my friends over a bottle of wine. 'It doesn't matter how many times you fall in the shit, you always come up smelling of roses. I hate you!' We'd laughed at the time, but I must admit her comments stung a little. I felt that she was jealous and having a go at me for my ability to pick myself up, whereas inside I still ached and grieved for everything I'd lost. But deep down I knew she was right – quite simply, I refused to be beaten. Not by the past, not by the present and certainly not by the unknown future.

So, after a relatively short time, my emotions had once again subsided, my head was back in charge, and I was ready to walk forward. I brushed myself down, dusted myself off and determined to find something better.

7

I am a Mother

Relationships, to be brutally honest, continued to be a bit of a mystery to me. Don't get me wrong, I had plenty of male interest and was rarely on my own for any length of time. But with promiscuity by then a thing of the distant past, I had my sights set on finding a meaningful connection. I had a number of on–off relationships after Yellow Pages, one that even lasted a couple of years, but I just never seemed to find the right guy. It has to be said, that nobody else could really cut the mustard after my doomed experience with Brett. He had awakened such deep feelings of love, that I doubted I'd ever find the same again. In any case, if the affair had failed in the end, despite my passion and devotion, well, perhaps I'd subconsciously stopped really looking for Mr Right.

All that changed in a most peculiar and unexpected way during the summer of 1994. I was 29 years old, running another business and pretty happy with my lot. This time it was a marketing business and, whilst it had its ups and downs, in the main I thoroughly enjoyed my work. I had plenty of friends, lots of hobbies, was financially stable and generally in a good place. It was a hot summer that year, and an old friend I'd known from my teenage years had invited me to the yearly barbecue organised by his workplace.

'You'll love it, Mel!' he'd enthused. 'The guys I work with are all great fun, and, anyway, it's free food and booze. Go on, you know you want to – pretty please!' He giggled and punched my arm before kneeling on the floor and pretending to beg. Dan was a natural clown and always made me chuckle. People generally loved having him around, and I figured that an evening with other people like Dan could be just what I needed. So I agreed, even though it meant I would have to finish work early.

I was dressed sharply that evening. I'd had an important business meeting in the afternoon and headed straight over to the barbecue in my business clothes. Short black skirt, fitted top, high suede court shoes and large statement jewellery – I certainly noticed a few admiring glances as I walked into the pub!

Dan lost no time introducing me to his friends. They all worked together as car designers, and most of them had started on the beers long before they'd reached the pub. The laughter and joking was infectious – these people clearly enjoyed each other's company, and the banter was flowing thick and fast. Within no time at all I was having a whale of a time and was glad Dan had persuaded me to come.

One of his friends, Paul, seemed a little different from the others. He appeared more boyish, was clearly a bit younger and had the cheekiest big blue eyes that twinkled with mischief. He was wearing a striped T-shirt and sported a heavy mop of auburn hair that fell around his face. He was no less vocal with the jokes and general high jinks, but he seemed to choose his moments to talk, which made him come across as a little more reserved than the others. His sense of humour was just a little bit drier and quicker, and his words somehow held more weight. But when he laughed – well, he just dissolved in to hopeless hysterics, curling up while tears streamed down his face! It was really quite appealing, and, although he wasn't my type at all, I found myself quite fascinated by this unusual stranger.

Soon, he and I were exchanging fast-paced jokes, teasing each other and ribbing other people in the bar as well. He had this ability to take a subject and concoct some weird story, taking people along on his imaginary adventures. One particular episode included the fantastical adventures of a pack of Corduroy Jupiter Moon Puppies – an endangered species who could only eat clock springs. With the advent of digital clocks and watches, the springs were in short supply, so now these Corduroy Jupiter Moon Puppies were in the process of developing mechanical clocks that could reproduce.

Dan, of course, shared the same kind of off-the-wall humour, and between them both the story continued and became more and more ridiculous as the night went on and the beer continued flowing. Near the end of the evening, Paul said he had an important question for me. He looked very serious, so I sat down next to him and waited for him to speak.

'I'm staying with Dan tonight,' he said, twiddling his fingers and looking nervous, 'and I know that you're giving him a lift home.'

'Yes . . .' I nodded, puzzled about where he was going with this. My friend (and temporary flatmate) had kindly agreed to pick us up, dropping Dan and his mate Phil off on the way home. 'Go on . . .'

'Well, you see, I haven't got a lift. And I wondered whether your friend would mind fitting me in the car as well? It's just that the Moon Puppies are expecting me tonight and I can't possibly let them down!' And with that he exploded with a huge guffaw and dissolved into uncontrollable laughter. He had been serious about asking for a lift but couldn't help making a joke out of it, fully confident that I'd say yes. He was such a cheeky monkey that I couldn't help smiling (and giving him a thump on the leg for good measure) and agreeing to give him the lift.

'You'd better give me an update tomorrow about how you got on with the Puppies!' I teased him. 'A few words by fax would be fine.'

When the time came for our lift home, Paul scooted into the middle of the back seat and the others got in either side. Hysterical laughter and shouts of 'That's disgusting!' soon filled the air as the back doors flew open and Dan and Phil burst back out of the car. Paul was the only one who remained in the back seat, paralysed with laughter.

Dan was on the pavement and standing upright, theatrically wafting at his nose and rolling his eyes. 'Serves you bloody well right that you're stuck in there! That fart of yours could kill an elephant at 20 paces. It's positively radioactive!'

Muffled giggles continued from the back seat. 'Must've come from Jupiter,' squealed Paul, only just able to control his laughter long enough to get the words out before once again collapsing back into the fume-filled car.

So that's the story of how I met Paul, the man who was to become the father of my son. Not exactly the romantic encounter I'd had in my head, but, as I'd learned a long time ago, things rarely turned out as planned – well, at least in my case anyway!

The next day, as requested, Paul did indeed send me 'a few words by fax' – literally. He'd photocopied a random page from a textbook and sent it over with his signature. It was this typically off-the-wall humour and fresh approach to life that had me intrigued from the start.

I never intended anything serious to happen. When he asked for my number, I agreed, mainly because I found him so funny. He was four years younger than me and didn't seem as mature as many of the other people he worked with. But there was something about him that I found quite fascinating. His laughter, for a start. He made such a ridiculous noise when something amused him, and within seconds he would be doubled up, screeching as the tears ran down his cheeks. He wasn't as suave or polished as Brett had been, and his humour was completely off the wall, but here, for the first time in years, was somebody who could push my giggle-buttons at any opportunity. It wasn't always his jokes that had me laughing. It may sound cruel, but sometimes I found myself chuckling just at his generally gawky behaviour or his embarrassment when he did or said something silly. There was nothing contrived or pretentious about him, and for that reason more than anything else I thoroughly enjoyed his company.

He got on like a house on fire with my sister, which was an added bonus. Paul seemed to understand the close bond between us and also appreciated our dark humour when relating anything to do with our childhood or our peculiar family. He also didn't mind our relentless ribbing. He was good-natured enough to smile at our barbed jokes, often giving as good as he got – much more in many cases!

Even though our relationship started off based on laughter and mutual fascination (we both agreed that neither of us was the other person's usual 'choice' of partner), our bond grew stronger and as the year was coming to a close we realised that our emotions had grown far deeper than we'd planned. That came as a bit of a shock to both of us, and we called the relationship off there and then. Yep, feel a bit of love, get scared, run away – a thoroughly mature and well-reasoned approach to romance, as I'm sure you'll agree!

But we couldn't maintain it and were soon back together again, agreeing that we'd just take things easy and see where it went. Well, a couple of weeks later, our pathway was made clear. It was Tuesday, 10 January 1995, and I was sitting on the toilet in my office. Holding my breath and biting my lip, I waited anxiously for the result on the pregnancy testing stick.

A couple of days earlier, my friend Kate had asked what I thought to be a most peculiar question after I'd complained of sore breasts and feeling a bit queasy.

'When did you have your last period?' she'd said in a matter-of-fact way, head cocked to one side as she fixed me with her beady stare. 'Because I think you could be pregnant. You'd better go and get a test, young lady!'

Of course I didn't for one moment think there could be any truth in what she was suggesting. I couldn't remember when my last period was, but then again my periods had always been irregular. I would often skip a month or two (sometimes more – it was just the way my body worked), so that was perfectly normal for me. Added to which, Paul and I had taken precautions. No, Kate couldn't possibly be right . . . but her words had been enough to start a niggling feeling in the pit of my stomach.

While I waited for the result to show, everything slowed down as my thoughts raced and tumbled over one another. My senses were sharpened, but it was as though I was underwater and moving very slowly. I could hear the beating of my heart – deep, deliberate and sluggish, yet rhythmical at the same time. I imagined the blood pumping around my veins as I sat there, certain I could hear the whooshing sound with each new slow thrust from my heart. The sun was shining brightly through the large window behind the toilet and I could feel the warmth on my back as I watched the dust particles leisurely dancing in the sunlight. Blinking was slow, and swallowing became an effort as my mouth became drier and drier with each new passing thought.

Supposing I am pregnant? What will I do? I really hope I am, it would be wonderful! But what if I really am? I hope I'm not! Oh my God, how did I get here? What on earth is going to happen?

Questions, answers and more questions continued crashing around as the slow tick-tocking of my watch counted down to the final verdict. And then it was time . . . time for the truth. Holding my breath, I turned the stick around to look at the tiny oblong screen.

There was a clear blue line. I was pregnant. There was no doubt.

Paul was on his way back from visiting his parents in the Midlands. I reached him on his mobile just as he'd driven away from their house.

'Oh God!' was his response. 'Are you sure? Oh no! What are we going to do? I'll have to go back and tell my parents!'

It was hardly the response I'd hoped for, but then again, it must have come as a huge shock for him. At least I'd had a day or so since Kate had first mentioned it to consider the possibility.

From the very moment the test confirmed my pregnancy, I felt a huge warm smile from deep inside of me. A smile that, for most of the time, showed itself on my face as well. I couldn't keep my hand away from my tummy, and although I knew the road ahead was not going to be easy, I had an overwhelming sense of completeness and safety. Here, at last, was something – somebody – who I could love with all my heart and all my soul. Here was my chance of having a proper family. Of recreating the bond I had with my own parents and this time making sure it lasted longer than childhood. My baby and I were a team, and nothing and nobody would ever come between us.

I realise, writing this now, that it might all sound a little melodramatic, but that was exactly how I felt. After years of mistreatment and cold distance from people who were meant to love me, I was going to give everything to the little soul who was now growing inside me. At last I felt complete. At last I felt worthy. At last I felt love.

It turned out that I was already over two months pregnant. I knew from the first moment that I was carrying a boy, even before the scan confirmed my suspicions. Paul got used to the idea and for most of the time seemed totally made up by the idea. Whilst we were not exactly well suited, and certainly not what anyone could call 'parent material', Paul and I decided to deal with the situation like responsible adults. We were far from being love's young dream, and Paul was even less mature and worldly wise than I was, so in fairness it was a pretty hopeless quest from the start. But we gave it a go. For the sake of our baby, we were going to be grown ups and do everything we could to make it work.

My flat, a ground-floor seafront apartment that Adam and I had originally bought together, only had the one bedroom. Paul had had a house but had been forced to sell it at a loss some time earlier and was staying with friends. So we decided that I would rent out my flat and we would both take out a six-month lease on a house in preparation for the arrival of our baby boy. I must say, the house was absolutely beautiful, and we knew we had been very lucky to get it.

Light and sunny with a perfect little nursery and room for visitors to stay, it was ideally situated far enough away from the town to be quiet, but near enough for us to walk to the centre in under 20 minutes.

The pregnancy went well. There were no complications and I absolutely loved my growing body. For the first time since I could remember, I was happy with the way I looked. I couldn't be accused of being fat, nor could I criticise my shape. It may sound crazy, but I just relaxed into the swelling of my tummy because it was something that was beyond my control. Yes, I was huge (I put on nearly four stone over the pregnancy!) and I was also firm – rock solid in fact. I carried the baby at the front, so from behind I looked no different. But sideways on – goodness me, I was enormous! But I loved it. I walked tall and I felt proud. And I was, quite literally, glowing.

There were many times during my pregnancy when I thought of my mother and desperately wanted her to be with me. Funnily enough, I also thought a great deal about my guardians. Gilly had been pregnant when we moved in, and in some ways being pregnant myself helped me to make sense of how she might have been feeling. Gilly had been only 26 or 27 when Abby and I arrived, she already had a toddler in tow and was probably feeling more vulnerable than I was now, expecting my first child at 30. Hormonal changes and a swelling body had my emotions swinging wildly at times, so goodness knows how Gilly must have felt with two orphaned girls to look after as well as her own family and, as I now realised, a husband who could be cold and distant. Yes, it helped me to understand more pieces of my fractured past, and at the same time it made me cross, my over-exaggerated pregnancy emotions causing me to miss my own mother even more. Had she been here, I would have been able to talk all these things through with her, and I was certain that together we would have made sense of the situation. But, of course, how could I talk with her? If she'd still have been here then we never would have had to live with Gilly in the first place . . . and anyway, she was dead. So there was nothing more to be done. And while we're on the subject, how dare she die and leave us? Didn't she care about us at all? How could she just up and go like that? At the same time, could it ever be possible that I might heal from the enormous sense of loss I still felt, now on almost a daily basis?

I know, there was no sense to it, but those were the kind of random conversations that went on in my head while my baby grew inside me. I found I would swing between enormous highs and lows, occasionally reaching moments of incredible clarity and peace and then conversely moments where I felt so confused I could hardly remember my name. But despite all that, my lasting memories of my pregnancy overall are those of happiness and contentment. My Cheshire-cat smile continued to grow, and I knew that whatever happened I was doing exactly the right thing.

The birth itself was another matter altogether. Although my son was born on exactly the day predicted by the doctors, his arrival was far from picture perfect. Abigail and her boyfriend came with me to the hospital, along with Paul of course. My sister became the grown-up during the process, while Paul just took huge delight in experimenting with my gas and air. He also seemed to need more soothing and reassurances than I did!

'This is just awful!' he wailed, pulling at his hair and looking worried. 'The worst day of my life!'

'Oh shut up, Paul, and pull yourself together!' admonished Abigail 'It's not exactly a walk in the park for Mel either you know! Now, breathe some more gas and air and then go out and stretch your legs. And behave like a grown-up, for goodness' sake!'

After struggling for hours, the baby's heart rate dropped perilously low and I was wheeled in for an emergency Caesarean. Actually, 'wheeled in' is perhaps not the right description, it was more like crash, bang and slam into the operating theatre! Terrified about what was happening, and totally out of control, all I could do was shut my eyes and pray. Pray that my son would be OK and that this would be over quickly.

It was, and he was – thank God. It was Sunday, 3 September 1995, just before 10 p.m. when my perfect son was handed to me, wrapped in a white towel. Dark, beady, questioning eyes stared out from a perfectly formed face framed with auburn curls and what I took to be a serene smile on his tiny little lips. Astonishing really, considering the trauma he'd just been through to get here! I held him while the medical team did whatever they needed to do behind the green screen that was masking me from my nether regions. I can say with all sincerity that I have never in my life felt such an all-encompassing envelopment of overwhelming love. It was indescribable. Honestly, if this was a Disney film, that would be the moment when the heavens opened and angels started singing! And the pain, fear and panic of the previous few hours literally melted away as I held my baby boy in my arms.

'Hello, you!' I whispered, finding his little hand and stroking his face. 'We made it, my brave boy! We made it. Welcome to the world! I have so been looking forward to meeting you. I'm going to take care of you and love you forever. You're beautiful and I love you with all my heart and all my soul!'

He and I spent nearly a week in hospital together. The birth had taken its toll on my body, and I had stitches everywhere. On the third day I felt dizzy and weak as I walked to the toilets. The nurses came to find out what was happening and discovered I was so weak that I needed a blood transfusion. At first I refused the idea – I'd read about people developing diseases from contaminated blood – and asked for an alternative.

'It's up to you,' said a kindly but no-nonsense nurse, 'but you lost far too much blood during the birth. Quite frankly, you shouldn't even be able to walk around, young lady! You're clearly a fighter. But if you don't take this blood, then the option is six months plus on strong iron tablets, with you feeling weak and dizzy until they take effect. I wouldn't recommend that to anyone, let alone a new mother! Trust me, you're going to need all your strength!'

So, after more questions, I finally agreed to the blood transfusion. And a couple of days later I went home with my son, Dylan Joseph Carnegie.

I adored my new role of motherhood – absolutely loved it! I have never felt so completely and utterly in love! Never felt so proud! So special! So content! So complete! Nothing else mattered any more – none of the past and none of the present worries.

Paul and I did our best, but it became clear fairly early on that our relationship was unlikely to work in the long-term – certainly not in the romantic way I had imagined. It wasn't going to be the ideal fairy-story ending I'd always hoped for, but it didn't matter. Whatever happened I had my son, and that was better than any knight in shining armour!

We both tried hard, don't get me wrong. Both of us adored Dylan, and we still enjoyed plenty of laughter and jokes together. But somehow our relationship just never developed a solid foundation and our differences continued to highlight the gaps, no matter how hard we tried as a couple.

After a short spell living in Spain (Paul secured a contract there, so the three of us went as a family, but the work fell through after just a couple of months), we all moved to London. We rented a house in Islington, north London, just around the corner from where my sister shared a house with a group of friends. Perfect! Abby and I were once again within spitting distance of each other! Paul took another contracting job abroad, and I found work in an advertising agency in south London. Dylan went to a preschool nursery and we had an au-pair living with us to cover the gaps when I was working. It should have worked out, and for a while I began to believe that perhaps we could make it after all. Abby was close by, so we saw each other nearly every day. Dylan was thriving at the nursery. I was happy in my job, and it was great to see Paul every few weeks when he'd come home. As I say, perhaps it wasn't ideal, but it was far from being a catastrophe. We just all muddled in and made it work!

But that Christmas, three months after we'd moved to London and with Dylan just fifteen months old, Paul announced that it was over and that he was leaving me for somebody he'd met in Sweden.

It may sound silly, because in hindsight the signs were all there, but I was shocked and absolutely heartbroken. I remember sitting in the bath the day he left, sobbing my heart out and wondering how on earth I was going to pick myself up this time. I was a single mother. Another statistic. I had once again failed to hold onto something that could be considered as 'normal' in the way of a family life. Worse, had I just created a broken future for Dylan, paving the way for him to have as dysfunctional a childhood as I had endured? Had I failed to protect the one thing that was more precious to me than life itself?

The questions taunted me, and once again in private moments I found myself sinking into the depths of despair. Where had I gone wrong? What could I have done differently? Could I have shown Paul more love and he would have stayed with me? Was I always destined to face troubles and disruption? But I refused to let the darkness take over. I couldn't. Previously, I had fought for Abigail. This time I knew I had to be even stronger – not just for me but for my son who depended on me.

So, drawing on all the skills I'd learned over the years, I slowly picked myself back up. At first the smile and confident walk were fake – they were just tools that I instinctively knew would help me to pull through. It was tough and I felt very alone, but my determination kept me pushing forward to do something about my situation and to take positive control. I may have been fighting for Dylan, but in the strangest way it was as though my small son was fighting for me. Because, just as Abby had been when we were both children, Dylan was now my reason to keep going. More than that, he was my reason to prove that I could make it, to prove my guardians and my family wrong. To prove that I was not a bad or worthless person. To prove that I was someone who could overcome and eventually shine out. *That'll show them!* I'd say to myself in the mirror, straightening my business suit and putting on my lip-gloss. That may have been my mantra, but the truth was I didn't want to 'show' anyone that what I actually wanted was acceptance and love.

One Saturday afternoon, a short while after Paul had left, I was browsing in a bookshop on Islington Green when a book fell off the shelf and landed at my feet. I remember thinking that it was a bit weird, but I picked it up and put it back. Straight away it fell back down again. So this time I picked it up and took a proper look at it – *You Can Heal Your Life* by Louise L. Hay.

Ever since childhood I've believed in the power of positive thinking (or constructive thinking as Mum's friend and guru Maisy would say) and I read many of the classics during my time at the flat in Preston Road. They helped me to find focus and hope, when everything around me was either falling to pieces, or seemingly attacking me. I also spent many years keeping a daily diary to help me make sense of things.

Whilst by that time I was no longer a regular writer, I would still occasionally scribble my thoughts down in a notebook and after Paul's departure I had taken to writing again. I had started asking myself how I could escape from the pain – not only of his leaving, but also the old pain that his actions seemed to be bringing up again: betrayal, abandonment, fear, isolation – so many of the old emotions left over from my childhood.

The book I now held in my hands promised to help me do just that. I had never heard of Louise Hay, but a quick skim of the back cover and a couple of pages inside explained 'If we are willing to do the mental work, almost anything can be healed' and promised that if we are willing to explore our thinking, we can improve the quality of our life – in some cases beyond recognition. I remember feeling the tiniest jolt of excitement in my tummy.

One of the first self-help books I ever read was *The Power of Positive Thinking* by Norman Vincent Peale, so I was familiar with the concept that our thoughts create our reality. I had never before, however, thought of myself as 'sick' or 'broken', so hadn't considered the idea that I could 'heal'. But reading more of Louise's words, I felt as if she was talking directly to me. The jolt happened again, so I bought the book.

That evening, after Dylan was settled, I curled up on the sofa and began reading. I didn't stop until the early hours. Louise's words – and her own story – reached deep inside me, soothing me and bringing me to tears at the same time. Such wisdom. Such straightforward solutions. Such easy-to-follow instructions. The next day I felt lighter and brighter than I had in months, and I knew I was on the right track.

Just a few weeks after buying the book, I happened to notice a tiny advertisement at the back of a copy of *The Big Issue*. I rarely bought that magazine, but for some reason I had willingly overpaid the vendor who was always outside Sainsbury's for a copy. At the back of the publication, the tiny advertisement, no bigger than a postage stamp, said, quite simply: 'You Can Heal Your Life – Louise Hay. Become a qualified trainer now!'

I picked up the telephone, asked questions and booked myself straight onto the course. It was a week-long residential course scheduled for the end of June and cost a good chunk of money. But it didn't matter; I just knew I had to be there. It turned out to be one of the most major life-changing events of my entire life, but I didn't realise that at the time of booking, of course! I just knew that I had to be there, strange as it may seem, and not for the first time in my life, I followed my instincts without question.

The training event quite literally blew my mind. It was intensive, emotional, healing, hard-hitting, enlightening, enlivening and rejuvenating. You may remember the famous 1970s Pepsi advert? Well, 'Lip smacking, thirst quenching, ace tasting, motivating, good buzzing, cool talking, high walking, fast living, ever giving, cool fizzing . . . You CAN Heal Your Life!' is a pretty apt description of how I felt about that course!

I left with a certificate confirming that I was competent to run weekend training workshops, sharing Louise's techniques with other people. Helping them, like me and all the other delegates who had shared the intensive teacher-training experience, to free themselves from boundaries, change their beliefs and create a life where they could be happy, whole and complete. Well, if it had worked so well for me, then I simply had to share theses techniques with others!

On my return, despite the fact that I'd spent much of the training in tears, along with most of the other delegates, people commented on how good I looked.

'I knew you were away, but I thought it was just a course. Have you been on holiday?' asked a work colleague.

'You look amazing!' beamed Abigail as soon as she saw me. 'Young, happy, alive and fizzy!' (I told you the Pepsi advert was relevant!)

She was right. I was alive. And for the first time I knew what I had to do. It may have seemed reckless to many, but my instincts were so strong that I just had to follow them. So the next day back at work I gave in my notice. My bewildered boss thought I'd lost my mind.

'I'm going off to heal the world,' I announced dramatically when he pushed me further about my plans. 'I've learned so much, and I know I can help people. I'm sorry, but it's my calling,' I continued, giggling as he shook his head and scratched his eyebrows.

'Well, I just don't get it, Mel,' he sighed. 'You must be crazy throwing this away! And when it doesn't work out, well, you can always come back here. I wish you well, but I honestly think you've lost the plot!'

He wasn't the only one. I was told some time later that a few people decided I must have been taken in by some strange cult. They imagined that I'd been brainwashed and were worried that I'd be led astray into goodness knows what sort of danger. Looking back, I can understand and appreciate their fears. It must have been strange. But I had never felt so sure about anything in my life. I knew this was where I was meant to be, and I was absolutely determined to follow my dreams.

After Paul left, I'd already decided to move back to Eastbourne and had secured a flat just up from the seafront. I moved in with two other equally inspired people I'd met on the training course, both as keen as I was to work in this exciting new field and make a difference to the world. So, yes, as I said, I can understand that my friends would have been a bit concerned!

But it worked. We set up a business and started running weekend workshops, and we also threw ourselves into further development training, including NLP, Reiki, Advanced Louise Hay Development, hypnotherapy and so much more. I devoured every book and CD I could find on healing and spiritual development, and I began to fine-tune my skills working with people, both through the workshops and by developing a one-to-one practice.

Dylan was at nursery during the days and because I was mainly working from home, it meant he and I had much more time together than we did in London. We also enjoyed a lot more fresh air and walks. In London, he had regularly suffered from coughs and colds, with the doctor at one point telling me he thought my son was asthmatic. I knew it wasn't true, and now we were back down in Sussex by the sea he was thriving. We both were.

In addition to the nursery, I had also kept up with always having an au pair living in the house with us. Our first au pair, Pilar, had been such a wonderful addition to the family that I determined I would always have an au pair while Dylan was small. With no family support, it was the perfect solution, and over the years we had some absolutely amazing young people living with us and sharing our lives. For me, it gave me a huge amount of security. I could carry on with my self-development and teaching studies (and build a solid future for myself and Dylan), and because much of the day-to-day housework chores were covered by the au pair it meant that every moment I had with my son was joyful and stress free. I always paid them over the odds and made sure they had as much time off as possible, with the understanding that there would be times when I would need them to put in extra hours if I had to work or study away. It was a great example of give and take, and the arrangement worked brilliantly for everyone concerned.

Happy and fulfilled, I knew I was finally in the right place.

8

Meeting My Soulmate

Saturday, 1 August 1998 is a date that will forever stay in my memory. It was a beautiful summer's day, the sun was shining and everyone seemed to have smiles on their faces, even at the crowded motorway services at Redhill where I had arranged to meet my friend Jack.

Jack and I had met a year earlier on a month-long NLP practitioner training programme. We had bonded during one of the exercises and since then had become firm friends. By this time I was working as a Louise Hay trainer, running workshops around the country based on her bestselling self-help book *You Can Heal Your Life*. Dylan and I had a wonderful Czechoslovakian au pair called Petra living with us at the time. She was a hugely important part of the family and ended up living with us for nearly two years – an unusually long time for a family–au pair relationship. We loved her and she loved us. Dylan was happy, Petra was happy, and I was happy too. For the first time in my life I felt that I was 'normal' and fulfilled, and well on the way to providing a stable future for my son.

I loved my work and was constantly on the lookout for more courses that would help me to improve my skills as a coach and workshop leader. I had attended a Mind, Body and Soul exhibition a few months earlier and had been blown away by a workshop demonstration given by a man named John Shango. Introducing himself as a firewalk instructor, he had gone on to explain the theory behind this fascinating process. He explained that the exhibition venue did not lend itself to demonstrating the process, so instead he said he would show us another skill that would prove the same theory of mind over matter. With that, he wheeled out a huge crate of broken glass bottles, took off his shoes and socks, and ignoring the gasps from the audience, he calmly walked across the jagged pieces of broken glass. I had never seen anything like it in my life, and I stayed behind to ask him some questions. I liked what he had to say, and when he told me that he was going to run a firewalking instructors training programme later that year, I knew that I had to attend. My Louise Hay and NLP training both focused on the power of the mind, but here was something that would actually allow me to bring practical elements of proof into my workshops.

Sure enough, the invitation came through a few weeks later, and I shared the information with Jack. Like me, he also worked in the field of training, but whereas I was working with individuals, he worked in the corporate world, running motivational sessions for business leaders and their teams. He was fascinated by the idea of firewalking and immediately asked me to book a place for himself and also for Campbell, his business partner.

That was how Jack and I we found ourselves driving towards Gloucester on the first day of August. The course was to be a week-long residential programme at a remote farm, with over twenty delegates all camping in one of the fields. I was both excited and apprehensive about the prospect, not only because I knew I would have to face my fears in order to walk over burning hot coals but also because I wasn't too keen on the idea of spending a week in a tent!

'I hope there are some good showers there, and since it's all going to be vegetarian food I also hope the toilets are up to scratch!'

I'd joked as we sped east along the M40, leaving London and the luxury of a proper bed behind us.

'Well,' Jack smiled, 'if it gets too bad, I'm sure we can find a local hotel, and there must be places we can buy proper food if we get fed up with beans and tofu!'

It was nearing 1 p.m. by the time we pulled up at a garage for a final stock-up on fuel – both for the car and for ourselves. I had brought a large family tent with me, and Jack had his one-man tent. Campbell was going to meet us just outside Gloucester, as he was driving down from Newcastle, and we decided that between the three of us we'd work out the most appropriate sleeping arrangements.

'Cam says he hopes there's not too much hippy-shit on the course or he'll leave. He just wants to be able to make money out of running firewalking courses,' said Jack as he keyed Cam's number into his car phone. 'He's a great businessman and the most amazing trainer, but he doesn't do the touchy-feely stuff very well. I'm sure you'll like him, though. He's great fun!' he added as the ringing tone flooded out of the speakers.

'Jack, my friend, how the devil are you and where are you now? I'm parked just outside a pub not far from the farm.' The car was filled with the most delicious-sounding voice I had ever heard. Campbell spoke with a gentle Scottish lilt and the warm chocolaty kind of tones you expect to hear on adverts for luxury food products – inviting and extremely seductive. I was instantly interested in listening more intently to his words. I introduced myself and jokingly said that with a voice like that I hoped he would be happy to read us some bedtime stories if we couldn't sleep. He chuckled and said we could discuss that when we met.

A few minutes later, we pulled up in the pub car park. Campbell had a maroon-coloured sports car. The driver's door was open and I could hear music coming from inside the car. When he saw us, he curled himself out of the car and came towards us with the widest grin and sparkliest eyes I had ever seen. Good lord, this was a handsome man! Tall and broad shouldered with an athletic body effortlessly dressed in a navy-and-red-striped Ralph Lauren rugby shirt and jeans, he sauntered towards the car, casually pushing his fingers through his thick shoulder-length hair as he got closer.

'Crikey Jack, you never warned me he was so gorgeous!' I managed to say just before Cam reached the car. Jack just grinned and warned me to behave, before bounding out to greet his friend. They chatted for a few moments before Cam came over and peered in at me through the sunroof. He beamed and nodded his head as he offered me his hand.

'Hi, I'm Cam,' he grinned. 'You must be Mel. Great to meet you at last. I've heard so much about you!' Those warm and inviting tones flooded my senses once more as I reached out to take his hand.

'I've heard a lot about you too, but you're not at all how I imagined,' I replied, noting a jolt of energy as our hands touched for the first time. Our eyes locked and I tilted my head in question and surprise. He did exactly the same.

'Hmm, this is going to be interesting,' he smiled, holding my hand a little longer than necessary, fixing me with an amused gaze until I looked away, embarrassed by the connection.

Jack seemed oblivious to this exchange, and we started up again and drove on towards the field that was to be our home for the next seven days. Cam was following us, and, although it may sound silly, I could feel him smiling at me from the car behind. Somewhat uncomfortable, I replayed what had just happened.

Don't be silly, I told myself. *And be careful. I'll bet lots of women throw themselves at Cam, so keep your guard up and stay cool.*

When we reached the farm, I got out of Jack's car to open the gate, so that both cars could go through. As I was undoing the lock, I had the sensation that I was being stared at. I could sense Cam's eyes boring into the back of my head, but I resisted the temptation to turn around. As his car passed through the gate, I dared myself to look at him. I was met with the hugest grin and a wink as he went past, and I felt the heat rising in my cheeks. Yes, I felt flattered, but I also reminded myself that he probably behaved that way with everyone he met.

'Don't be a wally, Mel,' I muttered under my breath, 'this is just a game. Stay calm, keep cool,' before climbing back into Jack's car and focusing on the fields ahead.

A few minutes later, we reached the campsite. There was a huge, green canvas, military-style mess tent in the middle of the field, a row of portable toilets and showers a short distance away, and a multitude of smaller tents, campervans and colourful people scattered around the edges of the field. We settled for a clear spot that was well-placed between the mess tent and the toilets, and began to unpack our tents and belongings.

'Bloody hell,' Cam teased, a cheeky twinkle in his eyes. 'This is looking like a hippy commune! It had better all be worthwhile. What do you think, Mel, can we make it?' he nudged my arm and flashed the biggest smile, and I couldn't help laughing.

The three of us soon relaxed into a playful pattern of teamwork and banter as we struggled to pitch the tent. Jokes soon started up about who was going to sleep where. First of all we talked about everyone sleeping in the family tent – Cam and Jack in the larger compartment and me in the other. Cam protested that he was no good at keeping tidy and said that he and I would both need to be inside the tent if he was to fulfil his role of reading bedtime stories. Jack could pitch his own tent just opposite so that we could all still chat. It was all a big joke, of course, but I couldn't help but feel a tinge of excitement, enjoying Cam's attention and wicked sense of humour. This was fun, and I was curious.

Since the sleeping banter drew no conclusions, we decided that we'd pitch both tents and sort it out that evening. Cam sidled up to me. 'I always get my way, you know,' he winked. 'You watch, Jack will sleep in the small tent . . .'

Later on that afternoon, the course began with just over 20 of us sitting around in a circle of white plastic garden chairs. There were all kinds of different people there – men and women, old and young, colourful and plain. We must have made quite a motley crew! Most of us had started to get to know one another while setting up our tents and getting acclimatised to our surroundings. Some were nervous, some were excited – all of us were curious. One particularly tall fellow in his early 30s walked around bare-chested with a streaming mane of sun-bleached hair and had announced himself as a healer who travelled the world and had already walked on fire many times. He had brought his own mini campervan and wore a uniform of multi-coloured Bermuda shorts, leather flip-flops and countless leather threaded necklaces. He went by the name of Skye, and Cam and Jack had already labelled him a Dippy Hippy.

'I'll bet he hasn't really done it before,' they'd giggled conspiratorially earlier in the afternoon. 'Anyway, we have, so we'll show him this evening!'

I reckon I must have been one of the more nervous people in the group, but I was determined not to let it show. Pulling on my skills as a workshop leader, I gave my introduction to the group. Explaining my profession as a Louise Hay trainer, I added that I'd hoped I could introduce some aspects of the firewalking theory to my workshops to help more people heal their lives. To my surprise, I was met by a small round of applause and a large 'whoop' and a wink from Cam, who was sitting across from me. Slightly embarrassed, I sat back down again and listened with interest as others made their introductions.

There were various different reasons for why people were here and how they'd heard about the programme, but most people already seemed to be working in the field of personal development. The two who stood out as being much more professional, however, were Jack and Cam. They stated quite clearly that the corporate world was filled with people who were ambitious but who didn't know how to fulfil their potential. Cam, in particular, shared his dream to run a worldwide training company that would encourage leaders to achieve their goals and motivate their teams.

'Firewalking is something I would like to bring to many more people,' he announced, passion and determination etched across his face as he held his audience with confidence. 'I already know I'm a pretty good trainer, and by becoming a firewalking instructor together with my good friend Jack here, I'd like to change the world for the better. Here's to the next level!'

Wow – I was impressed. Not only was he good looking, funny and successful, with the most amazing voice I'd ever heard, this man also cared about people in a similar way to me. I began to look at him in a different light and my curiosity grew.

After the introductions, we were invited to find a partner to start working on some preparations for our first firewalk together. There was no hesitation in his eyes as Cam marched towards me with his arms wide open.

'There's no other choice for me,' he smiled. 'Would you do me the honour of partnering me? And later on, can I talk to you about something? I am feeling the most incredible connection with you. It's peculiar, a bit frightening, and to be honest I've never experienced anything like it before. I'm just wondering whether you've sensed anything similar?'

By now he was holding me in a friendly hug. He was much taller than me, and looked down with an expression of hope and expectation in his eyes. All I could do was to return his hug and respond with a silent nod – there was nothing I could say. He squeezed me a little tighter and whispered a quick 'Thank you' before pulling away and getting two chairs for us. He offered me the first chair, insisting I sat down before he settled into his.

'Are you OK? Can I get you anything else – a drink of water perhaps?' he'd asked, his caring eyes looking at me intently for my response. I shook my head with a smile, somewhat taken aback by his good manners and thoughtful gestures. *Yes, this is indeed going to be interesting,* I thought to myself.

The afternoon quickly melted into the evening, and we started the full-on firewalk workshop. A couple of hours earlier, we had worked in a chain gang to build a heap of dried wood into a bonfire. It had been burning since then, the flames roaring against the darkening skies as we gathered around in a circle, careful to stay away from the immense heat and the choking smoke. I was terrified!

First of all we were all encouraged to talk about our fears – not only for the impending firewalk but also in our day-to-day life. John Shango, our intrepid course leader, told us that our limitations are usually self-imposed fears. Fears that are not real and are based purely on negative thinking. He asked us how much longer we were going to allow ourselves to be held back by our own thoughts, and to demonstrate his point he showed us the acronym False Evidence Appearing Real – instantly met by Jack's quickly whispered response 'or Fuck Everything And Run more like!', which made me giggle out loud.

John did a really good job of heightening my worries by pointing out that the fire was burning at around 1,200 degrees – a temperature that melts metal. He reminded us that there was no fire brigade or St John Ambulance on the site and that the choice we were going to make in a short while – to walk or not – would be entirely of our own free will. Only if we were really ready and committed to the walk could we achieve a safe passage across.

We carried on with exercises designed to tap into our feelings of power and certainty, much of it based largely on NLP processes with which I was already familiar. The difference was that all of these exercises, all of these discussions, were done with a much higher level of energy and enthusiasm. The idea was to get us into a state of absolute confidence and certainty. Whatever we did, though, I couldn't help but look at the roaring fire with fear. The crackling sounds seemed deafening, and the mixture of white, blue and orange flames appeared to offer the promise of burning and pain. I severely doubted that I would be able to do the walk and was somewhat comforted to observe the same look of confusion and fear on the faces of many of my fellow delegates.

But we carried on regardless, each time lifting our belief that

95

the fire was a friend and that if we put our minds to it we could achieve anything we wanted. The fear dramatically intensified when John announced it was time to rake out the fire. By that time the flames had subsided, but the extreme heat was just as unforgiving. He invited us all to remove our shoes and socks – whether or not we intended to walk the coals – and to each take turns in patting down the smouldering embers so they would make a comfy pathway.

Comfy! I screamed in my head. *Comfy! Are you having a laugh! This is sheer madness!* But I still took my turn first with the spade and then the rake, the heat from the fire pit burning the hairs on my arms as I pulled and pushed the coals into what could possibly be described as a level surface. The bigger bits of wood were pulled out and put to the side of the fire, and once everybody had done their bit and confirmed they were happy with the way the coals were arranged John announced that the time had arrived to face our fears and walk the fire!

I don't actually remember what I did at that time. I do remember the feeling of my stomach sinking, my heart in my mouth and my soul shooting out from the top of my head. I became an observer, hovering above the group too scared to move but also too curious to back out. This really was my opportunity to prove myself, to walk the talk and face my terrors, but I still didn't know whether or not I was going to be able to do it.

John walked first. Four or five confident, strong, calm steps towards the coals followed by seven equally measured steps on the fire before exiting the other side, letting out the most enormous whoop and receiving a huge cheer and round of applause from the group. He'd done it! I'd seen it with my own eyes! This man had actually walked across the same coals that had just burned the hairs from my arms! It was an incredible moment for me, and I found myself back in the group, eager to watch as everyone now prepared themselves to do the same.

Jack was quick off the mark. Both he and Cam had experienced a firewalk of a different sort, with the motivational speaker and trainer Anthony Robbins, a larger-than-life and hugely successful American, who focuses on positive thinking and 'Awakening the Giant Within'. Jack and Cam had recently attended one of his annual three-day workshop conferences in London, together with thousands of other fans. The first evening included a firewalk – ten pre-prepared lanes of smouldering coals in the venue grounds. Mr Robbins' method for getting people across is to use the mantra 'cool moss' as they march across the pits. John Shango's methods were totally different – inviting us to bond with the fire and take responsibility for our thoughts.

Jack decided he would add the 'cool moss' mantra and other techniques he'd already learned at the motivational conference to the tools we'd been learning that night. He walked across with a serene confidence I had never before seen in him. I was bursting with pride for my dear friend, clapping and cheering as he came off the other end, before running up to give him a huge hug. He was literally vibrating!

'Wow!' he said, his eyes blazing and his heart beating so loudly I could feel it against my own chest. 'That was different! No, that was AMAZING! What a rush! Mel, you've GOT to do this!' he enthused, beaming with energy and jumping on the spot.

But I wasn't ready yet. I was still keen to gather more evidence, more proof that it was possible, and, despite John's best intentions, I was still battling with a quiet, but determined, inner voice that was warning me this couldn't be possible. I remember shivering, but not because I was cold. The fire was still giving out an enormous amount of heat, but I was feeling lost and scared. *What if I can't do this? Suppose I start and I want to get off in the middle? What if I burn and end up in hospital? Suppose I'm the only one who chickens out of this?* Yes, to quote John's earlier advice, my inner critic was doing a really good job on me at that point, and I knew I was stuck.

All of a sudden I felt someone behind me and heard Cam's reassuring voice gently cutting through my thoughts. 'It's OK. I know what you're going through. Here, I thought you might like this,' and he gently wrapped his jacket around my shoulders, giving me a reassuring hug as he arranged the coat around my body. I remember turning to face him, deeply touched by his kindness and consideration. I don't think I said anything, but I know I had tears in my eyes. I was so grateful that he'd come to look after me. He'd deliberately come to help me. And at that moment I knew I was going to successfully walk the fire.

'Here,' he smiled, giving my shoulders a squeeze. 'I'm going to walk now. Watch what I do, and concentrate on what you're feeling, as you imagine that I am carrying you across with me. When I've done it, you're going to do it for yourself, and I'm going to walk alongside the fire on the grass next to you. I'll go at the same pace as you. I'll take your lead, but I will be walking every step with you. You're safe. It's OK, I'm here.' And with that he raised himself to full height, put his shoulders back, gave himself a shake and then purposefully strode towards the fire.

It was true. I could really imagine that he was carrying me. I believed that he was helping me, and when he came off I knew I was ready. He'd whooped and cheered like everyone else, but his eyes were on me. He came and stood next to me, away from the fire, as I walked towards the coals. 'I'm with you,' he nodded. 'It's OK. You can do this.'

And I walked.

That experience was one of the most mind-blowingly amazing feelings I have ever had in my entire life! As I walked safely off the other end of the fire pit, my eyes were wide as saucers and my smile would have put the Cheshire cat to shame. My entire body was vibrating with excitement, joy, shock and wonder, and I punched the air, jumped around and gave the loudest, biggest, happiest scream I could possibly muster before speeding off into the darkness of the field. Excuse the pun, but I was quite literally 'on fire'. I'd done it! I'd jolly well achieved the impossible! It was an electric experience and I knew this was a life-changing moment for me. I wasn't aware of anybody else, as I carried on jumping, running and whooping around the field, tears of joy by now streaming down my face. It was only as I came back to the fire, that I noticed the huge cheers coming from the group. They had seen my fears, and they were ecstatic for my achievement.

I do remember one face standing out from the crowd. It was Cam. He was looking at me with what I can only describe as pure love and pride, the smile on his face saying it all as he gave me a huge thumbs-up.

Of course, I had known in advance that this training programme was bound to challenge me, but let me assure you I had never in my wildest dreams expected anything like this, and on the first night for goodness' sake! I felt as though I was the luckiest person in the world, and I knew that my life was about to change for the better.

9
Of Love and Miracles

That night, we all spent a good couple of hours discussing what the day and the evening had meant for us. We had all grouped our garden chairs around the pit and re-built the bonfire to keep us warm. It was a warm night and the skies were clear, and it turned into a truly magical evening, that I will remember for the rest of my life. Each of us was buzzing from the firewalk. We were bonding as a group and the excitement was intense, though the atmosphere, at the same time, was relaxed. As we shared our personal experiences, the energy and bonding intensified within the group. Drinks were flowing, as was an enormously long joint that one of the group had made. Easily reaching two feet in length, it was passed around to anyone who wanted to partake. It certainly helped encourage relaxation, and, even for those of us who chose not to smoke, the very fact of passing it around, only added to the enchantment of the surroundings.

Cam sat next to me the entire time. He would continue to bring me drinks (making sure to top mine up before his), ask me if I needed anything (coming back with socks in case I was cold) and any time I went to get up, he would stand and hold my chair for me. He would do exactly the same thing on my return. I had never experienced such old-fashioned chivalry before, and it all seemed to come so naturally to him.

As the conversations quietened and people started going to their tents, Cam and I remained wrapped in conversation around the fire. Jack decided to go to bed just after 1 a.m. and said he'd sleep in his own tent because it was obvious we were going to be up chatting for hours.

'I'm tired,' he'd yawned, 'and I'm sorry if it seems selfish, but I'd like some guaranteed sleep without either of you two crashing in on me. We can change tomorrow if you like.'

During the hours we chatted, Cam and I found out lots about each other. I'm not usually one for spilling my life history, preferring instead to listen when somebody else speaks, probably compounded by my training experiences. Somehow, though, I felt that he understood me, and I found myself telling him all about myself – my hopes and fears as well as my unusual childhood experiences. Rather than judge or question me when I told him of my unarguably dysfunctional family influences, he in turn shared some deep hurts that he'd had to face in his past. He told me tales of woe starting from an early age, with his yearning for greater parental affection. His heart had been broken many times. As a result, he was driven to help people and wanted to make the world a better place. He said that it meant he tolerated unacceptable behaviour from girlfriends and that he tended to stay in relationships too long. His experiences mirrored my own, and I felt both understanding and understood.

He told me that he was afraid of being hurt again, and that the connection he felt with me was something he couldn't explain. Perhaps, he said, with tears in his eyes, this was destiny, but he didn't know whether he could trust his feelings.

This big, strong, beautifully handsome and caring man was opening up his soul to me, and I assured him that I was not like the other women he had described. I could never hurt him, although I wasn't sure about this whole idea of destiny! I was a little wiser than that . . .

But I couldn't help but be deeply touched – and reassured – by his words and his continued attentions. Polite, chivalrous, old-fashioned and well-educated, and he was interested in me – little old me, who had survived a good few life challenges of my own. I had always thought that I must have done something wrong for all these bad things to have happened to me.

'No,' he said. 'Not wrong and not bad. Just very loving, very open and very trusting. I know you don't yet know it for sure, but you'll see you can trust me. I'm here now and it will all be OK, whatever happens between us from here. It's up to you. You know how I feel, and I will always tell you the truth.'

We finally went to our tent at around 3 a.m., and by that time the conversation had returned to banter and laughing. He had the cheekiest, off-the-wall sense of humour that had me in fits of schoolgirl giggles that only encouraged him further. He went to his compartment of the tent and I went to mine. We carried on joking and laughing for a bit, and each time I felt myself drifting off to sleep he would burst into laughter or start singing a ridiculous song. It was hysterical – I don't know if I've ever laughed quite so much or for quite so long! I remember seeing the sun coming up through the canvas of my tent and pleading for some peace so I could get some sleep.

'It's your fault!' Cam teased, bursting into giggles again. 'You're encouraging me to keep going, you know!'

In the end, exhausted from giggling, my tummy hurting and my cheeks almost in cramp, I did manage to get some sleep, even if it was just a couple of hours. I dozed off with a big smile on my face and full of positive expectations for the next day and the week ahead.

The next few days were equally as amazing as the first. John Shango proved himself to be a passionate and determined workshop leader, teaching us skills and experiences that were both challenging and liberating. Every day I was collecting more exercises and ideas I knew I could incorporate into my Louise Hay workshops, and every day my bond with Cam was growing stronger.

By the second day, people had started assuming we had arrived as a happy couple, and by the fourth day we were openly declaring our love, freely referring to each other as soulmates. On the last evening, we went through a private ceremony exchanging personal vows confirming our love and our intentions to stay together forever – 'infinity and beyond' had become our personal mantra. The ceremony was overseen by the Dippy Hippy who had since become our friend. While this was all new to me, Skye seemed to know what he was doing, and Cam somehow remained supremely confident and relaxed as usual.

I admit I was a little nervous about the ceremony idea. It had been Cam's suggestion, an incredibly romantic gesture as he got down on one knee and asked if I'd be willing to marry him. I, of course, said yes, but since his divorce wasn't finalised, we would need to wait for the real thing. That was when he suggested we create a ceremony of our own, a public declaration of our intentions that was to consist of an exchange of chosen vows that would bind us together. We had asked Skye if he'd be kind enough to act as a witness and to add a few words of his own. He, of course, said yes, since it would allow him to use some of the many spiritual rituals he had learned over his time as a healer.

To calm my nerves, I reminded myself of a story about friends my mum had known – a couple who had met and married within two weeks of first meeting each other. Thirty years and two children later, they were still together and as blissfully happy as the day they first met. I had shared the story with Cam during one of our many long discussions, and he said that true love, true soulmate love, is something that is pure and everlasting. He said that he too had found it hard to believe but that now he knew it was meant to be and he asked me to embrace our love as fully as he was. Mindful of the number of times he had been hurt by women, and touched by his brave declarations of love for me, I was reassured that I really was involved in a modern-day miracle, and I swept my doubts aside.

The vows ceremony took place with just Skye, Cam and myself. We stood a good way from the rest of the group and the huge bonfire, by now a nightly occurrence along with countless firewalks, each of us holding a candle. Skye was clinking some Indian bells and burning a strong incense stick to create the scene. I'm not one for religious ceremonies, and I hoped that this would not make me feel uncomfortable. As usual, Cam took control and gently guided me towards the spot where we were to make our vows.

'It's OK, you're with me now,' he whispered. 'I won't let anything hurt you. Trust me. I love you more than I ever thought was possible – stuff all the romantic books and films, this is real!' he added, squeezing my waist and encouraging me to walk forward with him.

The ceremony proved to be one of the most romantic occasions I have ever experienced. We held hands as Skye opened with a poem he had written and a blessing. Gazing into each other's eyes, we did our best to put into words how we felt about each other and made a promise that from this moment on we would always be together. Cam took his candle and held my left hand, gently pouring some of the molten wax over the third finger of my left hand.

'We may not have rings for the moment, but this feeling will stay with you for ever,' he said, as I felt the hot wax solidifying on my skin. I did the same to him, and then Skye rang his bell, waved the incense stick and announced that now we were together, nothing could ever separate us again.

I have never felt so lucky in my entire life. I could hardly believe my good fortune. This beautiful man had chosen me as his soulmate, and I knew that he'd be true to his word. I knew that from this moment on we would be together through thick and thin, and I couldn't have been happier if I'd tried.

Nobody seemed able to believe that we had only met on the day we arrived and, to be honest, neither could I. Looking back I realise that it may all seem unusual to say the least, but I had never before felt so safe, so well understood, so perfectly matched and so loved. Blessing my lucky stars that destiny had worked its magic and brought me to the man I believed was my soulmate in every sense of the word, I knew that finally I could look forward to a positive future filled with love, joy and contentment. I was alive, I was happy, and I was in love.

The programme finished in the early afternoon of Saturday, 8 August. I had gained so much over the course of the previous week. I was a qualified firewalking instructor, I had learned countless new tools that would help my workshops, I had a wealth of new friendships among the group I first described as a motley crew, and I had found my true soulmate. A man who understood me better than anyone had ever understood me before. Someone who made me feel as if anything was possible and who showered me with so much love and affection that I felt safe and secure for the very first time since my father had been alive. I even dared to think that if Cam was my prize for all the heartache I'd suffered, well, it was almost worth it. I couldn't wait to introduce this amazing man to Dylan and my friends and family. I knew they'd all love him as much as I did, and I knew they'd be overjoyed to see me so happy.

Cam and I had decided to spend our first night away from the field in a seaside hotel to let the dust settle and make our plans. We all packed up our tents and started to say goodbye to everyone. It was an emotional parting. The training course had been an extraordinarily powerful event, and the group had formed a tight bond of trust and friendship as we'd witnessed one another's fears and triumphs together. Tears were shed and hugs were shared. We all made promises to stay in touch and gave one another thanks for making the week so special. The goodbyes stirred a huge mixture of emotions for me because, although I was sad to be leaving behind a group of people who had become immensely important to me, I also knew I was heading off for a new start with the love of my life. So, with the Republica track 'Ready To Go' blaring out of the car stereo and our hands linked together while we waved our goodbyes, Cam turned and smiled at me. 'Thank you for choosing me,' he said, clearly overcome with emotion. 'It's you and me against the world now, babe, and nothing and nobody can stop us. I promise that I'm going to make you feel so loved and so special, each and every day. Infinity and beyond!'

He accelerated hard as we span away from the field and into a world filled with possibilities.

10

Living the Dream and Waking to a Nightmare

Immediately after the course, Cam moved down to Sussex and we set up home in a quirky rented house in a village just outside Eastbourne. Dylan had taken to Cam straight away, perching happily on his lap and offering to share his bottle. Petra moved on just a couple of months after Cam joined us – like me, she had met someone she had fallen in love with and had gone to make a life for herself. It was heartbreaking when she finally left, but at the same time I was pleased for her – how could I be anything else but happy?

It just so happened that a distant young cousin of Cam's was looking for somewhere to live, and it didn't take much for him to convince her to come and stay with us. Almost too good to be true, Amy fitted in straight away and hit it off with Dylan immediately. Within no time they were rolling around the floor together, singing songs and dancing. Petra was always going to be a tough act to follow, but Amy brought a different set of skills to the party. She was taking some time out from her training as a paediatric nurse, and her love of small children was plain to see. Her playtime with Dylan always included an element of teaching – almost in the same way my father had shown me when I was a child. Everything just fitted into place so perfectly, I could hardly believe my good fortune!

As for Cam, well, true to his word every day was amazing and our love grew stronger and stronger. We fitted together so well in every single way and I continued to thank my lucky stars that I had finally found someone I could share my life with – fully, openly and honestly, in ways that I would never have dreamed could be possible. We had the same taste in music, we laughed at the same jokes, we cried at the same films and we got on like a house on fire. There was never a cross word, and, quite simply, I adored every single moment we were together.

He also adored Dylan, who turned three just after Cam moved in with us. Cam was working as a freelance trainer for a local company (a project that he'd already started before the firewalking course), and on the day of Dylan's birthday he came home with a brand-new bicycle brightly wrapped and with a huge red bow attached to the handlebars. It was Dylan's first 'big boy' bike, and I remember his beaming face as he pedalled it around the house.

'Ha-shah!' he'd squealed, doing his best Power Rangers impression with an imaginary sword. 'Look at me! Look at my bike! Ha-shah!'

Cam would read him stories, buy him toys, encourage family outings and want to involve him in everything we did. He also supported my decision to lie quietly on the floor next to Dylan whenever he couldn't sleep.

'Hey, I can't do it for my daughter. Your son is the most important thing, and I think you're a wonderful mother!' he would smile, tussling my hair in the same way he did to Dylan.

There was only one small fly in the ointment. The first time I introduced Cam to Abby, I had cooked lunch at home for a handful of friends. My sister had hardly spoken to him, choosing to stay tucked away in the kitchen with her boyfriend rather than come out and join in with everyone else. I felt hurt and thought she was being rude, and, anyway, why couldn't she be over the moon for me? After everything that had happened before, couldn't she just be pleased that I was clearly so happy at last?

'It's OK,' soothed Cam. 'She's just jealous. She can see how close we are and she feels shut out. She's probably scared that I'll take you away from her. But she'll get used to it in time. She'll see how happy you are, and she'll be pleased for you – for us both. In the meantime, just give her space and let her come to terms with whatever she's feeling.'

It made sense and, while I felt upset by Abby's apparent coldness, I decided that perhaps she really did feel threatened by my love for Cam. I decided also to let sleeping dogs lie and not to say anything to her about my confusion. She'd realise soon enough that my love for her would never diminish, and in time perhaps she'd become comfortable with the situation. After all, as far as I was concerned, Cam and I were going to be together for the rest of our lives, so she'd have all the time in the world to come round! So I shrugged it off and didn't say any more about it, although in quieter moments the thought sometimes niggled at me . . .

In addition to this, Cam told me early on that he had a few debts that he had to clear up, debts from a previous marriage which he claimed were nothing to do with him. I wasn't in the least bit worried. After all, I had been through some pretty tricky financial times myself, and I knew that Cam had the ability to earn much more money than I had ever been able to achieve. I reassured him that together we would take care of everything and that, as far as I was concerned, it wouldn't matter if we lived in a cardboard box under the pier. As long as we were together, I would be happy, and I meant it.

The first few months proved to be a huge financial strain. I had stopped running the Louise Hay workshops because they just weren't paying well enough. Cam's freelance work had also ground to a halt, and he'd pulled away from his business plans with Jack because he said he was tired of carrying the bulk of the responsibility. I didn't quite understand the ins and outs of it all, but I believed everything that Cam was telling me and supported his decision. So, yes, for a good few months money was a huge issue. But that wasn't the only blot on the horizon.

Every two weekends or so, Cam would head up to Scotland to see his daughter from his previous marriage. It was hard, because the way Cam told it, the breakdown of the marriage and the distance from his family wasn't his wish or his fault. I realised that there are always two opposing sides in a marital dispute, and his wife likely had good reasons for any decisions made, but of course I felt desperately sad for Cam. I knew exactly how it felt when you can't keep your family together. I understood the feelings of failure and self-doubt, and I reassured him that it wasn't his fault. That relationships break down for any number of reasons. That none of us is perfect. And that, anyway, we were together now and we could provide a good solid base for his daughter as well as my son, and perhaps for children of our own one day.

I was bursting to meet his daughter, but there were always reasons why that never happened. He told me he was allowed only limited access, but I never knew the details and he was not more forthcoming when I pressed him on it. Having been through such emotional upheavals in my own childhood and now with a child of my own, I simply couldn't bear the fact that Cam was so desperately unhappy about the situation. I was keen to find a solution – any solution – and we would talk about the situation for hours at a time until Cam would become too emotional and ask me to stop.

'I know you're only trying to help, Mel,' he'd say, 'but this is very painful to me and you just don't understand.'

And it was true, I couldn't understand. For Dylan's sake, I had maintained a healthy relationship with Paul, and it didn't make sense to me why a mother would be anything but positive about nurturing a positive connection between her children and their father. Surely there was something we could do? Surely this was wrong?

I desperately wanted to help and asked Cam on many occasions whether I could talk to his ex-wife myself. Perhaps mother-to-mother I might be able to understand the situation better and be a useful and objective mediator. I had no axe to grind with her and suspected that Cam might be presenting her position unfairly

'Surely,' I reasoned, 'there must be something I can do? I'm pretty good at reaching out and helping people, you know. It's what I do. And with my own experiences of a difficult childhood, I'm certain I can reach out and appeal to Eileen as well, perhaps even help her?'

'Don't you understand, there is nothing you can do here, Mel?' he'd say, holding back his obvious anger. 'I know you want to help, and I understand that you think you can. But you can't. Eileen will never ever talk to you, and in fact it would just make matters worse. So you're just going to have to let me handle it in my own way. It may not be the perfect solution, but I'm doing my best, OK? So please, just leave it!'

And that's how the cycle continued – Cam in obvious pain, and me unable to do anything to help him or to ease the situation. I felt powerless, and it hurt me to see the man I loved being eaten up by the fact that he was distanced from his child. I was so keen to help heal his relationship with his family that I muted we could relocate to Scotland if that would help. Aside from Abigail, who lived in London and had a life of her own, I had no other family ties or obligations that held me in Sussex. But Cam would just ruffle my hair, call me a 'sweet thing' and tell me once again that this was more evidence that I just didn't understand his situation. His words stung, causing me to bite my tongue and blush with embarrassment. I had no choice but to back off and instead just offer my support whenever Cam asked and only in the way that helped. More than that, I had to accept, was beyond my control.

But even those issues could not dampen my happiness. I loved every moment we spent together and adored the fact that finally I had been able to create a secure and loving family unit for myself and for Dylan. Every day brought its own magic – Dylan's peals of laughter when we all played together, Amy's imaginative stream of fresh ideas for fun and games, and Cam's constant messages of love (he would leave stickers around the house, bring me cards and small presents, and send a constant stream of texts messages on my phone, even when we were in the same room!). The house was full of love and romance, and it was real. I was living the dream.

After a few months of financial hardship – which I felt actually made us stronger as a unit – we both managed to land ourselves some very well-paid freelance work. Almost overnight, we went from being as poor as church mice, to bringing in thousands of pounds a month. It was an astonishing turnaround, and I could hardly believe the sudden and successful change in our fortunes.

'Of course, that was always going to happen, you know that! And, yes, this is now the life we're destined to lead,' Cam grinned one evening as we opened an expensive bottle of wine at our kitchen table. 'Didn't I tell you we can do anything together? Didn't I promise you I'd make you happy? Isn't this what being a soulmate is all about? Did you ever have any doubt? It's you and me against the world, babe, so the world had better watch out, eh?' He always had a way of holding me with his eyes and talked in a manner that made things seem magical. I felt supported, safe and loved, and believed that together anything was possible.

'We deserve success. We deserve all the good things in life. We deserve to be happy and we deserve to be successful. All you've got to do now, Mel, is believe that's the case, and together we can achieve anything we set our minds on – OK? I love you, and I am so grateful you chose me. Now come on and let's start living, really living, eh?'

So we did. Just a few months later, and less than a year after we first met, we decided to set up our own training company. We reasoned that our combined skills – his years of experience in the corporate world together with my passion for helping people – provided an offering that was unique in the training business. And it worked. Our first client was a major blue-chip communications company. From there the work just piled in.

We married in a registry office on 9 October 1999, 14 months after we first met. We laughed at those few people who had said it could never work, delighted to prove that our love was real and that we were indeed destined to be together for ever. Shania Twain's song 'Looks Like We Made It' had long been a favourite track, regularly cranked up to full volume at home while Cam and I sang along together. We weren't quite *X-Factor* material when it came to talent, but nobody could criticise our enthusiasm!

The wedding itself was an amazing day filled with love, laughter and happiness. Dylan smiled happily with us for the wedding pictures in the registry office and then in the car, where he posed behind the wheel as our chauffeur. We held the reception at our home, another rented house that we'd moved into some eight months after the first. We had a marquee in the garden and were joined by a hundred or so friends and family. It was a gorgeous sunny day, surprisingly warm for October, and we had asked people not to buy us any wedding gifts. Instead we asked them to bring food and champagne to share, so that we could all enjoy ourselves together. And we did! Shunning the traditional wedding themes (both of us had been married before) we asked guests to dress casually and did away with the usual formality, seating arrangements and wedding speeches. Instead, people were encouraged to stand up during the meal to say a few words whenever they felt like it. After the meal and later on in the afternoon, Cam chose to serenade me with Joe Cocker's 'You Are So Beautiful'. Watching the smiles on the faces of our guests, I brushed away my embarrassment and bathed in the love he was sending me. He'd had a few too many glasses of champagne by that time, so the singing was somewhat off-key, but I didn't care.

We partied way on into the evening. Cam, myself, Abigail and her partner Steve carrying on together until the early hours after everyone else had gone. Abby and Cam had put their differences behind them, and I was now officially married to the man I loved with all my heart and with all my soul. I couldn't have been happier.

Life continued to improve. Business was booming, we were

gaining a terrific reputation for the work we were doing, and our money worries were nothing but a distant memory. Dylan was thriving, and I had come to accept that my life was truly blessed. Cam and I continued to get closer, and his constant messages of love and affection never failed to touch my heart. I remember one time we were both running a workshop with a management team when my mobile rang. Embarrassed, I apologised to the group and went to turn it off, but Cam said it was OK and told me I'd better take it, as it could be important. This went against my professional judgment – when we're with a client, we're with a client, even when they're discussing things among themselves, as was the case at that moment – but I did as he said and took the phone into the next room. The number was blocked. I answered the call to find it was Cam.

'Just to say you look beautiful and I love you,' he said. 'Thank you for choosing me.'

We hit a big glitch in the business at the end of 2001. By that time we had invested in offices, vehicles and a team of trainers. Work was continuing to come in, the bank loved us, and we had the promise of two major contracts that would potentially boost our turnover to millions. It was exciting and scary at the same time. This would mean moving into the big time, and I wasn't sure we were ready. But we went for it and made plans and preparations as best we could. But at the very last minute both of the contracts fell through. It was devastating. It was a typical case of too much too soon for a young business. We had overstretched ourselves and had to pay the harsh consequences.

To cut a long story short, we had to close the business, move out of our offices and make the team redundant. It was absolutely soul destroying to see our hard work going down the drain, to lose our loyal team, and most of all to see Cam's utter devastation at the realisation that his business dreams had gone up in smoke.

'It's OK, we've still got each other,' I'd say, holding him tightly. 'We can get through this – you'll see. Didn't you say we could do anything together? We've done it once, we can do it again!'

In those moments, I was supremely grateful for some of the bad things that I'd been through, because it meant that I could use my experiences to stay calm and focused. I knew how to survive – I'd done it before. This was just another 'tough time' and, just like everything else, it would pass. I felt that I had to be tough for both of us, so it was me who contacted the bank, the liquidators and the lawyers, and together we worked to find a solution to our problems.

By then we were living in a beautiful home that we'd bought by selling my flat on the seafront and topping up the proceeds with a hefty mortgage. Luckily enough the house had a small thatched building in the front garden. It sounds very posh, but it really wasn't. The tiny structure had been there since the 1930s and was originally built as the sales office when the council was dividing up and selling off neighbouring plots. It measured no more than 12-foot square, but it did have a sink and a toilet. The lady who owned the house before us had used it as a studio for creating her artwork.

It would be perfect for a new, downsized business. We decided to keep our secretary, Kitty, on and to work with our team on a freelance basis. I contacted all our clients to let them know that we were restarting the business, and within a very short time work once again started coming our way. We had created such a great reputation that people were happy to refer us on, and once again the business grew. This time, though, some tough lessons had been learned, and I swore we would never again try to run before we could walk. This time every penny would be accounted for, and we would make sure we always had a financial cushion should we encounter any future problems.

The whole episode, however, seemed to have taken its toll on Cam. Halfway through 2002, he became withdrawn and silent. Little by little he slipped further away, and for the first time since we'd met I just couldn't reach him.

It culminated in a conversation the night before a team-building event we had planned with one of our major clients. We were settling into our hotel bedroom before meeting the client for dinner. Against my better judgment, I pressed Cam to tell me what was really happening and how I could help. He had just spent the past couple of weeks working with one of our international clients, so this was the first opportunity we'd had to be together since then. He looked washed out. Exhausted. His face was grey and he had dark circles under his eyes. He sat on the edge of the bed, his back towards me and his head in his hands. He was clearly troubled, and yet he couldn't even look me in the eyes. My heart broke to see him that way. But nothing could have prepared me for the words I was about to hear. Level, measured and with no emotion, his voice pierced my heart.

'Mel, the fact is that I haven't missed you since I've been away. We have major issues, and I am not prepared to paper over the cracks. Don't push me or I will run. I need time to sort myself out.'

What? He hadn't missed me? But all the time he was away he'd been sending me the usual messages of love and adoration. We have major issues? But each time we'd spoken on the phone he'd told me how much he loved me. I knew he'd become distant, and I realised something was wrong with him, but I honestly thought everything was fine between the two of us. What on earth was this about? What was going on? What signs had I been missing? Why hadn't I known he was feeling this way?

But no matter how many times I questioned him or went to hold him, he would push me aside and tell me he needed his space. He said that he believed he was having a nervous breakdown and that there was nothing I could do to help. He asked me to respect his feelings, saying that if I truly loved him now was my chance to prove it.

Quite simply, I didn't recognise the stranger sitting on the bed in front of me. The man I knew and loved, my soulmate who was always full of so much fun and energy, had vanished. In his place was a cold and distant stranger who clearly didn't know what he was saying. A shell of a person who looked worn down, wiped out and full of nothing but darkness. He was empty. What had happened to make him this way? Had the troubles with the business taken more of a toll on my husband than I had realised? What could I have done differently? Why hadn't I been able to help?

Questions raced and crashed around inside my head, while hot and cold tremors of fear and confusion raced up and down my body. I knew there must be something seriously wrong with him, and all the signs were there to confirm that he was indeed in the grip of a serious breakdown. My beloved husband was quite obviously in dire trouble, so my questions would have to wait. I decided instead that at this moment in time the only thing I could do was to respect his wishes. He'd told me clearly what I could do to help, so that was what I was going to do. I stopped pushing, painted on a smile, and throughout that evening with the client and the whole of the following day I just acted as if everything was normal, even though my heart was breaking with worry and fear about the damaged health and mental state of the man I loved.

Immediately after the course he left and headed back up to the tiny flat we were renting in Manchester. We had landed a major long-term piece of work there and it had worked out cheaper and more comfortable to rent an apartment on a short-term basis rather than live out of hotels. Cam would spend most weeks there and he would either come home to Sussex at weekends or I would go up to visit him. It wasn't ideal, but we made it work. It had been a sure fire way to revitalise the business and get us back on track financially.

He said he wanted his space, so it made sense that he should go there for the next few days. We already had a holiday booked in Corfu for just the two of us, so that would give us plenty of time to talk and find out what was going on. All I wanted was for him to get better, but he wasn't ready to let me help. Once again I felt powerless, and echoes of the ongoing situation with his daughter once again came to the surface. No matter how many times I had tried to help or talk about the situation (by this time the relationship between Cam and his ex-wife had completely broken down, and the visits had stopped along with the telephone calls), I just couldn't get through. It was a problem he was determined to keep to himself, although his heart was breaking. Mine was breaking too, not least because I could neither soothe him, nor help the situation, but also because this was a little girl whom Dylan and I had still never met. I wondered how she must feel, being cut off from her father and also having no idea that there were two other people here who were just bursting to welcome her into their lives. It was tragic, but, exactly the same as now, Cam just pushed me away and said he'd deal with it in his own way and in his own time.

On the plane over to Corfu, I watched Cam quietly slip off his wedding ring and slide it into his rucksack. He was still cold and distant, and physically he looked like absolute hell – grey skinned, gaunt and with dark-circled eyes in an expressionless face. I felt chilled and was bursting to just shake the stranger in front of me by the scruff of the neck in the hope that my old husband would return. But of course I couldn't. It wouldn't have done any good and in any case I would likely have been arrested in the process!

It was as though my beloved soul mate had disappeared…he'd somehow just gone away and had been replaced by what? Or by whom…? While my imagination started running on overdrive, Cam still wouldn't talk to me and could barely even acknowledge me. Whenever he looked my way there was nothing in his eyes. They were cold and emotionless, like a shark – he was empty. Gone was the laughter and love I knew so well. I knew beyond doubt that he must be very ill with some kind of emotional trouble, and I feared that I might have lost him for good.

The holiday proved to be a roller coaster of emotions. The first night we arrived, Cam started to open up to me, a little of his colour returning to his face as he told me that he thought he was losing his mind. Sitting at the small wooden table in our holiday apartment, he explained that even though it made no sense, the strength I had shown over the difficulties with the business had caused him to lose confidence in himself.

Well, you could have knocked me down with a feather at that one! My intention during that time was to find ways to save us – both of us – and to keep our heads above water. How on earth could that have caused him to lose confidence? Surely it should have made him feel more confident that we could overcome even the toughest challenge together?

He carried on with his explanations, saying that the male role is to protect and provide, to be the hunter-gatherer in a partnership. To make sure that his family is cared for and safe. He said that he'd failed to do that when we lost the business and then had been shocked to find that I was able to demonstrate what he described as 'a super-human strength that made me feel worthless as a man and as your husband'.

Horrified, I began to understand that I was more than slightly to blame for his sickness. I was appalled to think that my power had perhaps caused him to feel less capable, but as he explained in more detail it made perfect sense. How could I have been so blind? Why could I not have seen this? Was I so focused on what I was doing, confident that I could pull us through, that I had lost sight of the one person who meant the world to me?

The guilt started kicking in, as well as all the old messages from my childhood. Well, once again I'd gone and made a right royal mess of things, hadn't I? The inner critic took over, castigating me for my folly. *Clearly it wasn't enough to stick your stupid neck out and lose your blood relatives, now you've gone and cocked up your marriage as well, and look what that'll mean to Dylan! Goodness me, Mel, and you call yourself a behavioural trainer – well, you jolly well missed that one didn't you? And it was going on right under your eyes! You're beyond help, you know that? You've brought this all on yourself! I wash my hands of you. I hope you're happy now!*

Feeling a miserable failure, I was desperate to help and make amends. But I felt torn between the devil and the deep blue sea. How could I now step up and do something when he'd told me so clearly that it was this same drive to 'make things better' that had in fact contributed to the broken soul that now sat before me? Like a rabbit caught in headlights, all I could do was watch my beautiful, beloved husband sobbing into his glass of wine, bent double with his pain and anguish. I couldn't just reach over and help in the way I had before – that had made things worse, and he was telling me loud and clear that I was to back off. He had to sort this in his own way and reclaim his dignity.

I knew I must find a new way to support him. Find different ways to respond. I had obviously missed the signs last time, and so this time I had to do everything within my power to 'get out of my own way' and truly understand what he was asking of me – and do it. I'd got it so hopelessly wrong last time. I'd better make darned sure I got it right now. So I listened and I asked questions, biting my tongue whenever I was tempted to offer solutions and instead gently prompting him to continue when his words tailed off. And I promised him (and me) that I would do whatever it took to help him heal, even though it was contrary to an approach I would normally expect to use. I had no choice. Here in front of me was my husband, a stranger who was clearly in the grip of some dreadful breakdown – a loss of self-esteem for which I had been partly to blame, despite my best intentions. I felt wretched, and I knew it was absolutely critical that I listen and act on the information he was giving me. It wasn't going to be easy, but I was determined to do everything within my power to help – yes, even if that meant doing nothing and letting him just get on with it.

As the week progressed, I learned that Cam had some deep-seated childhood issues that he hadn't resolved or shared with me before. He felt these issues were the reason behind his own constant disappointment with women. How could he know how to show love if he'd not felt it when he was young? That made sense to me, of course, because it mirrored many of my own experiences, and I began to understand.

He also told me, his voice cracking under the emotional strain, that he thought I didn't love him. He thought that he'd let me down with the business, and that when I became so strong it was because I didn't believe he could do it himself. He said that my actions had hurt him so deeply and brought up so many past emotions, that he simply couldn't tell me. He said that he hated staying in Manchester and couldn't understand why I hadn't insisted that I stay with him every night. Those, and many other things, had brought him to the conclusion that I just didn't love him. He couldn't bear the thought of losing me, so instead he'd shut himself away, and in the process he'd hurt himself so badly that he didn't know how he could get back.

We talked about counselling. We talked about medication. We talked about all manner of therapies. But however much we talked, Cam was still having none of it. He just couldn't bring himself back, and because of that we had to make some changes.

'All I want,' he'd say, 'is for you to be my friend through this. I cannot be your husband at the moment. Will you please just be my friend? Just support me? If you really do love me then you'll understand.'

We were sharing a bed, of course, and even though Cam said he couldn't be a husband to me for the moment, we regularly made love during that holiday. It was confusing for me and hurtful at the same time, particularly when Cam wanted to be a bit more experimental. I went along with most of his wishes, but I didn't feel good about it. Our love life had always been so tender and so special. Yes, OK, some occasions were steamier than others, but always there had been a wonderful spiritual connection between us. Sex in Corfu, however, was just that. Sex. And it varied between 'going through the motions' to what I would deem pushing perverted. I was doing as he had asked by respecting his need to heal in his own way, but no matter what we did together, I just couldn't connect with him. We slept in the same bed, but I was isolated and alone. Feeling useless, drained and exhausted, I wondered whether I could ever have the strength to see this through. Perhaps he was right. Perhaps I didn't love him enough after all?

In the evenings, he always wanted to go out on the town. Just a few kilometres away (a good 40-minute walk) was a thumping resort town filled with the kind of tacky scenes of drunken debauchery that are regularly flashed across our newspapers and TV screens. I hated it. Cam had always been an enthusiastic drinker, but on these evenings, as we tottered through streets littered with cheap bars, garish nightclubs and scantily dressed young holidaymakers, his thirst knew no bounds. Lurching from one bar to the next, throwing shots down his neck like there was no tomorrow, he took on a whole new persona, and I didn't like it. In fact, it frightened me. He'd become wild and unpredictable, greedily devouring drink after drink.

'Come on, Mel, this is fun. This is helping me. Don't leave me now!' he'd scoff, glaring at me as I did my best to keep up with him. One night, to my shame, I confess I was so drunk that I couldn't put one foot in front of the other. Disorientated, frightened and feeling totally out of control, I realised the danger that we were in and reached to Cam for support, begging him to come back to the apartment.

'Don't be such a pussy!' was his spittle-slurred response, the fire of defiance burning brightly in his eyes and a sneer on his face. 'The night's only just started!' and with that he staggered off, leaving me to follow along behind as best I could.

No matter what I did, no matter how much I tried to understand and support him, I simply didn't recognise my husband any more. The kind, gentle, caring man I had fallen in love with, had turned in to someone unfamiliar to me, someone I didn't like and who scared me. I couldn't understand what was happening.

He'd choose moments to confess his concerns and worries, but many of his stories were contradictory and made little sense to me. He had shown none of this anguish over the four years we'd been together, and try as I might, I just couldn't comprehend what was going on. Yes, I was with him in person – physically we were never more than a few feet apart – but I felt so alone and frightened, and increasingly helpless. I was terrified of saying or doing the wrong thing, convinced that this illness or breakdown might get worse. I was desperate to have my husband back and for things to just return to normal, and I had hoped that this holiday would have produced some answers.

One morning, after another particularly boozy evening, I'd slipped out of our bed to have a shower. I remember curling up in the corner of the shower tray, my head thumping from the alcohol while the cold water pounded hard and fast on my back. I had turned the water to full power, to make as much of a noise as possible to muffle my strangled howls of pain as my body shuddered with the force of my sobbing. I remember stopping for a moment and looking up to notice Cam standing in the doorway. He was leaning against the wall. His arms were folded and I couldn't read his expression – it appeared cold. I was shocked by his intrusion as well as by his expression. Instead of any trace of concern or compassion in his face, I had the distinct impression that he was faintly amused by the scene.

'What on earth do you think you're doing?' he'd sneered, locking his cold stare on to my puffy eyes and looking up and down my naked body as I hunched shivering in the corner. It felt like a kick in the guts, a slap in the face, a punch in the head – and I felt stripped, exposed and very, very stupid. Averting my eyes from his gaze, I stood up, wiped the tears from my face and picked up the bar of soap.

'Having a shower, that's all,' was the only response I could manage, as I turned my back to him and started lathering my body. I don't know why, but I never even mentioned that episode to him again, so it was never spoken about between us, but the memory of it is branded so deeply into my soul that to this day I can still remember it and feel the burning shame with vivid, livid clarity.

As I've said, it was meant to be a holiday where we sorted out our differences and moved forward together. But by the time we got back to England, I was no nearer to finding any solutions; in fact,

I just felt numb and exhausted with the effort of trying to understand. The taxi dropped us off at the house and Cam got straight in his car and headed back to Manchester. It was late at night, but he wouldn't even come in for a cup of tea let alone consider staying the night in what was meant to be his home. Promising me that he'd find a counsellor, he thanked me for giving him his space and said we'd continue texting and talking and then get together in a couple of weeks so we could discuss things further. No kiss, no cuddle, no reassurance, no clues. He just span off into the night, leaving me on the doorstep to take in the bags and unpack my suitcase together with my raw and jangled emotions.

That discussion never happened. He'd send the occasional text or business-related email but refused to talk on the telephone other than to tell me that he was exhausted, confused, frightened and still in need of his own space while he worked through his problems. Fraught with worry about what was happening to my husband and desperate to find the answers, I configured our computer server so that I would be blind-copied in to his business emails. Consumed with guilt, I felt dirty, cheap and disloyal for betraying my sick husband's trust. I hoped and prayed with all my heart that I might discover some more information that would help me to understand and help. Perhaps, even though he couldn't talk with me, there was somebody out there who he'd been able to confide in. I knew I was being dishonest, but I was at my wits' end. I was desperate for information.

It didn't take long – less than 48 hours in fact.

It was the morning of Friday, 20 September 2002, and I was in the office, as usual, chatting away with Kitty, who was well aware of what was going on. Alerted to the arrival of a new email, I opened another blind-copied message. It was a reply to an email he'd sent the night before to an old school friend I'd never heard him mention before. Reading through the email, my cheeks flushing with guilt, I discovered it was someone he'd found on Friends Reunited. I knew the email was from Cam, but I just didn't recognise the tone of his writing. It was boastful and blokey, cocky, almost like he was trying to get one up on this newfound childhood friend. Confused and somewhat taken aback by the unusual manner of his writing, I carried on reading until I reached the second to last paragraph:

Business is good and keeping me out of too much trouble – but still keeps me in fast cars and women! And because I'm so damned good at relationships I've just left one in Brighton to go and live with (AKA shag!) another in Manchester.

There and then, my entire world came crashing down around me. It all happened in slow motion. It was like a nuclear blast – the flash of white light, the rush of wind, the heat of the blast and then the deadly impact of the explosion. I felt every single shudder and screamed in silence at each shooting pain that fired up and down my body. Worse than the death of my father, worse than the death of my mother and worse than the shock of being thrown out from my guardians. I gasped for breath as I heard the groaning sounds of nerves and sinews stretching and tightening before snapping with a deafening crack as my heart broke in two.

I remember mumbling my discovery to Kitty before getting up from my desk on autopilot and somehow driving around the corner to the house of Monica, my best friend. I remember falling through her front door onto the hallway carpet and waking up a short while afterwards lying on her sofa while she passed me cups of hot sweet tea. I remember her driving me home later on, to find Kitty playing with Dylan in the front garden, keeping him occupied while I stumbled up to the house. I remember hearing Monica and Kitty talking together and I also remember my sister turning up that evening, but the rest of the hours after finding that email are a blank.

To be honest, the next couple of days remain a blur. I have no idea what I did or how I got through, but with the help and support of people who loved me, and with Dylan my priority, I managed to keep going and keep my discovery hidden from Cam, who called at least two or three times that weekend. On the Monday morning, I booked an appointment with a divorce lawyer.

It turned out that the woman he was having an affair with was not just any old person. She wasn't someone he'd picked up in Manchester but was one of our clients. Worse than that she was a coaching client, someone he'd been telling me about just a few weeks earlier (although it might as well have been a lifetime ago), describing her as 'a poor broken soul who has no confidence'. I remember I had shared some hints and tips with him about how he might be able to help her. I usually took the role of coach within the business, but since she was part of a team from a Manchester-based client, we decided that Cam would be the coach on this occasion. Putting the tools I shared with him into practice, he had been very proud to tell me about the positive effects his coaching was having on her life. He even thanked me for my help, telling me how much he loved me!

The lawyer was a lovely lady who welcomed me with a kindly smile. 'It's OK, dear, I've seen worse,' she'd said in a matter-of-fact way. 'Even the best marriages can break down. Don't worry, I'll get you through this,' she continued as she started asking about the financial details of our marriage and business.

'But you don't understand!' I'd wailed. 'I'm not like the other people you've dealt with. It's different. We're different. I love him! We're soulmates! He's having a breakdown and I don't understand what's happened!'

'Believe me, Mel, I hear this all the time,' she replied, handing me a tissue as my eyes filled with tears. 'You're not the first to say those things, and I'm afraid you won't be the last. I know it's hard for you to hear this, but the fact is your story is far from out of the ordinary. I'm sorry, my dear, you married another of those men who just can't keep their trousers zipped. I know you loved him, but I'm afraid these are the facts. So now we need to safeguard your position and get the best possible deal for your divorce.'

And there it was on the table. The dreaded 'D' word I never imagined I would have to hear again.

So it was that we came up with a plan. I was to call Cam and tell him that I knew about his infidelity. I was to keep the conversation calm and business-like, letting him know my intentions and warning him to stay away while I worked with my solicitor on our divorce.

That night, that is exactly what I did. In the office, away from Dylan, Monica sat with me and got me to take long deep breaths to compose my shaking hands and quavering voice. Finally, calm and in control, with a page of carefully planned notes in front of me, I called Cam's mobile. He was working on a residential training event, so I deliberately chose a time when I knew he'd have a few moments to spare. I'd wanted to shock him, so as soon as he answered I gave it to him straight.

'It's over between us, Cam. I know about you and Sophie. What have you got to say for yourself?'

I don't know what I was expecting, but his immediate, monotone response took me by surprise. He hardly even skipped a beat!

'OK,' he said, matter-of-fact. 'So what do you want to do about it?'

I laid out the facts as my solicitor had guided me, telling him that I was divorcing him, and that he'd be receiving a letter stating the terms of our separation within the next couple of weeks. I would be taking over the running of the business until we reached a settlement, and that in the meantime he would be allowed to keep the company credit card and the car, and that the business would pay him a modest monthly salary. Again, I asked him whether he had anything to say for himself.

His cold reply cut me dead. 'Nope. I've got to get back to the delegates now. Get on and do what you want to do with your solicitor. Goodbye, Mel.' And that was it. No explanation, no emotion, no remorse. No nothing.

Life as I knew it had once again changed forever.

11

No Going Back

The next few days and weeks saw me back in fight mode. Business-like, efficient and determined to pull through, I had to break the news to the team of people who worked with us, as well as to our clients. I had decided to continue the business on my own, believing I had the right people around me to continue delivering great training. Cam, I knew, would also continue by himself, and I decided to pre-empt him and visit each of our clients to tell them the news and give them the choice – stay with me or move to Cam. To my utter amazement, every single client that I approached pledged support for me.

'There's no question, Mel. You are, and always have been, the heart of the business. You're going to do so much better now you're on your own!' It was a shock to hear those words from so many people, and I dared to start believing that perhaps I could succeed with the business, even though he wasn't there any more. To a very large extent, I know now that I was still operating on autopilot. But with all my clients secured, the team around me, a very healthy bank balance and my lawyer's promise that I would be able to keep the house, I pushed forward with the divorce.

So, on the face of it things were going well. I had heard no more from Cam on the matter since the night I'd confronted him and had stopped receiving his emails just a couple of days later. There was no point being copied in to whatever he was doing now. There was nothing left to learn. The fact was that my husband had been having an affair and had deliberately deceived me. He'd shown no remorse when confronted, and it appeared that he was not going to contest the divorce. He had stayed in Manchester and our only communication had been a few curt business emails that required both our involvement – that was it. I pushed on, stayed strong and kept my head held high.

But in the quiet moments, on my own, I was in pieces. I had taken down the montages of wedding and holiday photographs that had hung on the walls, but his clothes, belongings and other reminders of 'us' were everywhere. Sometimes I would find myself staring at his wardrobe, the smell of him still on every item of clothing, the memories of our life together flooding towards me, vivid and cruel in their clarity. Oh, how I had loved that man! I remember pulling the navy-and-red-striped rugby shirt towards me, the one that he'd been wearing the day we first met. Holding it in my arms, I drank in the scent of him and, despite my best intentions, allowed my memories to flow free. I imagined his voice whispering in my ear, his laughter and the warmth of his embrace, knowing that I would never enjoy those sensations again. Never again would I hold or be held by the man I loved. Never again would I enjoy the seductive sense of safety and security it gave me, his warmth enveloping me, the low and exquisitely soothing vibrations of his deep voice caressing my soul as he stroked me and whispered in my ear how much he loved me. All of that was gone. Gone forever. In just a few short weeks, my dream had shattered and been replaced by an exhaustingly excruciating nightmare from which I could not awaken – for this was now my reality.

My toughest challenge was telling Dylan. He had just turned seven years old, and in the weeks leading up to and just after the fateful holiday in Corfu he had started waking up and wailing during the night. Frightened and covered in sweat, he would tell me about monsters and dark things chasing him. While I did my best to soothe him, I knew he'd been picking up on my own anxieties even though I'd done my level best to keep him protected. So once the truth was out, I knew I had to tell him what had happened. There was no going back.

It was the first Saturday after my telephone confrontation. Dylan and I sat face to face on the sofa together as I held his hands and asked him to be very brave while I explained something important. Taking a deep breath to steady my nerves, I told him that bad things sometimes happen in life, and that a bad thing had happened to me. I reassured him that it was nothing to do with him, that he'd done nothing wrong, but that his life was going to be affected as a result and so he needed to know the truth. I explained as honestly as I could that Cam had done some very bad things. Things that had hurt me very deeply when I'd found them out. I went on to say that because he'd hurt me by doing the bad things, I'd asked him to leave, because hurting other people is not what family life is about. I reassured Dylan that he still had and would always have Paul, his own father who loved him very much and would always be in his life. Cam, however, could no longer be a part of our family. I promised Dylan that I would do everything within my power to make him know every single day that he was safe, secure and very, very loved.

When I'd finished, there was silence. Dylan just sat there looking at me, his little face showing confusion rather than fear or sadness.

'But why did he want to hurt you, Mummy?' was all he said.

I shook my head, the tears pricking at my eyes. 'I don't know the answer to that, darling, but I do know he's a silly man and he's made a very stupid mistake. Because now he's lost not just me but you as well in the process. And that's just plain silly! So perhaps he'll learn his lesson and won't ever hurt anyone ever again, eh?' And that was that. The truth was out, and Dylan had no more questions – for now.

Believing that we could now start to rebuild our lives together, little did I realise that this was far from the end of it. I had thought that Cam was going to accept the divorce as a done deal, and I considered that was done and dusted. How wrong could I be?

The texts started happening as we approached mid-October.

'Sorry' came the first one, late one evening after I'd put Dylan to bed. I had been feeling confident and strong, determined that I would be able to build a new life without Cam, so it came as a bit of a shock.

After a few minutes, I texted a terse reply: 'For what, precisely?'

'Being horrible. Being me. Being hurtful. Being unsupportive. I just want to talk. Maybe soon? Sorry. X'

And there it was – a Judas kiss from the man who'd broken my heart and shattered my life. I shook my head in disbelief at the cheek of it. How dare he try to make any demands on me? How dare he?

So I fired out a clear response: 'I will talk to you if and when I feel like it. For now I need my space and I don't want to hear from you. Please respect that.'

'OK. X' came the immediate reply.

There it was again. He was sending me another kiss. The bare-faced cheek of the man! I wondered what Sophie would think if she knew he was texting me.

But I confess it had rattled me. I knew of course that at some point we would have to meet, but I hadn't wanted to even think about it. I realised that the divorce would need to be finalised and that at some stage he would want to collect his belongings from the house. So, yes, I understood that I hadn't got away entirely. Not yet. But I hadn't expected those texts for goodness' sake, and so out of the blue! Why? Why now? What was he planning?

The texts continued. Slow at first but then more frequent. He'd ask to see me. He'd ask about Dylan (the nerve of the man! Didn't he realise how much damage he'd caused?). He'd ask if I still felt anything for him. He'd tell me that he knew he'd blown it but that he'd always love me. Most of the time I just ignored him, but when I chose to reply my messages would be short, telling him that it was too late and that it was over. There was no way I was going to let myself be hurt by him again. He'd broken something that was so precious, so special, and I knew there was no going back.

But I hadn't reckoned on his persistence.

It was Wednesday, 23 October, the day after he'd received my solicitor's letter outlining the divorce settlement. Kitty and I were in the office together as usual and the phone had rung. Answering with her usual greeting, she had said no more before replacing the receiver and turning to face me. Her face was white.

'It's Cam,' she stuttered. 'He's driven down from Manchester and will be here in less than 15 minutes. Mel, what are we going to do?'

The last time I'd seen my husband was outside the house when we returned from that awful holiday in Corfu. How on earth was I going to deal with him? What did he want? How was I going to keep my cool?

I had no time to think about a strategy because, sure enough, 12 minutes after the phone call, his car pulled up in the driveway. I was waiting for him outside the office, the door locked behind me, with instructions to Kitty to call the police if there was any trouble.

'You can stop right there,' I commanded, pulling myself upright as Cam climbed out of the car. I was surprised by the authority in my voice and continued in a steady tone. 'Fine, so you want to talk. But not here. It will be on neutral territory. Kitty is in the office, and I don't want her involved or worried. So get back in the car and we'll go somewhere else.' Reinforced with adrenalin, I kept my face expressionless, placing my hands on my hips and stubbornly standing my ground.

'I want to see the accounts, Mel. It's my right,' he countered, but his face betrayed surprise at my defiance.

'I hear you, Cam. And we'll discuss that once we're away from here.' I held his gaze, pleased with my small victory.

We drove to a local pub, not the cosy one where we used to

spend our Sunday afternoons, but a large modern bar that had both space and anonymity. Plenty of opportunity for me to escape, or at least get some help if things got nasty. The short journey passed in silence, and I kept my eyes firmly fixed in front. I didn't want to look at him. I couldn't. How could I now look at the man I had loved with all my heart and soul? The man I thought I'd grow old with? The man who'd betrayed me and then abandoned me for someone else? My mind was churning, and I was struggling to keep my composure. But I had to. Reminding myself that I'd come through worse, I took deep breaths, gritted my teeth and clenched my fists until we arrived.

I sat down while he ordered two coffees and brought them over to the table. There was an uncomfortable silence as our eyes met. For a moment I imagined that this was just a normal meeting, but the sudden churning in my tummy announced the stirring of emotions buried deep within me. He smiled at the same moment. I blinked and pulled myself up straight.

'What do you want?' I asked.

Cam's smile went, but I sensed something in his eyes. What was going on here?

His responses were short. The conversation was prickly, and his explanations were peppered with conflicting messages. He said he wanted to see the accounts and was deeply sorry for the pain he'd caused me. Then he added that he knew his rights and that he'd be contesting my claim on the business and would never let me keep the house (even though the courts were almost duty-bound to award it to me). At one point he attempted to put his hand over mine, saying that he'd missed me and that it was good to see me.

I wanted to shout and scream at him. I wanted to slap him around the face. I wanted to hurt him. To kick him. To punch him. To make him understand the pain he'd put me through. But I didn't. I decided that it would do me no good, and, anyway, just as I'd learned from childhood, I'd become pretty good at keeping the 'bad stuff' buried deep within me. I couldn't show that much pain, because it would make me vulnerable. And anyway, if I started, I might never be able to stop . . .

So, after half an hour of stilted exchanges, I suggested we get something to eat. I wasn't hungry, but I needed some kind of distraction to help me keep my feelings under control. Here was my estranged husband talking about divorce, business and legal rights in one breath, and then telling me how sorry he was and that he missed me in the next. This wasn't what I was expecting, and I didn't know how to react.

As I got up to go to the Ladies, he also got up to place our order at the bar, purposely brushing against my shoulder as he moved past me. A jolt of electricity shot through me, and I reprimanded myself on the way to the toilet.

Stop it, Mel. Stay strong and don't let him get to you. Remember what he's done. Remember how cold and calculated he's been. This is all just a game to him. Remember how far you've come. You've got to get through this.

Washing my hands I stared at my reflection in the mirror, hardening my eyes and imagining my heart to be made of steel. *Come on, Mel. Stop it. He's hurt you. He doesn't love you. You've got to get through this – you've just got to, whatever it takes!*

But underneath, the questions had already started to gnaw away at my resolve.

Picking at the ploughman's lunch in front of me, I decided to ask him questions – this could be the only opportunity I would have to find answers to the uncertainties that still kept me awake at night. I needed to know what had happened. I had to understand why. I just wanted to get some answers. When I asked why, and whether he loved her, he immediately held his head in his hands.

'No, Mel, she's just a symptom. I don't love her, not at all – I never have done. Can't you see? It was just that I thought you didn't love me any more. It's like I told you in Corfu – that, at least, was all true. I just couldn't tell you what else was happening. I couldn't, Mel, I just couldn't. I wasn't brave enough.' He looked up and his crumpled face mirrored the torture I'd grown to know so well. 'I've made the most stupid mistake, and I know I'll continue to pay for it for the rest of my life,' and with that his voice cracked as his shoulders started to shake, and he bowed his head once more.

I felt an enormous pang of pity in my heart, but I shook my head and took another deep breath. Squinting my eyes and gritting my teeth, I willed myself to stay strong. I wasn't going to allow myself to be swayed.

'So why did you wait until today to come down? Why not before? And why unannounced? You got my solicitor's letter yesterday, so what's your game?' I continued, steeling myself against any desire to comfort him. It was tough. I knew he'd done me wrong, but my entire career was based around showing care and compassion for people. And here, suffering right in front of me, was the man I'd loved with all my soul. It was a huge struggle, and I fidgeted on my seat before sitting up even straighter, cocking my head and waiting for him to reply.

'Mel, you have no idea what I've been going through. I've been such an idiot. When I opened the letter, I was immediately sick. I threw up on the carpet – right there in the hallway. Then I must have passed out. It was horrible,' he said, screwing his face up in pain and embarrassment. 'I haven't slept a wink, and I just had to come and see you. I didn't announce my visit because I thought you'd refuse to see me. Do you have any idea how much strength it's taken for me to come here? Do you? I wanted so badly to come down before, straight away in actual fact. But I knew you wouldn't see me. I've missed you and Dylan so much, Mel, and I'm so, so sorry,' and with that he just dissolved in front of my very eyes. His fight was gone, together with his talk of rights and legalities. Instead I saw a crumpled and broken man, folded and sobbing over the table, and again I felt a familiar twang at my heart.

I still wasn't going to let him get to me, but at the same time I felt embarrassed for him being in this kind of state in public. Leaning over the table, I put my hand on his arm. 'Come on, let's get you out of here,' I said quietly, gently encouraging him to get up. It was that pitiful look in his eyes as he lifted his head that caused my resolve to melt just a teeny-weeny bit more. Because in that moment I saw in his face a carbon-copy reflection of all the pain and hurt that I'd been feeling myself over the past few weeks.

We got to the car, and he opened the passenger door for me – his impeccable manners had clearly not changed. As I moved past to get in, Cam suddenly put his arm around my waist and pulled me towards him, his sobs suddenly coming back with a vengeance as a deep moan of pain rose up through his body.

'You see, Mel, even our bodies are such a good and natural fit. Look – it just works. We fit together. Feel it – I know you can. Don't you see we were never meant to be apart from each other? I'm so sorry for hurting you. I'm so, so very sorry.' The sobs wracked his body, and he just collapsed into me, holding me tightly while he dissolved.

There was nothing else I could do. Returning his embrace, I let my head lean against his shoulder, desperately fighting against the churning in my tummy. But he was right. It was true. Our bodies were indeed a perfect fit. I'd said so myself many times before. Once again I felt the powerful connection and ached for the pain we were both feeling, longing for everything to be as it was before. But it wasn't. It could never be the same. And I wasn't going to be taken in that easily.

We got in the car and just sat there for a while, and I called Kitty to let her know I was all right and that I was going to be a little bit longer. Cam and I had decided to go for a walk along the seafront. I needed to get some fresh air and I hoped that walking in the sea breeze would clear my head and bring a fresh perspective on the situation. He continued to apologise and tell me how bad he was feeling about the whole situation. He went to hold my hand, and the desperately conflicting sensations were almost too much to bear. It felt so incredibly good to have my hand in his once more, but at the same time it just reminded me of the pain he'd caused. Everything had been broken – everything. It was beyond repair, because I knew things could never go back to how they were before, no matter how sorry he was. I remembered the feeling of my heart breaking in two as my rising grief at the hopelessness of the situation seemed to break it all over again.

In the car on the way home, Cam smiled at me and pushed the play button on the CD.

'This is for you. It's all I've been playing on the way down to see you. Please listen carefully to the words,' he pleaded, his bottom lip quivering. It was a new track called 'If You're Not the One' by Daniel Beddingfield, and it took my breath away.

Music and songs had always had a huge significance in our life together. We would often play tracks to each other to express our deepest feelings, and this one seemed to reach right into my soul. I stared out of the window and listened to the words. I felt their meaning cut through my barriers. I ached for what I'd lost and yearned to wake up from the nightmare. For everything to go back to the way it was. For the chance to show Cam, really show Cam, how much I'd always loved him. Why hadn't he known it all along? Why had it taken until now? What could I have done differently? The questions continued as the music played. And Cam kept holding my hand, squeezing it and looking at me as he implored me to listen to the lyrics

'This explains how I feel better than I could even begin to. Please keep it and listen to it over again and know that every word is true,' he whispered as the final bars of the song faded away. Taking the CD out of the player, he reached under his seat before placing it in a pre-written envelope: 'For Mel, I love you forever xxx'

As he drove away back up to Manchester, I felt that I was once again being ripped in two. The past few weeks had seen me get strong and clear. Yes, I'd missed him and grieved for our lost relationship, but I told myself that it was all part of the mourning process. And I'd come a long way. But now my emotions were once again thrown into confusion. I felt raw and exposed, but, while he'd got to me, I certainly wasn't prepared to trust him or make any move to let him back in.

It was true, however, that I had loved this man deeply and honestly, with all my heart and all my soul, and now those feelings I'd worked so hard to either dissolve or bury were beginning to stir within me once again. I knew I was in for another sleepless night.

The text came at 11.30 p.m.:

Thank you Mel. Home now. Great to see you and chat. I love you and still really fancy you too. Lots of steps to move forward and today's was a big one. Sleep well and talk tomo xx

12

forgiveness and Paradise found

Cam is a man who is used to getting his way. But I am also a determined force when I put my mind to it. There was no way I was prepared to take any action or change my decision as a result of our meeting, so I decided that I would carry on as before, although I was willing to keep talking, in my own time. But he wouldn't give up. I received cards through the post, flowers when I was working on-site with clients, emails every day and literally hundreds of text messages. The texts came at all hours of the day and night, and were often very emotional. But it seemed he was experiencing the same depth of pain and confusion that I was, so that, at least, was comforting.

For me, I was least uncomfortable communicating by email or text. This allowed me the space to consider what he was saying and think carefully about my responses. So, yes, we were talking, but on my terms, although his onslaught continued, mainly by text:

22.24hrs: I love you . . . remember that I want you girl. Xxx

22.26hrs: God these emotion things really fuck your head! Feelin really positive about us . . . just missin you and want to hold you. Xxx

22.29hrs: Honesty all the way now...I messed up . . . we messed up . . . and I hope
        you are giving me a potential second chance . . . I won't mess this one
        . . . you are too special to me. Xxx

23.10hrs: I love you more than ever . . . and I will prove it and make you feel loved
        again and I will always let you in. xxx

My responses were always less emotional, still standing my ground, explaining that I just wanted to be happy but was willing to talk. But regardless of how cool or infrequent I kept my responses, he just kept on coming. After that particular barrage, I replied with a text I thought would make things clearer:

23.20hrs: We are working with the small window of opportunity you asked for
        because we are talking. I don't know if this is retrievable Cam . . . the
        damage runs deep and long . . . yes I still totally love what I believed we
        WERE and that nearly killed me in the process. So it's going to take
        time. I need time, ok?

His response was immediate.

23.25hrs: Cool. OK. I hear you. I know I love you. I know you love me. I hope
        that I am part of making you happy and that you want to make me
        happy too xxx wish you were here xxx I want to talk and I want to listen
        xxx

23.30hrs:I love you and always will. My heart body and soul wants to make us work.
        I want you and I want us. Thanks for supporting me. Xxx

The beginning of November was looming, together with Cam's birthday. His texts continued to be full of feeling and he'd begged and pleaded for us to meet up. His words came from a place I recognised from deep within him, the person I had known and loved so well. He was once again speaking a language I was familiar with. The cold stranger had disappeared without a trace, and I began to look forward to his texts. He was back to normal, and I felt that

I'd absolutely made my point clear. He'd hurt me, I was not to be messed with, and I would never be messed with again. I also believed him when he said he was sorry, and I knew that forgiveness was an incredibly powerful step towards healing. Hadn't I taught about the power of forgiveness and run countless workshop exercises during my time as a Louise Hay Trainer? Hadn't I witnessed, first-hand, how liberating it could be to let go of hurt and blame? Well, hadn't I? Perhaps this was my own opportunity to experience that feeling for myself. After all, everyone makes mistakes, don't they? And anyway, when you scratch beneath the surface, I was hardly perfect myself! So I finally agreed to meet up with him for his birthday on 5 November. We decided on Oxford, as it was halfway between Manchester and Eastbourne. He was delighted.

29th October 21.07hrs: I can't wait to see you . . . what a birthday present that is just being in your company! I love who we are and what we can be . . . may take time and be a different shape . . . let's explore with open hearts . . . talk soon xxx

I planned my moves during the drive from Eastbourne. I'd stay cool. I'd stay calm. I'd continue to press him for answers to all the questions I still had in my head. I'd be honest about my feelings. But I'd promise nothing. And although he'd made it clear he wanted a second chance, there was still a long way to go before I'd give it any serious consideration.

It was late afternoon by the time I pulled into the car park at Oxford services. I knew the place well, as it had been a regular stop-off for me and Cam when we were travelling and working away together. This time it was different, and once again I felt a kick to my stomach and an aching void where there used to be certainty and love. But I was absolutely determined to stay strong.

Nothing, though, could have prepared me for what I saw when I found him sitting in his car. It had been just under two weeks since the day he'd turned up at the office, but in that time he'd lost tons of weight and appeared tired and drained. In short, he looked absolutely terrible. His face was grey and he had huge black bags around his eyes. He had been hunched over the steering wheel but quickly leapt up and got out of the car when he saw me. The smile was a forced bravery and his eyes were red raw. He moved towards me cautiously, searching my face for clues. As he got closer, he opened his arms and the tears started to fall down his face.

'Thank you so much for coming, Mel. You just don't know what this means to me. I'm so very, very sorry for all the pain I've caused us. I haven't slept properly in days because I've been so nervous. I honestly thought you wouldn't come. Thank you. Thank you,' and with that he wrapped me in his arms and started sobbing.

Yes, he got to me. I was overwhelmed with pity and compassion for him. My Cam, the once strong and powerful man who I had fallen in love with four years earlier was now an emotional wreck. He was broken and his heart must have been breaking the same way as mine had. His performance reached me and, against my better judgement, I felt my own heart bursting open for him as I squeezed him back, holding him tightly as I breathed in the scent of him.

He'd booked an early dinner in a small country pub. It was one of those olde worlde buildings with heavy flagstone floors, chunky wooden tables and real ale on tap. I'd agreed to a meal but wasn't sure about staying the night. The choice, he assured me, was mine, and he'd support my decision either way.

There was a huge roaring fire in the corner that crackled and danced as I leaned up against the bar and surveyed my surroundings. I'd always loved real fires since I was a child. Now, of course, flames had the added depth and meaning associated with the firewalking programme. I remembered the magical evenings when we'd sit together in the group, all of us telling tales and sharing our hopes and fears. I smiled at the memories and then stopped as the void in my stomach once again reminded me that those times were gone and that things could never be the same again.

Cam ordered a bottle of wine and nodded for us to head towards the fireplace. There was a small table with two red leather armchairs right next to it. 'We can pretend we're back at the firewalk, eh, babe?' said Cam, smiling nervously as we headed away from the bar. He can't have noticed me flinching at his words, because he strode ahead while I caught my breath to stay balanced against the sudden wave of grief and anger at a treasured memory that had been vandalised and ruined forever. This was not going to be easy, and I began to wonder whether I'd already made a huge mistake.

Settling the wine and glasses on the table, Cam as usual pulled out a chair for me.

'Thanks,' was all I said. His manners were still impeccable, and he looked to me for my usual response of gratitude and love. But I was still smarting and nowhere near ready to be swayed by shows of chivalry. 'You'd better sit down. We have some serious talking to do.'

Yes, his tears at the service station car park had moved me, but I still had a barrage of questions, and I wanted full explanations. Why hadn't he come to see me earlier if he knew he'd made a mistake? If he still loved me, why hadn't he told me? If he was hurting, why had he kept his distance for so long?

His response was somewhat puzzling. 'I wanted you to come after me as soon as you found out, but you stayed strong to yourself and that really hurt. Nothing, I know, compared to the hurt I've caused you, but I love you to the core and nothing will stop me. You have to know that. And know that I want you.'

What, so he was concerned that I'd stayed strong to myself? What on earth was he talking about? What did he mean? I just didn't understand.

'I thought you'd come up to Manchester and get me out of there. But you didn't. The only reason all this happened was because I thought you didn't love me any more, and when you didn't drive up to get me when you found out the truth, it hurt me even more. You have no idea of the pain I've been going through . . .'

And so it continued, though I was left none the wiser. I interrogated and he replied, many times with answers that just confused me further. No matter how many times I asked, or in how many different ways, I still could not comprehend how he could have felt unloved by me. Had I failed in some way? Perhaps I hadn't understood him properly in Corfu. Was that when I lost him?

'No, Mel, you'd already lost me before then. It was too late. You asked me all the right questions, but I was too shut off from myself. So I certainly couldn't let you in. Surely you must be able to see that now?'

His responses were baffling. OK, I was willing to take responsibility for my part in the problems, so I wanted to know what I should I have done differently. More importantly, if there was to be even the smallest glimmer of hope for us in the future, did I have the strength to dig deeper and change the way I behave?

It didn't really matter to me what would happen at that point. Regardless of the outcome, I was willing to explore all possibilities, for whether or not we were going anywhere together, I saw this as a learning opportunity for me to develop as a person. It seems pitiful to me now, looking back at that time. Yes, I can understand the 'noble' intention to learn through difficult circumstances. I also acknowledge that this was a hugely difficult situation, and I can appreciate a level of bravery in choosing to take that route. But for goodness' sake, did I really have to put myself back into the line of fire in order to grow as a person? Hadn't I already proved myself enough when I was growing up? Now, of course, it's all so much clearer, but at the time I thought I was doing the right thing. And looking back, I still believe that it was exactly the right route to take, even though it was painful and perhaps slightly masochistic. It may seem a bit daft and unnecessarily gung-ho now, but hey, it's all part of what got me to where I am today . . .

So, settled in front of the fire, I continued probing Cam about what he thought I could have done differently. He was only too willing to oblige, explaining exactly how my actions had made him feel unloved and giving me countless examples of when those occasions had happened. I was too close with my sister and he felt shut out; my encouragement to renew contact with his family showed I didn't understand the situation – or him; I'd spent too many long evenings getting Dylan to sleep and he'd felt abandoned. The list went on and on.

'But why didn't you say something at the time?' I asked, perplexed by his long list of specific examples. But his response was always the same.

'Because I didn't think you loved me any more, so I was afraid and started shutting down. You don't know what it's been like for me, but now, I hope, we can make progress together. We've both messed up here, and it's up to us both to make this work. Because we both want it.'

That night we shared a bed for the first time since Corfu. It was strange and uncomfortable. He wanted to hold me, kiss me and touch me. But I wasn't ready. Wearing my pyjamas, I agreed to be cuddled, but that was it. My emotions were churning, and I felt lost and bewildered, confused by the conversations we'd had before. But he'd got me thinking in a different way, and I reconsidered the examples he'd given. Perhaps he was right. Perhaps I had been too wrapped up in my own thoughts. Perhaps I had been to blame. It was tough. But my overwhelming desire was to find the truth, so I was prepared to explore every avenue, however unpleasant or uncomfortable.

Lying beside him late that night – or early the next morning – I watched him sleeping, making soft snores and at last with a more peaceful expression on his face. Could it be true that I'd been responsible for hurting this man I had loved so dearly? Perhaps my strength of character meant that I'd become too blinkered and could no longer read the deepest feelings of those close to me? These new questions turned and grew in my head, until eventually I gave in to yet another night of restless sleep and disturbing dreams.

On my drive home the next morning, I felt a little clearer. Yes,

I could understand lots of the points Cam had raised. While I didn't agree with many of them, I could accept that perhaps – perhaps – I had been blinded by my own dogged determination to make things right and to help others. The text arrived just as I pondered whether or not I might be willing to take things a little further with Cam:

> I love you. Please be with me. Life without you is soul less . . . Life without you is nothing. You are my light. Help me find it again. I love you so much and I will spend my life telling you and making it up to both you and Dylan. I love you. Xxx'

It worked. By the end of November, I was regularly meeting up with him and by the first week of December I decided to re-introduce him to Dylan. My son had been very matter-of-fact when I asked him how he would feel if we were to consider letting Cam back in.

'If Cam is going to come back, he has to stop being grumpy. And he's never to hurt you ever again. If he loves you, he won't. So make sure you're certain before you let him back, OK?'

His terms were clear, and on that basis Cam started paying regular visits to our home. My questions continued, because, as Dylan had so rightly said, I had to be certain before committing to anything more permanent. It's true, I still couldn't get my head around some of his explanations, but he never complained at my relentless questions. His responses were always clear – if puzzling – and by the end of December I decided I was ready to give us another chance. Although the scars were still raw, I knew that the magic we had shared together for the first three years was worth fighting for. I knew it wouldn't be easy, but I was willing to forgive him and move on.

Cam moved back into the family home at the beginning of January 2003. He continued to be attentive, gentle and caring, showering both Dylan and I with treats and presents at every opportunity. One day he came home with a top-of-the-range piano keyboard for me, 'Because I know you love to play and I want you to be happy. I want you to be who you want to be because I love you.' He'd also bought the sheet music for Daniel Beddingfield's 'If You're Not the One' and he looked coyly at the floor as I opened it up. 'I hope you like it, Mel. I hope you think of me and remember I mean every word in the lyrics each time you play the music. I never meant to hurt you or Dylan, and I will spend the rest of my life making it up to you both.'

My friends had been supportive of my decision, though many of them had taken Cam aside to warn him against ever repeating his mistakes, and all of them said they just wanted what was best for me.

'If you're happy, then I'm happy,' my friend Kirsty had said to me one evening over a bottle of wine. 'I can't say I'm pleased with Cam, but I do respect your willingness to forgive. It can't be easy, and I'm here to support you. Good on you, girl, you're stronger than I could have been!'

With everything that had happened, I was keen on making a clean break. A new start in a new home – that, for me, was the only way forward. A few years earlier, we'd spent a fun-filled family holiday in France, and we'd enthused that we'd love to retire to the area. So, one evening at home by the fire, watching yet another episode of the popular TV series *No Going Back*, we discussed the idea of moving to France.

The programme followed the highs and lows of families who decided to escape the rat race and move abroad to a new way of life. The programme we watched that evening was of a couple with a young child who had made the move across the Channel and were now happily living in an old French house and running a successful gite business.

'Why not?' asked Cam. 'Don't we deserve the chance to live life to the full? We've always loved France, the property's cheap and we can start afresh. No memories, no people to judge us – just you, me and Dylan. A whole new start!'

It seemed like a crazy pipe dream at first, but after a further discussions and plenty of research on the Internet, the idea started to make a lot of sense. At seven years old, Dylan was the perfect age to embrace a new language. The property prices were ridiculously cheap and with the exchange rate at a high of 1.6 euro to the pound our living costs would also be greatly reduced.

We researched the Charente area, where we'd holidayed. It boasted a micro-climate and most importantly it was serviced by three airports that all offered cheap and regular flights to London. It would be easy to commute, which meant we could continue with our training business. If we sold our house, we could buy a property outright and, yes, we could start afresh. I was excited!

'Well, I hope you know what you're doing,' was all that my sister said when I phoned to tell her of our plans. She had never warmed to Cam in the way I had hoped she would, and, while she supported my decision to give it another go, she had distanced herself even further from him since then. 'You'll be away from friends and family, Mel. What happens if Cam does something stupid again?'

Disappointed by her response to my excitement, I brushed her comments aside and went ahead with my research. I could understand that people would be dubious about what seemed like a far-fetched plan, but I was becoming more and more certain this could be a wonderful opportunity for all of us to live life to the full.

It was the middle of February when we first saw and fell in love with the old Charentaise farmhouse that was to become our home. Nestled on the bank of the River Charente, it was a collection of stone barns attached to a 'habitable' two-bedroom house. Yes, it needed lots of work, but it was in a fair enough state that we could move in almost straight away.

The details had been far from promising on the website, and it was the very last house we looked at. To be honest, I had wanted to cancel the viewing because the photographs looked shabby and it was well below our budget. 'I don't think it's worth it,' I'd said, shaking my head as I re-read the scant details we'd printed from the

Internet. 'It'll take us 40 minutes to get there, and we've already got some good choices. We're going home tomorrow, so can't we just spend the time getting to know the area a bit better?'

Cam convinced me to at least give it a chance. 'We've got nothing to lose, Mel,' he'd countered, 'and who knows, it might be just what we've been looking for!'

He was right. I was intrigued as soon as we drove into the tiny hamlet. A winding country lane took us along a burbling, tree-lined river. Passing two stone-built houses on our right, we turned a corner and parked up in front of a huge set of light blue double gates. They were chained with a large padlock and the buildings were clearly deserted. The estate agent, Terry, worked the lock with a huge grin on his face.

'This one's an absolute treat,' he enthused. 'Just wait and see!'

He'd already explained that the house had been empty for a good while, but as we walked into the huge grassed courtyard there was something about its appearance that grabbed my attention. Was it the creamy-coloured Charentaise stone that reminded me of the village I had loved so much as a child? Was it the whisperings of previous families who had lived here? Was it the location? I don't know, but as we continued further into the garden, I was taken aback by the size of the place. Beautiful old stone buildings ran around three sides of the courtyard, and right in the middle was the most enormous cherry tree.

'You'll get fantastic cherries,' Terry continued. 'And the great thing is that you can be totally secluded here if you choose. This place actually belongs to me. I bought it last year because it has so much potential and I love the location, but I'm just too busy to do anything with it,' he continued, bounding up to the house.

Inside, the house felt empty and cold. The decor was dated, but the house had certainly been someone's pride and joy at one point. It had a fairly modern kitchen (not to my taste, but perfectly clean and functional), a downstairs toilet and bathroom (both were hideous – one of the first things to change I thought to myself!) and two large front rooms. Terry was still chatting away in the background, but neither of us was listening.

By now I was totally enraptured by the place, poking into the old cupboards, peeking behind the peeling wallpaper and imagining where our furniture would go. As well as the house there were numerous barns, all with good roofs and so many possibilities it was almost mind blowing! The whole property had such a great feel about it. It held so much potential and was absolutely perfect – and, more to the point, I felt totally and utterly as though I'd 'come home'. I checked in with Cam, who, by the smile on his face, was clearly having the same reaction as I was, and we silently nodded to each other. We'd finally found our new home. But the best was yet to come.

Terry took us back out through the front gates and down to the river, where we continued along the little track by the side of the bank. It took us past a walled garden area ('This comes with the property as well by the way. The previous owner used to grow tons of vegetables here') and along the length of two fields where the small river on our left suddenly gave way to a huge expanse of water.

'Now this,' continued Terry, barely able to control his excitement, 'is the *pièce de résistance*. Check this out. You've got your own little ferry!' and with that he started pulling at the wires that traversed the river. They were attached to an old, wooden-slatted, oak ferryboat, known as a barque. We all climbed in, and Cam and I slowly pulled our way across the river. It was very wide and clearly very deep.

'You should see this place in the summer – it's great for swimming and canoeing!' winked Terry. It was absolutely breathtaking, and we stopped in the middle to drink in the scenery. The water was tranquil and a beautiful deep turquoise green, with tree-lined banks stretching out either side. I could see our house from here (because by that time it was most certainly ours, there was no way I was letting this one slip through my fingers!), its beautiful creamy yellow stonewalls and light terracotta-tiled roof beaming and calling out towards us.

'It's perfect, I love it!' I whispered, squeezing Cam's hand

'It's where we're meant to be, Mel. It's where we were always meant to be,' he murmured into my hair, wrapping his arms around my body and lifting my chin to kiss my forehead. With one final nod between us confirming what we were about to do, I turned to face Terry.

'OK, we'll take it. No nonsense, what's your best price?' Less than three minutes later and the deal was done. It was Saturday, 15 February 2003.

We collected the keys on Thursday, 17 March, the beginning of the Easter weekend. We had driven down with Dylan, packing as many essentials as we could possibly fit into our Land Rover Defender. A removal lorry was due to deliver more of the bigger essentials – mattresses, a few chairs and a garden table that could be used inside or out – and we planned to buy a fridge and cooker while we were there. The plan was to take a few working holidays over to France, decorating the place ready for us to make the permanent move that summer. Our house in the UK was on the market, and once that was sold we would transport all the rest of our furniture. So, for now, the idea was to make the place liveable, that was all.

Dylan, like us, absolutely fell in love with the place, and his face was a picture when we showed him the river. 'Wow!' he exclaimed, his eyes just about popping out of his head. 'This is so much better than a swimming pool! Can I go and explore?' With that he paddled across the rocks and earth banks and climbed onto the small island that sat between the main river and the shallower part that went past our house.

'I'm the king of the castle!' he shouted, while Cam and I waved back.

'Now this is what I call magic, don't you think, Mel? He's going to have a whale of a time here. I'm so glad we decided to do this!' We had our arms around each other, and for the first time in a long while I felt the magic taking hold again. Yes, Cam was right – this was absolutely the right move.

That night I made tomato pasta (we'd bought a microwave and a tiny fridge that same afternoon), and the three of us sat in the front room on rickety old chairs around a rusty old table we'd found in one of the barns. We hadn't realised that there were no bulbs in any of the light-fittings, so we ate by candlelight and the glowing flames from the huge open fire. It was incredibly romantic, and I couldn't keep the smile from my face. Dylan tasted his first drink of Orangina during our simple meal and he shook the bottle with obvious enthusiasm. 'I LOVE France!' he'd squealed as he gulped down the brightly coloured fizzy drink.

I still have the photographs from that evening, and, seeing Dylan's smiling face and remembering the sheer delight of that first night, I always get a warm feeling in my tummy whenever I look at them.

Later that night, with Dylan asleep in his blow-up sleeping bag we'd bought from Woolworths before we left, Cam and I curled in each other's arms in front of the fire. I couldn't have been happier.

'See you in dreamland, babe,' Cam whispered as he started drifting off to sleep, but as far as I was concerned I was already there. The dream had become my reality, and I was busy imagining a brilliant future for all of us.

Over the next couple of months, we took regular trips down to the house, the car stuffed full of DIY equipment and bundles of smaller essentials for the house. The place had been sold as 'habitable', but there was a huge amount of cleaning and decoration to be done before we could realistically live there. But a few personal bits and pieces and a fresh lick of paint and the once deserted house soon started to feel like a cosy home. I grew to love our visits more and more. We were usually exhausted, filthy and covered in paint by the time we got home, but it just didn't matter. We were shaping our new home together.

I also used the trips to continue making peace with myself and with Cam over what had happened. Forgiveness, I found, is not as easy as I had imagined, although I had been under no illusions in the first place. I knew it would be difficult but, crikey, the process was really tough going!

Cam seemed completely clear and settled with the whole episode, but I was still struggling to make sense of it all. I still couldn't get to the bottom of what had made him change. What had triggered his belief that I didn't love him any more? When had it happened? What had I been doing differently? Where were the signs, and how had I missed them? I would torture myself with vividly imagined scenes of him with Sophie, the agony compounded because some of those times had happened way before I knew anything was wrong. It meant that even my most precious memories of the time when I believed we were happy together were now tainted. Cam, however, had become less keen to answer my questions.

'This is your stuff now, Mel,' he'd tell me each time I had another barrage of questions. 'I've dug deep and managed to clear my issues. Perhaps yours are more to do with your past than with what happened to us. We can find a counsellor if that would help, but I think you're doing really well working through it on your own. I'm proud of you.'

After he'd made it clear that the issues I continued to struggle with were largely my own, I began to find respite through the DIY work we were doing on the house. Stripping wallpaper allowed me to metaphorically strip away the bad or confusing memories. Cleaning stained surfaces allowed me to wipe away my imagined scenes of Cam with Sophie. Painting walls and skirting boards encouraged me to deliberately invite brightness into my life. And, yes, I also used the opportunities to wash away older hurts from my childhood as well. Inch by inch, room by room, I slowly and purposefully continued working silently through my pain.

By the time we made the permanent move on 26 July 2003, I was once more happy and contented. I'd done so much work on myself and was so in love with the whole new adventure, that any remaining doubts or pain had all but disappeared. I was simply focused on creating the best home and an idyllic lifestyle for my family. Cam was once again the person I had fallen in love with – perhaps more so. He was attentive, thoughtful, considerate and caring, and he told me every day how much he loved me.

'You mean everything to me, babe,' he'd say. 'You are my light, and I am so grateful for our second chance. Every day, for the rest of my life, I'm going to keep reminding you just how much I love you and Dylan.'

The move, however, had not been without a few hiccups. Despite our best efforts, we'd been unable to sell our house in the UK, so instead we'd found tenants with a view to marketing the house again a year or so later. We'd secured a small loan on the French property and remortgaged our UK house to pay the balance. Although it was pretty stressful while we were going through it, the whole process ended up being the best solution in the end. It afforded us usage of the tiny thatched building that had been our office for the past couple of years, meaning that Kitty could still base herself from there and also keep an eye on the house in the meantime.

'It's OK!' she'd said. 'I love working here. I'll look after the business for you, you know that. I may not be seeing you both as often, but I'll be on the phone every day and over to see you as soon as I can!'

We felt at home in France sooner than I could have imagined, and I would happily tell people that I had found my own piece of paradise (in actual fact, I still use those very words when describing where I live!). Life was once again good, and now it held the added bonus of becoming so very much better as Cam, Dylan and I concentrated on settling into our new country, new relationship and new way of life together.

13

La Vie En Rose

The next few months were akin to living in paradise. The simpler way of life suited me perfectly. I was born and raised in a tiny village, and I felt almost instantly at home from the moment we arrived in our French hamlet. I had studied French at A level, so, although it had been more years than I cared to think about since I had practised the language, I soon found the words flooding back – albeit my accent, tenses and vocabulary were far from perfect!

We were very quickly accepted into the village, which was made up of a total of twelve old stone houses, four of which were inhabited by English people (two holiday homes and one other permanent residence), the rest by French (again, three holiday homes). We loved the hot weather and the opportunity to live most of the time outside. Barbecues were no longer an occasional weekend treat, they became a daily occurrence, and we never tired of sitting outside enjoying the peace and tranquillity and feasting on good French food.

'Wow!' said Cam, tucking in to his third piece of barbecued meat. 'Who'd have thought that pork could taste so different and so thoroughly and utterly delicious! I'm loving this life!'

And as for the wine – well, we'd always enjoyed a few glasses in the UK, but here the wine was so much cheaper and of much better quality. I confess there were some evenings it slipped down far too easily.

One such evening, we'd invited our English neighbours over for dinner. Robert's wife, Sylvie, was off on a walking holiday, and we thought it would be nice to get to know our neighbour a bit better. Since he had retired some years earlier, we thought it would be an early evening. Oh no. At 1 a.m., Robert, a slender fellow with enormous eyes, a great sense of humour and a wealth of fascinating stories to tell, let slip that he played the saxophone. Happy to oblige our invitation to play, we all sat round for the next couple of hours with Cam accompanying the hauntingly beautiful notes of the saxophone by strumming his guitar and me singing along to the music. It was magical, although I'm quite sure in reality that 'magical' could only really be applied to the atmosphere rather than our combined sound! It didn't matter. We all had a lovely time, and long after Robert had tottered off home Cam and I were still sitting outside wondering at our good fortune.

'A perfect home, a perfect evening and a perfect wife. I must have done something pretty good in a previous life to deserve all this richness!' Cam whispered softly, emptying the remains of the last bottle into our glasses.

'It's as though all my dreams have come true,' I replied. 'I am so lucky and so blessed, and this was the best decision we ever made! I love you more than I can begin to explain. I hope you really know that now.'

Dylan started school in the September. He had just turned eight and the first day I'm really not sure who was more nervous – him or me. It was a tiny village school just four kilometres from our house, a one-storey building consisting of two large classrooms that housed just twenty-eight pupils ranging from six to twelve. I remember that first day as if it was yesterday. I had been told to bring a pair of slippers for Dylan, together with two serviettes. These, it seemed, were the most important items for the start of term. I could just about understand the slippers idea – after all, I remember needing indoor and outdoor shoes when I had been in junior school. Slippers, though, were much more quaint. But the serviettes?

Cam and I were heavily into DIY, working hard on the house in our attempt to gradually turn it into the dream house we had visualised. So, even though I'd washed and scrubbed myself before turning up at the school, I was still covered in paint splashes and I wasn't wearing a scrap of make-up. I dared to ask Dylan's teacher, a petite dark-haired woman about my age, who was immaculately dressed and made-up, why we needed two serviettes.

She looked at me in absolute horror. 'Why, so he can use it at lunchtime, of course!' she retorted, her eyes widening as she scanned me up and down, obviously less than impressed by my paint-splattered hair and face, lack of make-up and scruffy clothing.

'He will need a clean one every day, which is why he must have two. You will of course be expected to wash them every weekend,' she said, her lips tightening at the stupidity of my question.

Feeling suitably castigated for my ignorance and scruffy appearance, I gave Dylan a sheepish kiss goodbye and watched her march him off to introduce him to his classmates before sloping back to my car with as much poise as my decorator's clothes and paint-splattered trainers would allow. I chuckled to myself as I imagined the staffroom discussions about this wild-looking foreigner who hadn't understood the significance of the daily two-hour lunch breaks, the focal point of which was a three-course meal.

'These English women! How can they show themselves looking so scruffy and without even a scrap of eyeliner? Oh, that poor boy, what must his life be like at home?'

Her name was Jacqueline, and as it turned out, we first became allies and eventually good friends over the coming weeks, as Dylan's French improved day by day. Each evening I would sit with him and help him with the language and his homework. Understandably, he became hugely frustrated at times, and there were many occasions I questioned my wisdom at uprooting him from his school in

England where he had been very popular, top of the class and head of his house. So I started writing notes to Jacqueline, explaining the extra language homework we were doing and asking for additional French resources so that Dylan and I could do more to get him used to this new way of life.

To start with, though, he refused to speak to anyone in his class. 'I can't!' he wailed. 'Whenever I say anything, they all want to talk to me at once, and I don't understand!' But his comprehension improved at a dramatic rate. It was mainly a confidence issue. So, to combat this I thought it might be a good idea to find a way for him to feel more in control of communication with his peers. My solution might raise a few eyebrows, but I provided Dylan with a comprehensive list of English swear words that he was encouraged to swap for the equivalent in French – one at a time – with his friends in the playground. This seemed to give him an edge, a certain *je ne sais quoi*, and all of a sudden he became the cool English kid that everyone wanted to know. He quickly gained friends and confidence as well as an impressively wide vocabulary of slang and swearwords to rival any adult, French or English. My left-field plan had paid off, and within three months he was totally fluent. Good – we had arrived!

The business was ticking over very nicely at this point. We'd taken our foot off the gas, because the prime focus was to settle into our new home, but the work was still coming in, including design work that could be completed from home. We'd made a pact that we wouldn't spend another night apart unless absolutely necessary, so we had associates taking on much of the face-to-face delivery work. On the odd occasion that a trip back was necessary for either one of us, we'd make sure it was as short a trip as possible. With a regular TGV service to Paris and then to King's Cross, plus three airports within easy drive and plenty of flight times, it meant this was easily achievable and everything went to plan. We were earning enough money and living a proper life as a family for the first time. On more than one occasion I'd heard Cam boasting to friends and clients alike that he'd got it all.

'I'm in my mid-30s, semi-retired and living the dream!' he'd enthuse. 'And I have the most gorgeous, sexy wife in the world to boot – ain't life grand?' I couldn't have been happier.

Cam continued to be the perfect husband and family man, and was also proving himself to be pretty handy on the DIY front. Electricity, plumbing and building work were all within his grasp. Reminding me that he'd done all of this before, he seemed to delight in proving his range of hidden skills. He'd playfully tut at me whenever I tried to join in, and he thought I was out of my depth, either on DIY conversations or on one of the many jobs we had started within the house. He'd laugh when I put forward an innocent suggestion and raise his eyebrows when I explained my future plans and the timescale I thought we should work to. Patting my shoulder, my leg and on the odd occasion my head, which I found rather patronising, he'd gently remind me that he knew about all this stuff and that I should leave it in his hands.

'I know what I'm doing. Trust me. I've done this before, remember?' he would say, giggling whenever I moved my head away from his hand. 'I'm here to look after you now. I told you, I want to be the best husband in the world, and you're not to worry about a thing!' His winning smile told me he meant it, so I would shrug my shoulders and get back to simple manual labour – painting, sanding and, of course, cooking.

We continued along in that way for the next few months, our house gradually taking shape and our relationship becoming stronger by the day. So much so that by the end of the summer the following year, we agreed to renew our wedding vows. It had been five years since our marriage, and after everything we'd come through we thought it would be a fitting testament to our new-found love and happiness together.

So it was that on Saturday, 9 October 2004, we led a colourful procession of more than 60 friends and family from the UK and France through the village and up to the twelfth-century church that takes pride of place at the top of the hill. We were accompanied by the haunting sounds of pipes and drums played by a local band of costumed young men who had their roots in Breton music. Not dissimilar to the sound of Scottish bagpipes, the group had been only too pleased to oblige my request for them to accompany us to and from the church.

A couple of weeks earlier, we had dutifully been to the Mairie to ask permission from the mayor to use the church for a couple of hours. We knew it was a radical request as the church is very rarely used, and we were asking if we could conduct our very own ceremony to celebrate five years of marriage. Nothing religious, no need for any priest or legal representatives, just the opportunity to create something very personal to us that we'd like to share with a handful of friends and relatives as witnesses.

I hadn't known how our request was likely to be received. '*Bah oui, bien sur! Pourquoi pas?*' the mayor had replied, accompanied with the traditional Charentaise shrugging of shoulders and a wide smile, and word soon got out among the commune about what we were planning to do. To my astonishment, the local committee des fêtes, a small group of locals who organise the handful of annual celebratory get-togethers for the nearby villages, immediately rallied round. It was really quite astounding. They told me they'd lend us the village marquee together with tables, chairs, lights, cutlery and crockery. They'd even come and set it all up for us at no charge whatsoever because we were part of the commune! They'd also arrange a spit-roast lamb – a local speciality that requires a crack-of-dawn set-up and dedicated anointment with herbs and oils for the next ten-plus hours while the meat cooks through to perfection. On top of that, they would set up in our hangar with all their cooking pots and equipment, so they could prepare and serve the five-course meal for us – soup to start, followed by salad, then the lamb and beans, a cheese course then apple pie and coffee to finish. No matter how may times I offered, they would only accept payment for the raw ingredients. Everything else – the shopping, the preparation, the cooking, the service and even the washing up – was all to be done just because they wanted to. No money was to change hands because we were part of the commune and because looking after one another is what people do around here. The gentle, relaxed and caring Charentaise attitude I'd already grown to love in this simple farming community warmed my heart and made me glad to be alive.

'*Bah, mais c'est normale!*' shrugged Bernie, a kindly rounded lady in her mid-60s with a weather-beaten and wrinkled patchworked face, the typical slippered feet and Charentaise blue chequered apron her daily uniform.

'Don't worry about a thing, Melanie. We're family now, eh?' Lowering her voice, she then nudged me in the ribs, her mischievous black eyes sparkling as a knowing smile crept across her face. 'After all, it's your wedding. You've got much more important things to take care of with that handsome young husband of yours, eh?' and with a conspiratorial wink she let out a huge belly laugh and bustled me away so she could continue with her preparations.

If ever I had wondered whether or not we could be accepted, there were no doubts now!

The day was absolutely perfect. The shining sun and unusually warm weather only added to my feelings of love and happiness. Everyone else settled themselves on the old wooden church pews while the band continued to play. It was only after they'd finished that Cam and I then went inside. Just as we were about to enter, I turned to him.

'Isn't this just magical?' I asked, squeezing his hand, the emotion already catching in my throat.

'Yes, babe,' he replied, 'and it's all the more amazing because you're here with me. I never thought this day would happen. Thank you for loving me.'

And with that we went in. I took a deep breath and held my head as high as I could as we walked together across the ancient white cobbled floor and in between the two rows of wooden benches, all eyes following us as we made our way to the front of the church where Dylan and our dear friend Matt were already waiting. We'd first met Matt when he was a client some eight years earlier, but since then we'd become the best of friends. He'd supported me through the earlier storms and been one of the closest allies for Cam after we got back together again. He worked in radio, his earlier years having been spent as a voiceover man. Just as we'd asked Skye to oversee the ritual in the field all those years ago, we wanted Matt to take that role during this, a much more poignant ceremony. We'd written our own vows, and Matt was to introduce us in English, with Dylan, also at the front of the church, reading out the French translation. It was to be a personal, bilingual family affair.

The ceremony itself was charged with emotion. After Matt's welcome and introduction, his beautifully theatrical voice resonating around the entire building, it was my turn to read the very first vow. Matt had already cued it up in English, and my job quite simply was to say it in French, to Cam. This is the English version of what I had to say: 'I have learned that a choice, once made, is not necessarily completed. I have chosen you many times since our wedding day. I choose you still.'

I'd read the French translation to myself a thousand times before; indeed, I'd read the whole ceremony a thousand times as I was pulling the scripts together. So I knew exactly what to expect. Which is why I was so shocked when I faltered at the very first hurdle. Opening my mouth to speak, no sound came out. Instead, a nauseous feeling rising up too swiftly for comfort forced me to shut my mouth again very quickly and very firmly. My throat closed up. I could feel the heat in my heart pumping tension around my body as I fought with all my might to get my raging torrent of emotions back under control. Dizzy and swaying, I blinked furiously as I continued looking down at the floor, desperate for some inspiration to guide me through.

All eyes were on me as Cam gently took my hand and squeezed it. 'It's OK,' he whispered. 'I love you babe.'

162

I could feel everyone in the congregation holding their breath and willing me to regain my composure. It was an astonishing sensation. My increasing anxiety was by now spreading throughout the whole church, and I could hear a few sniffs and rustling of tissues. Still unable to meet anyone's gaze for fear I would dissolve completely, I took a deep and determined breath, raised my head and pulled myself up as tall as I possibly could. And then from somewhere, I don't know where, I found my voice again. Speaking loudly and clearly I repeated the same vow in French: '*J'ai decouvert qu'un choix une fois decider n'est pas toujours accompli. Je t'ai choisi mille fois depuis notre jour du marriage. Tu restera toujours mon choix.*'

The mass sigh of relief was enormous, and everyone relaxed and started breathing normally once more. We completed the rest of the service without any further hitches, and when it was done Dylan lit the candle lantern we'd brought with us. Holding it high in the air, he shouted for everyone to follow us and start the party back home.

I simply cannot describe the depth and breadth of emotions I experienced as we paraded back from the church, the pipers playing once more and everyone full of smiles and congratulations. I truly felt as though I'd come home – properly this time. Not only to the place I loved but also to the husband I had always loved with all my heart. Despite the odds, Cam, Dylan and I had made it. We were a proper family at last and the past was well and truly just that – the past. Now we were free to live our lives in the way we'd always dreamed...

The renewal ceremony ushered in a new vibrancy and love – not only to our relationship, but to life in general. And it carried on that way. The next four years were a continuation of the dream. Yes, we had a few ups and downs, and a few uncomfortably difficult financial glitches, but we made it through. Cam and I were living, loving and working together, Dylan was thriving, and I couldn't have been happier – or so I thought.

14
Pushed to the Limit

2008 was a big year. We celebrated ten years of being together as well as Cam's fortieth birthday. At the beginning of the year, we had survived a financial meltdown that had driven both of us almost to the point of no return. It had all started the previous summer when we'd agreed the sale of our house in the UK. The tenants were buying, at a price we had agreed between us, and we were all there bar the final paperwork. We'd moved Kitty out of the thatched cottage and into a modern office closer to where she lived. On the day we moved, the tenants had brought a bottle of champagne for us all to share in celebration of their impending purchase.

Cam and I had often talked about where the business was going and how we could plan for a more secure future in our old age. We had always avoided the pensions route, mainly based on Cam's knowledge of the financial industry.

'It's a fool's game,' he'd told me on numerous occasions. 'The return is practically worthless and there are no guarantees in any case. We'll be much better to plough our money into property or other investments.'

I agreed and with the house sale going through we would have a healthy chunk of capital to invest – somewhere in the region of £85,000. This is what drove our decision to investigate property options. We made up our minds to re-invest our money in a property in Edinburgh, Cam's old hometown. It was near his daughter, with whom he was desperately hoping to reconcile, and if we bought the right type of property in the right place we were confident that we could offer it out as an executive let to cover the mortgage. On top of that, we'd also committed to a new build buy-to-let property in Derby that was one of those no-cash down deals and more or less guaranteed income return through rental.

Scottish law is very different from English law when it comes to property. In Scotland, as soon as you say yes to buying, you have to follow through, or pay a hefty fine based on a percentage of the property value. Confident and reassured by our solicitors that the house sale in Sussex was all stacked up and ready to go, we chose to make an offer on a reasonably priced modern apartment at the top of a refurbished block near the centre of town. The spacious penthouse flat was bright and airy, with a balcony that ran right along both the back and front of the building. It had three double bedrooms, two bathrooms and a huge open plan living/dining/kitchen area – perfect for renting out on short-term executive lets, both because of the layout, and also because of the location. It was a no-brainer. We would have plenty of money to cover the deposit as well as re-vamp and furnish the place to the necessarily high standards for top-end rentals, and the mortgage would be covered at least twice over with the income we'd receive. Perfect!

So, after checking one more time that the purchase of our old home was on track we went ahead and signed the purchase agreement documents.

And that was our mistake. Because the house sale in Sussex fell flat on its face. The tenants, it turned out, were merely stringing us along. They then refused to pay the monthly rent and kept quoting us their rights. We subsequently discovered that they had done exactly the same thing to previous landlords. We had no option other than to turn to the law for help. Little did we realise, however, just how ineffective the law can be when it comes to the rights of a landlord. It took until just before Christmas to even secure a court hearing, and that was after completing reams of forms that had us feel that we were the criminals! At that hearing, the judge decided that the tenants could stay in our house, believing their sob story that they had found an alternative place to buy and had nowhere else to go until the sale was completed. The fact that they'd ruined our plans and were not paying rent seemed to have little sway in his decision.

'These are decent honest people who cannot be made homeless over the festive season,' he said. 'I hereby rule that they may stay, and we will reassess the situation at the beginning of February.' Unbelievable.

We had to go ahead with the purchase in Edinburgh in the meantime – there was no choice. It was either that or lose some £35,000 if we backed out. It was nail-biting stuff, as we did everything we could to raise money on our home in Sussex. The home in which our tenants were living in rent-free. The same tenants who had rights as to who could or couldn't enter the property. Neither Cam nor I were permitted to go near the place, and it took hours of careful negotiations to organise a visit for the surveyor so we could secure a re-mortgage. Even then the tenants were surly and unhelpful, pointing out real and imaginary defects on the property that may have swayed the valuation. It was pitifully low, and we had to pull out all the stops to secure enough money for the deposit on the Edinburgh flat. As well as the loan, we racked every single credit card right up to its limit – my credit cards, of course, since Cam had never recovered his credit rating from his previous financial problems.

But by hook or by crook we did it, although we were totally up to every single financial limit, with no cushion, and very little work coming in. Stress levels built, we were finding it difficult to sleep, and we often took to drinking wine to dull the growing feelings of desperation.

Both of us were knocked out by a debilitating attack of flu over Christmas, and by the middle of January I just didn't know how we were going to get through the growing financial crisis, which was made worse by the fact that we felt powerless to deal with the sitting tenants who were clearly mocking our situation.

'I'm going to do something about this,' Cam had slurred, downing yet another large glass of red wine. 'Just you watch. I know how to get out of this. You're just going to have to trust me, Mel. Leave it up to me, OK?'

I agreed. I had always been the one who more or less took control of our finances, and I was relieved to see Cam willing to step up and take responsibility. He'd been a very successful financial adviser in his youth, and I had often asked him to get involved with our business planning, but he'd brushed me aside, reminding me that he was the one in the front line.

'Mel, I'm the one who delivers the training and keeps our reputation shining. I can't get involved with anything else,' he'd tell me, ruffling my hair and giving my shoulders a squeeze. 'And anyway, with you doing invoicing and all those little jobs, well, it keeps you occupied and feeling part of things, doesn't it?'

I don't know what he did, or how he did it, but somehow he went about arranging an unsecured loan in the region of £40,000. He wouldn't tell me the details but just kept telling me to trust him and got angry when I pushed for too much information.

'You don't need to know,' he'd shout, slamming his fists on the table. 'Do you have any idea how much pressure I'm under with this? I'm running the gauntlet here to take away the stress from you, so you'll just have to trust me. Is that too much to ask?'

He'd taken to drinking early in the afternoon, whether he was too stressed, too angry, or had made some level of progress. Any reason for opening a bottle of wine.

'A day without wine is a day without sunshine!' he'd trill, as the red liquid glugged in to one of our oversized wineglasses.

He'd also agreed to completely take over the company finances, and again I breathed a huge sigh of relief. Perhaps now he'd curb his spending. Perhaps now, if he was the one in charge of balancing the books, he'd stop pushing for more and more expensive gadgets, toys or unnecessary office equipment.

He'll learn just how difficult it is now, I thought to myself, pleased that he wanted to step up and take responsibility.

The unsecured loan, as it turned out, was something that made me feel increasingly uncomfortable. It reached the stage where we got an offer through and I was required to co-sign the documentation. I balked.

"This is far too risky, it just doesn't feel right!" I cried as I read the paperwork, horrified at the information given to the lenders. "I'm not doing it! No way!"

'Don't overreact, Mel,' he countered, his voice calm and reasoning, his arm around my shoulders. 'It'll be fine. I know this market. Just trust me, OK?'

Feeling uncomfortable, I pushed and questioned for ages, but eventually he wore me down. Unhappy and uneasy, I felt I had no option but to sign the form, so finally I did just that.

Call it divine intervention, call it circumstance, it really doesn't matter. But the loan, thank goodness, was turned down at the last minute. There was one more piece of paperwork they needed in order to make it go through. Cam couldn't make it in time, and we were denied the money. Cam was furious, but I was relieved beyond words. And I focused all my energy on finding an honest way to get us out of our troubles.

Based on my Louise Hay experience, I knew one of the first things I needed to do was to get my thoughts back on track. We had both been under so much stress that it was a daily struggle sometimes even just to function, never mind keep my thoughts positive! So that very same evening, I sat in front of my computer and composed an email asking for help from all our friends. It went something like this:

Most of you know our situation, and many of you have lent us an ear and a shoulder to cry on as we've battled through our problems – thank you!

I'm writing now to ask you for help. I don't want to talk about our issues any more, neither do I want any advice. We are at rock bottom, and I don't know what else to do. All I want right now is some kind of message of support. Something that will give us a lift. Anything to remind us that we're OK, that we'll get through.

Thank you, my friends, and I look forward to hearing from you.

It took every ounce of courage to press the send button, and as soon as I had I switched off the computer and went to bed, crying myself to sleep. How could we have got into such a mess? What have we been doing wrong? Now all our friends knew we'd hit rock bottom, and yet we were meant to be motivational trainers and coaches? Hah! Ain't that a joke?

Cam, on the other hand, stayed downstairs drinking yet more wine. He was watching television and refused to come to bed with me. 'We deal with things in different ways, babe,' he'd mumbled, his eyeballs flickering back and forth from the effect of too much alcohol. 'I'll be fine here for a while. Don't you worry about me. I'll be up soon.'

But I was worried about me, and I felt desperately alone, empty and scared to the pit of my dark, cavernous stomach.

The next morning I nervously switched on my computer, squinting as the screen flickered in to life. I could hardly believe my eyes. My email box was flooded with responses from our beloved friends. Some had sent poems, others had sent photographs. Some had written out reminders about who we were and how we'd helped them in the past. Others sent a ream of motivational quotes. It was astonishing and overwhelming at the same time, and the tears that blurred my vision as I read through the emails were, for the first time in months, tears of joy and gratitude.

I printed out every single one of the messages and stuck them all to the fridge. I wanted to have a daily reminder of what people thought about us, so that we could both get our own thoughts back on track and find a positive solution out of the stifling negativity that had bound us for so long. And it worked. From that moment on, things started to change – fast.

We got the tenants out of our house in Sussex and secured back-payment for the rent they owed. We received enquiries from two brand-new clients, both generated by people who had worked with us in previous years. Both were huge companies who were calling us to help them on major projects and it wasn't a question of 'if' they were going to work with us, it was a questions of 'what' we were going to do. We secured a short-term business loan with our bank, which I had to guarantee since I was still the only director of the business after Cam's affair, and we finally put the house on the market. All was good, and I once again felt able to breathe and enjoy life.

Cam was still adamant he would take over total control of the company finances, and because of that I insisted that we finally change the company paperwork and add him back as a director. It seemed only right and, after all, with everything we'd been through and the way we'd pulled together and got over so many challenges over recent times, surely he deserved to be shown that I trusted him?

'It doesn't mean anything to me, babe,' he'd said, when I brought the subject up. 'I understand why you didn't want me as a director before. I fucked up. I know I did, and I'm spending every minute making it up to you. I know you trust me, it's OK. I don't need to you make me a director. It's your choice, I want you to know that.'

But I was determined. And as soon as it was done, Cam took over everything. We changed bank accounts, and Cam insisted we buy some big filing cabinets so that he could keep proper control of finances and client records. 'We're doing things properly now, girl', he grinned. 'You've never seen this side of me. I'm bloody good!'

He'd make a big show of going through invoices and old receipts, labelling and numbering things and putting them into separate hanging folders. It was a system that I hated – in my opinion it was far too prone to mistakes and far too complex, with nothing easy to find. And the labels didn't make sense either! But he was having none of it, shooing me away and telling me he knew best.

I was exhausted from the fight of recent months, and, to be honest, a huge part of me was relieved that I wouldn't have to worry about that side of things any more. So I stopped asking questions and just let him carry on.

Some time after that I had a call from Kitty, late on a Friday afternoon. I knew something was up as soon as I heard her voice, but I wasn't prepared for what she had to tell me. She'd been for an interview with a much bigger company and was phoning to give me her notice. It was a decision that had been really hard for her, but after nine years with us she felt she needed to experience more and have a bigger challenge. I was gutted, and both of us were in tears on the phone. I knew it was the right move for her, and I supported her decision, but I didn't know how on earth I was going to survive without her in the business. She was my rock, and she was the one who kept everything in order. More than just an employee, she was a confidante and a friend. I saw her as my little sister, and I was heartbroken to see her go.

Cam and I decided not to replace her. Instead we redirected our 0845 number to a remote handling centre and packed up all the office in to a self-storage place near Stansted airport. This would mean we could easily drop in and collect anything we needed whenever we arrived or left the UK. It seemed to work, and Cam was on overdrive to make sure he was in control of things. To be honest, I felt a little bit like a backseat passenger. I'd lost Kitty, and now Cam was in charge of finances, delivery of training and decisions on how we were going to move forward. My only role at that time was to be the main point of contact for existing and new clients. But as the months went on, that slowly changed as well. Cam seemed happier to deal with clients and I began to withdraw, even staying quiet during the rowdy team-building sessions we were known for delivering.

We spent as much time as we could in Edinburgh. School holidays and half-terms were great because the three of us could be there together. But we sometimes tagged on an extra day or two when we were working in the UK. Dylan would stay with friends whenever we were away, so it meant Cam and I had some free grown-up time together. I must say, I absolutely loved it there! The atmosphere, the hustle and bustle, the beautiful buildings and the breathtaking countryside made my heart sing. I also loved the fact that it was somewhere Cam knew so well. He was finally at home, and I was pleased to see him spreading his wings and even starting to catch up with some old school friends he'd found on Facebook. Most of them he hadn't seen or spoken to in years, and he revelled in the idea that he could re-connect with his old gang. Of course, this was his personal trip down memory lane, so I wasn't invited, but I was just pleased he was going out and about. He'd never done that before, as we'd always mixed with either my friends or people we'd met as a couple.

'It's great having a boys' night out!' he'd giggle, grinning from ear to ear when he returned home. 'We had a whale of a time going to old haunts and chatting about the old times. We're doing it again as soon as possible and are talking about organising a boys' weekend!' Whenever Cam was out I was happy spending time with Ann and Tim, friends of ours we'd met on the firewalk and who lived close to the flat.

All was going well and I was happy – work was coming in, we could enjoy two very different places to call home, and Cam was enjoying his role of company accountant. He'd write out lists, showing me the details of bills he'd paid and what was due to come in. Everything was being paid on time, and I finally relaxed. We were on top of things. Good.

We celebrated our ten-year anniversary in Edinburgh and booked an exotic holiday in St Lucia to mark Cam's 40th birthday. I was a little worried about the expense; after all, we'd only just clawed our way out of an extreme financial pickle, and I was keen that we didn't overstretch ourselves and put ourselves in that sort of situation ever again.

'Stop worrying, babe!' Cam would say anytime I brought the subject up. 'I'm running our finances and I've got everything under control. Don't you trust me? This is all for you and me, girl. All for you and me. You are everything to me. I love you, and we both deserve the best.'

The holiday was at an all-inclusive health spa that we both agreed would provide an ideal wind-down and treat after working so hard to get ourselves out of trouble. It was billed as a 5-star resort and considering what was included – health treatments, sports, massages and all our food and drink, and – the total price for 11 days, including airfare and transfers, was a pretty good deal. It was his 40th birthday, after all, and I wanted him to feel special.

When we got there, it was just breathtaking! Cam said he'd been to the island once before, but had stayed at a different hotel (he seemed to have travelled to lots of luxurious places before he knew me!). The resort was set on its own private beach offering all manner of water sports. The hotel was clearly upmarket, and the rooms were cool and airy with beautiful creamy marble floors and walls. It was luxurious and extremely stylish. The health and treatment centre was set away from the main building, at the top of the resort and up about a thousand steps. 'Well, this is the start of our health regime!' I'd joked as we climbed our way up on the welcome tour. There we would get one treatment every day – different kinds of massage, body scrubs, health jets, relaxation sessions and all manner of pampering were on the menu. Anything on top of the one pre-booked session would cost extra, but we didn't care about that, one session per day was going to be plenty for us!

It was paradise, and for the first day or so it was all we could do to drag ourselves from the pool to the sea and to a multitude of restaurants for food and drinks. We had quite clearly been exhausted, and we simply turned to jelly. As Cam began to pick up energy, he started exploring the water sports and other things that were on offer. It suddenly wasn't enough that we had an all-inclusive holiday, he wanted to book more things. To me, it seemed he was doing it just to show off in some way – exactly as he'd chosen a more expensive menu on the first evening we were there, complaining that he didn't like the look of any of the other dishes. It was five-star cuisine, specifically designed to be healthy as well as tasty. I kept quiet – it wasn't worth the fight. But when he started talking about wanting to arrange trips, hire boats, book more pampering sessions and goodness knows what else, well, I put my foot down.

'Don't you think we've already spent enough?' I asked, feeling the same old fear rising in my stomach. 'After what we've been through, can't we just enjoy what's here and – most importantly – enjoy just being with each other?'

'You're such a spoilsport,' he sulked 'You know it's my birthday and, anyway, it's because of me that we got out of the mess in the first place! Perhaps you should take a closer look at your own failings before telling me off!'

His accusations stung. On a logical level, I knew what he said was completely untrue. But my emotions told me something else. He was right, on some level, I still felt pretty bad about my management of the company finances. I had never had accountancy training, so how could I possibly think that I could run the accounts of a company that was turning over hundreds of thousands? It was a ridiculous idea. Who on earth did I think I was in the first place? No wonder we had hit financial hardships! I felt ashamed and decided to back off. I knew I wasn't going to win.

The holiday ended up costing us nearly double the original price. The most expensive 'extra' was a private sunset boat trip on the day of his birthday. It was a ridiculous price, but he said it was what he wanted, so we did it. The adventure was meant to be romantic, but by that time the only true emotion I could feel was fear – fear that we were once again pushing financial boundaries and that there was nothing I could do to control the haemorrhaging of our hard earned money. The photographs from the trip send shivers down my spine. We were both there, posing with glasses of champagne on a private speedboat that was taking us away from the shore and into who knows what. My fear about safety, based on the continual financial pressures had manifested so much by then that I even questioned whether the (very polite and charming) young men who were manning the boat had actually planned to kidnap us and slit our throats. I know, I know… I've always had a fertile (and sometimes unhealthy) imagination. But heavy dread was becoming an ever-present emotion – for the most part for no apparent reason. I just knew I was scared.

After the boat trip, we returned to the hotel for a specially booked meal in their exclusive restaurant. It was a lovely meal, and I remember smiling, but for some reason I just couldn't connect with myself. Cam was smiling like a cat that had the cream, but I felt alone. I felt he was distant, that I just couldn't reach him (or myself) and I had the feeling that he was pushing me away.

Earlier in the day I'd asked him how we could become closer. His unexpected response shocked me.

'Well, you could get your knickers off a bit more regularly!' he'd sneered under his breath, walking away from me while smiling at the people around us, leaving me open mouthed and speechless. Our sex life had always been healthy and honest. We had a great connection, and I really didn't understand what he was talking about. True, we'd quietened off a bit over the months that we'd had severe financial pressures, but we were right back on track – at least, as far as I was concerned. Was I being blind again? Was I really that stupid? His comment threw me into turmoil.

After the very tasty meal in the restaurant – with more champagne and more wine – we went straight to the bar. There we met up with friends we'd made since we'd been there, and I was hurt to notice that Cam's smiles seemed far more genuine with two of the women we'd met than any he'd shared with me throughout the whole evening. The alcohol had gone to my head, and this time I decided I was not going to swallow my feelings. Stifling the pricking of tears and keeping my voice strong, I asked him what was wrong – had I done something to offend him?

'You are doing my head in!' he spat at me, slamming his drink down on the bar and running his fingers through the thick glossy hair that I loved so much. 'Honestly, I'm exasperated, Mel! This is my birthday, for God's sake. Are you going to ruin this for me as well, just like everything else? Just get a grip and get over yourself.'

And with that he turned his back and lurched off to the Gents' toilets, winking, joking and twirling one of the women around in his arms along the way.

The evening got no better, and we finally got to back to our room in the early hours. I fell asleep straight away. I was tired, drunk and feeling shamed by what had happened. So far as I was concerned I had done everything I could to make sure that his 40th was memorable, but all he seemed able to do was to berate me. His unpredictable behaviour was getting to me, and I realised I had once again started walking on eggshells. In public he'd usually appear warm and affectionate with me, yet in private he was becoming more and more distant. I couldn't put my finger on what was different. His smile was the same, his words of love were the same, and we were physically no different from before, but somehow the bond just wasn't the same. I began to think that perhaps I had just exhausted myself with the pressures of the past few months. In the end it had been my strength and positivity that carried both of us through. I suppose I had every right to be tired. Perhaps, as well, my strength had once again made Cam feel less than capable. I was too tired to care. If that was the case then he'd have to get over it.

Something Cam didn't know, was that I was organising a surprise birthday party for him the night we were due back home in France. Dylan had been helping, and we'd been emailing and telephoning people with the details during the two weeks before the holiday. We'd confirmed more than 30 guests, many of who were coming over from the UK. We'd also been collecting countless goodwill messages from others who couldn't make it. So it made his strange behaviour all the more difficult to bear.

I awoke in the morning, after a night of troublesome nightmares, to find I was alone in the bed. Cam's side didn't even look like it had been slept in. Worried, I got up and looked in the bathroom – perhaps he might have passed out? But he wasn't there. He wasn't on the balcony either. Throwing cold water over my face and the nearest clothes I could find on my body, I hurried down to the main part of the hotel – the restaurant area where I would be certain to find people we knew.

To my total astonishment, I found Cam sitting eating breakfast with our friends from last night. He looked worse for wear but was clearly engaged in animated conversation. I could hear his laughter as soon as I entered the restaurant!

'What happened to you? Where on earth have you been? I was worried!' I exclaimed. His face dropped the moment he saw me. Gone was the laughter and back was the cold, empty stare.

'I couldn't sleep thanks to you,' he said flatly. 'If you must know, I spent the night sleeping on the beach. Some birthday. Gee thanks, Mel.' Giving his apologies and a huge smile to the others at the table, he then got up and started heading towards the exit. I followed, furious that he could behave so rudely towards me.

'Do you have any idea how stupid you made me feel last night?' he continued when I pressed him for answers. 'You have become so judgmental and distant, and then you accuse me of flirting with other women! How ridiculous is that? These people are our friends, Mel, and you made everyone feel uncomfortable. Of course I couldn't sleep! I was worried about what people might be saying about us – about you in particular. You were out of order, completely out of order. I went to the beach to clear my head and I fell asleep on one of the deckchairs. I feel like shit. Thanks to you. Well done.'

It was a barrage of accusations, exaggerated stories that twisted the truth. Shaking my head in disbelief, I struggled to make sense of what he was going on about. Yes, I'd been upset that he'd been flirting with other women, but as for being distant? And as for everyone thinking my behaviour was out of order . . . How and why had that happened? Maybe the drink had gone to my head. Maybe I had been wrong. But I was certain that I didn't actually make a big fuss about it . . . did I? Perhaps I did… And, therefore, maybe there's some justification in his feeling that I'm cold to him. After all, this explosive reaction I'm getting has to be based on something . . . doesn't it? This was all so out of character! I just couldn't understand what was happening.

The rest of the day was a little prickly between us, to say the least. The mood was eased by the constant jokes and smiles from our friends who were never far away and seemed to enjoy our company – so could it really have been true, as Cam had said, that they'd been upset by my 'bad behaviour' the night before? My emotions were becoming so ragged, and I had started to question my judgment. Cam's ability to flash a smile and become the life and soul of the party whenever other people were around was increasingly unnerving. I started to feel that my husband was becoming a regular Jekyll and Hyde, and I couldn't make any sense of his changing attitude towards me. I just knew that, even though we'd successfully weathered a furious financial tornado that had threatened to destroy us, I felt neither the safety nor the calm that one would expect after a storm. Nor did the sense of relief come; it had become an elusive dream that stayed just beyond my reach.

And I was tired. So tired. The fight had taken so much energy, and for much of the battle I had been keeping focused and positive for both of us, as well as keeping strong for Dylan, of course.

'Come on, this is no good. You're worth more than this!' I remember saying to Cam months earlier one evening when he'd dissolved into tears one evening at the kitchen table, frustrated by yet another financial setback. 'We can get through this. Come on, you know we can!'

'But you don't get it, Mel,' he'd replied. 'Maybe I'm just not good enough! I'm falling to pieces here and your constant positive mantras are not helping me in the slightest. I just feel worse.'

But, of course, I'd held fast to the positive focus – it was the only thing I knew how to do to get us through. And, from where I was standing now, I felt confident that it had been my determination to stay optimistic in the face of potential devastation that had enabled us to claw our way out of the mess! That was how we'd managed to win against the tenants and finally get the house on the market. That was how we'd secured a short-term loan from the bank. That was how we'd won a heap of well-paying projects out of just a couple of enquiries. That, I believe, was also what made Matt and Karen, two of our dearest friends, insist on lending us a serious chunk of cash when we were on our knees. They knew they'd get it back, but would they have been quite so willing had we both been wandering around peddling doom and gloom?

It hit home as I watched Cam now, literally turning on charm, lighting up with charm and charisma in public. No matter what was going on between us, he just flicked a switch and – bang – it was show time! Now, I understand that this kind of self-management is a hugely useful skill, particularly when presenting to groups as we regularly did. Standing in front of delegates means you need to be flexible in your style and approach. Great. That makes sense. But to suddenly notice Cam doing it here, on holiday, with friends? Switching his outward behaviour towards me in public as well?

Still analysing the unsettling events of the past 24 hours, I was reminded of the conversations with Matt and Karen around our kitchen table in France. For weeks before they had arrived, Cam had become a despondent and lacklustre Eeyore-type character, next to my encouraging Tigger. And yet, and yet . . . Once we'd all sat down and Matt had made his incredibly generous offer, it was Cam who had suddenly gone off in to a PR spin about how good things were going to be. It was such a change of character! I hadn't noticed it at the time, I'd just been pleased that at last he was beginning to buy into the vision that was so clear in my head. Although, I must say, some of the things he was spouting were, to say the least, a little exaggerated.

'We're heading for our best turnover yet this year!' he'd said, slurping his wine and giving his best movie-star grin. 'Mel's doing a great job generating new leads, and I'm at the top of my game in terms of training delivery. We're going to need to expand the team and we're really going places this year!' This had all been news to me. As far as I was knew, we were just concentrating on getting ourselves back on our feet. I had thought we'd agreed that a more family-focused lifestyle was where we were heading. I had also understood that we'd do the vast majority of the work ourselves – keeping overheads low and making the business more profitable. So it came as a bit of a surprise. Still, I was just glad to see Cam being enthusiastic after months of misery.

It was only now, sitting in this beautiful holiday resort, which should have provided the ideal surroundings for a relaxed and romantic getaway for the two of us, that I began to think about things in a different way. I couldn't get close to Cam – no matter what I did, what I said, or how I said it, I felt as if I was being met by a void. I couldn't read his feelings any more, he was distant to me. Despite the smile he would still flash, his expression had become flat and he had become more critical of me. He was distant and moody. Friendly and smiling with the people we had met on holiday, I saw him once again being the life and soul of the party. Clever, witty, charming, attentive and incredibly charismatic – this was the person I had fallen in love with and knew so well. This was the Cam who charmed me and who made me feel so special, so loved, so adored and so able to achieve anything! This was the Cam I loved with all my heart and all my soul.

So what was happening? How had he turned away from me? Why was he being so distant? And more to the point, what was it, exactly, that he was doing differently to make me feel so isolated? No matter how hard I tried, couldn't put my finger on it, but I knew I was feeling more and more unsettled and more and more unsure of myself. What should have been an idyllic holiday had turned in to a lonely, unnerving experience that left me feeling wrung out. Looking back at the photographs now, it's true that I had a great tan, but the strain and uncertainty is plain to see behind my over-smiling expression.

On our return, the surprise birthday party was a roaring success. Cam had absolutely no idea what was happening until the second we arrived at the restaurant and he was greeted by a huge table full of well-wishers, cheering and whooping as we came through the door. It was a fantastic evening, and Cam was clearly touched by all the attention and love that our friends showed him. Lots of people came home with us after the meal, and we continued partying and making merry until the early hours. Cam, as usual, drank far too much, but I had not seen him look so happy for a long time. Dylan and I were chuffed to bits – between us we'd managed to pull off a complete surprise for the man we both adored. I hugged my son and told him how proud I was of what he'd achieved.

'You're a superstar, Dyl, you know that?' I grinned, planting a huge kiss on his cheek.

'Aw, get off, Mum!' he squirmed, while also squeezing me back. 'I know, it was great fun and I'm so pleased it worked! Welcome home, Mum. I'm glad you and Cam had a good time!'

Cam had seen what was going on and immediately shushed the room, tapping against his glass with a spoon for attention. 'I'd just like to say thank you to my beautiful wife and my gorgeous boy for arranging this surprise for me!' he said, to another round of cheering and applause. 'I am very lucky, very blessed and very happy! And as for all you lot of bastards keeping it all secret from me, well, thanks to you too! But mark my words, I'll be watching you all much more closely in the future!'

Guffaws, laughs and a few rowdy obscenities were exchanged between the gathered audience, and a series of emotionally charged toasts carried on around the room. My smile, I noticed, was more real and relaxed than it had been in a long while.

That was why I was so taken aback by Cam's words just a couple of days later. It was the Monday morning. All our guests had disappeared and Dylan was at school. I'd just made Cam another cup of tea and some toast. He was standing in the doorway between the kitchen and the office, leaning up against the wall as I made my way towards him. He looked drawn. And cold. And empty. Instinctively I stopped in my tracks and held my breath.

'The thing is, Mel,' he said, dark eyes boring into my soul as he shifted his position to make himself taller. 'The thing is, I just don't feel loved or supported any more. That's all there is to it.'

We both stood there in the deafening silence.

15

Counselling, Confusion and Confessions

You could have knocked me down with a feather. How on earth could he say that? What was he thinking? How much more could I do for him? Surely this was some kind of sick joke?

But it wasn't. We both sat down in the office and Cam started to explain that he'd felt distant over the past few months. He told me that he felt I didn't love him any more. That I'd become strong and was pushing him away. He said that he felt isolated and that whatever he did just wasn't enough.

'You always get into bed with your back to me!' he complained. 'And then you go to sleep. How do you think that makes me feel? It's been going on for months, Mel. You can't deny it!'

He clearly felt very strongly about the things he was saying, but they just didn't stack up to me. I never got in to bed with my back to him. In fact, I was the one who always went to cuddle him and he would be the one with his back to me! What was he talking about?

The rest of his grievances didn't make sense to me either. Of course I loved him, couldn't he see that? What else did I need to do, for goodness' sake?

I knew it was no use arguing. He'd obviously got himself into a really strange place. So I just listened and asked him what he'd like to do about it. He said he thought that our only hope was to go for marriage guidance counselling.

Fine, I thought. *Let's do this. Let's find out what's at the bottom of all this. Let's get to the truth and work it all out. Perhaps a professional can make more sense of this total madness than I can!*

That's how, at the beginning of December 2008, we started seeing a professional counsellor whose practice was not far from Stansted airport. It meant that we could book sessions to fit in either side of our business trips – no matter where in the country the work might take us, we always entered and left the UK via Stansted.

It had been left to me to find the counsellor, but Cam rejected my first choice of a woman therapist who, I had thought, sounded ideal on the telephone.

'I don't really want to be airing our dirty linen in front of another female,' he sneered when I told him of my find, 'and anyway, you'd probably only feel threatened. I'd much rather work with a man.'

So a man was exactly who we chose. His name was Bill, and he'd been working as a therapist for over a decade. When I made contact with him, I gave him an outline of the situation as I saw it, and he assured me that he would be happy to help guide us through our storm.

'Marriages often hit choppy waters,' he said, 'even the best ones! There's no shame in asking for help – quite the contrary, in fact. You have both chosen to come and work out how to make things better, so that's a major part of the battle already won. It won't be easy, and it may be painful at times, but if you both keep an open mind then you'll be amazed at what you can achieve!'

I did feel ashamed, though. I felt stupid for not noticing that my marriage was falling apart around me, blind for carrying on regardless and for failing to push Cam earlier about his underlying feelings. I also felt scared. Suppose we were about to fall apart? Suppose this was the beginning of the end?

The first session was exactly as I had expected – uncomfortable, emotional and also enlightening. Shocked by the vehemence of Cam's words, and his confession to Bill that he had been walking on eggshells around me for months, I sat open-mouthed at the totally alien picture he was painting of our marriage. Had I really been that blind? Was he really that scared of me? Could it be true that my behaviour was so extremely divorced from my intentions that I'd once again inadvertently caused my soulmate to shut down?

I asked Bill how that could be. I wanted to know how it was that my reality was so totally at odds with that of my husband.

'It's often only through talking with a third party that we let our true feelings out,' he replied, calmly and with a particularly irritating smile on his face that I'm sure he intended to be reassuring. 'You are both clearly strong characters. Perhaps because of your childhood you have become stronger and more resilient than you had realised, Mel? And perhaps Cam has been unable to adequately flex his male muscles in the process? It doesn't make anything right or wrong – it's just a matter of exploring real feelings. Then we can start re-building.'

I saw Cam bow his head at that, though I felt like screaming. This whole session seemed like a pantomime to me, and I felt that both Bill and I were being manipulated. Then again, as Bill had said, it was more than likely that I had a host of unresolved childhood issues to work through.

That's rich! I thought, annoyed by Cam's pity-play in front of a well-intentioned therapist. *I've done more work on resolving my own issues than most people do in a lifetime, and I've come out pretty darned well, thank you very much! When are we going to start looking at why my husband is giving you a totally different account of reality? When are we going to start delving into what's going on for him? When are we going to get to the real issue?*

We were both given some 'homework' to do before the next

session, which was to be on 18 December, my birthday. I don't remember the details, but it was something along the lines of defining what was important to us as individuals. Forget the other person, we were each just to take some private time to clarify what makes us tick. We were not to discuss the homework but were to bring it with us to the next session.

That evening, Cam and I went out for a pizza. I was looking for some kind of reassurance, as the session with Bill had unsettled me. But there was to be none.

'I just don't have any feelings any more, Mel,' Cam said, stabbing at his pizza and greedily gulping at the Diet Coke in front of him. 'I'm empty. Worked out, worn out and just numb. I don't hold out much hope for us, Mel. I can't continue like this. We've grown apart, and I don't feel the same way about you. I need to find myself now, because I've lost myself being married to you. That's all there is to it.'

'I don't understand,' I replied, the empty pit in my stomach gnawing at my already reeling emotions. 'Why couldn't you tell me this earlier? When did it all start happening? What stopped you from bringing it up before if you felt so bad?'

'Have *you* ever tried talking to you?' he spat, slamming his knife and fork down on the table. 'Honestly, Mel, it's sometimes just impossible! You are so damned focused and blinkered that reality just doesn't come into play! You regularly cut me out, and lots of your friends too – go on, ask them, plenty of them are too scared to ever disagree with you – and you make me feel inadequate. Useless. Worthless. Nobody is allowed to have real honest feelings with you. Oh no, we just have to stay happy and smiley. Well, Mel, that's not reality, and now I'm standing up for myself.'

Oh my God, was that really the case? Am I really that scary? Do I really shut people down? The questions continued in my head, and we ate in silence.

Following Bill's instructions, we kept our homework to ourselves in preparation for further exploration at the next session.

Cam had been running a project in the UK, and Dylan and I had come over to join him on the afternoon of 17 December. Dylan was spending Christmas with his dad, and Cam and I were flying home on the 19th for a quiet time with just the two of us. It would be an ideal opportunity to relax and be gentle with each other.

We spent the evening and stayed overnight with our friends the Brightmans, our neighbours in France who were also back in the UK, and had a lovely time eating and drinking at the local gastro-pub. We'd toasted my birthday, the beginning of the school holidays, the start of the festive season and also the deep bond of friendship that we all shared. I loved being in the company of my warm and generous friends, and they clearly had no idea about the truth behind Cam's mask of jolliness and frivolity. Neither, of course, did Dylan. Disconnected and emotionally detached from my surroundings, I desperately wanted to scream and shout. I wanted to let people know what was going on. I wanted to cry and sob and ask for help. But I couldn't. So instead I kept my own mask on, staying silent and going along with the charade, hoping and praying that we would make some positive progress the next day – my 44th birthday.

The second session was worse than the first. We shared our homework, and I was once again shocked by the things that Cam had written down. He said that he needed to do more sport but that he felt hemmed in by me. He said that he wanted more freedom to be himself, that he felt he always had to live up to being someone when he was with me. That I pressured him to become something he wasn't. He also said his ideal scenario would be to get away for a few days before Christmas, on his own, skiing, so that he could start to sort himself out.

'That's all I need right now,' he'd said to Bill, with tears in his eyes, 'but I'm scared that Mel won't let me, it would be the same as with my first wife.'

'But of course I don't mind!' I blurted out, a little more forcefully than I had intended. Now he was comparing me to a woman he claimed had controlled and manipulated him, accusations I was now beginning to doubt.

'How could you even think such a thing! You go if you want to. If it's what you need, then I support you. I thought you knew that? I'd never stand in your way!'

I spotted the 'do you see what I mean?' kind of look that went from Cam to Bill, but I decided to ignore it. I didn't know what sort of game he was playing here, and I was confused by his unfounded accusation. Fine, if a couple of days' skiing was what he needed and would make the difference, then great. He could take the car and drive down to the Pyrenees and come back in time for a quiet Christmas with just the two of us.

On the night of my birthday, the three of us had tickets to see *We Will Rock You*. Cam had booked the seats a couple of weeks earlier, and we checked into a hotel in the West End to make it more special. I had brought my black dress to wear for the evening, teamed with brown leather boots and a statement necklace.

'Do I look OK?' I'd asked Cam and Dylan just as we were leaving the hotel room.

'It's not your best look, to be honest. You're much better off in jeans,' Cam replied, squeezing my arm and hanging on to Dylan at the same time. 'But never mind, let's go and have a great evening together, shall we?'

Back home in France, Cam quickly found and booked a little B&B in the Pyrenees.

'Thanks for doing this, Mel,' he beamed, giving me a hug. 'Here are the details for the hotel, so you know where I am. I'll be back on the 23rd, so let's have a nice few days chilling out and getting to the bottom of this, shall we? I do love you, you know that. And I really do want us to work through this. Thanks for being so understanding. This is a really positive start, babe.'

I was pleased to see him go, and pleased with myself for being so supportive. Surely it proved I was not the scary person he'd made me out to be? Surely he must be able to see that I loved him? That I trusted him? And that I only wanted the best for him?

I was still confused by the accusations he'd made during both counselling sessions and was doing my very best to understand how it might have been that he got to feeling so alone and unloved. I was determined to do everything within my power to make our marriage work. We'd been together for ten years, everyone experiences a blip or two, and perhaps I had become stuck in my ways and blinded to my actions. This was our opportunity to work together, to explore openly and honestly, and to create a marriage that was even stronger than before. Whilst the process was uncomfortable, and was causing me to reassess things about myself and about my expectations that I didn't like very much, I knew this was a healthy road to be following and that only good could come out of it. A love like ours was something worth fighting for. We'd just become a bit lost along the way. That was all.

I made the most of my time alone. I bought and wrapped presents. I played my music CDs really loud. I took long walks and even longer baths, soaking away my cares and nurturing my body. I ate mince pies and drank wine snuggled up in front of a crackling fire. I spoke to friends. And I imagined how it would be when Cam came home.

The evening of Monday, 22 December rocked my world in a way I least expected. Christmas music was playing on the stereo and I had just made myself a cup of tea to enjoy by the fire, settling down for my last evening before Cam came home. I'd fired up the computer and decided to log in to Facebook. I hadn't quite got the hang of it at that stage, and Cam had been showing me how it worked, so the account on my computer was still logged in to his page. I was about to log out when I saw a message pop up.

'Hey there's a pity! Ha ha,' it said. 'How's it going? Have been out of macbook land for last week, too blinking busy!'

It was from a girl I didn't know, and for some reason I prickled a bit. I don't know what made me do it, but I decided to go into the message inbox and find out more. The history had been hidden, but with the arrival of this new message I had the option to view history. So, feeling a little guilty, but unable to stop myself, I clicked to see what had been said between them. The previous message, sent by Cam on 17 December, the day before my birthday, said: 'I am what you call in married land – for now! So please do not get out of hand! It's all harmless banter . . . He he x'

Oh please, dear God, not again. Surely not! With blood pumping loudly in my ears, I went backwards through the history to discover that Cam had been flirting with this girl, Vicky, since the beginning of December. She had been a guest at his friend's wedding that we'd both attended. That was another night where he had flown off the handle at me, accusing me of being boring and embarrassing him in front of his friends because I hadn't wanted to dance. That hadn't been the case at all, and in fact I was having a good time chatting and getting to know people who'd known my husband from years ago. At last I was getting to learn more about Cam's life, some real-life history with some real-life people, and I had loved the way he was introducing me as his 'beautiful, sexy wife'. So I had been flummoxed when his mood suddenly changed and the accusations started out of the blue. We had left immediately after his outburst, and I had cried myself to sleep, confused and distressed by his unreasonable and aggressive behaviour. Reading the messages he'd been exchanging made my entire body freeze up, but I had to read on. I had to understand.

Campbell Deveraux

12 December at 14:09

And I missed a chance for a dance eh! Another time I hope!!

X

Sent via Facebook Mobile

Vicky Eames

12 December at 15:43

Yes where was my dance?!!

Campbell Deveraux

12 December at 15:52

It was very poor of me – but I might have been less of a gentleman had we danced! I kind of found myself staring at you a lot! Sorry! You looked very gorgeous by the way! X

Vicky Eames

12 December at 15:56

Thanks and yes I noticed but I always spot the cute guys ;)

Campbell Deveraux

12 December at 16:08

That's a good thing then! Hope to see you next time I am up?? X

Campbell Deveraux

12 December at 16:24

And I tend not to notice anyone but you kind of grabbed my attention! What's that about eh?! ;-)

Campbell Deveraux

12 December at 16:27

And . . .happy birthday to you! X

Vicky Eames

13 December at 14:34

Thanks Cam. All over now and got the worst hangover - goodness it must be my age!

Campbell Deveraux

13 December at 21:39

Can't be – you are only 21! X

Campbell Deveraux

13 December at 23:13

And . . . are you flirting with me Ms Vicky Eames? I need to know!!!? X

Vicky Eames

14 December at 14:59

Campbell Deveraux – more to the point are you flirting with me??!!!!

Campbell Deveraux

14 December at 16:50

I think I might be...What about you?!!!

Vicky Eames

15 December at 17:57

Yes well I can be a terrible flirt when provoked – can't help myself. But let me check before I get out of hand. Are you a married man?

Campbell Deveraux

17 December at 06:57

I am what you call in married land – for now! So please do not get out of hand! Its all harmless banter . . . He he x

Vicky Eames

Today at 18:26

Hey there's a pity! Ha ha.

How's it going? Have been out of macbook land for last week too blinkin busy.!

There it all was. In black and white. In front of my very eyes. There was no denying that my husband was up to his old tricks again. This particular flirting session might not have gone any further – for now – but the fact remained that he was behaving in a totally inappropriate way. Perhaps that was why he'd turned so cold? Perhaps that was why he seemed to be doing his utmost to push me away? How could he want to punish me so much? Why did he want to hurt me? What was the point behind all the psychological games he'd been playing in front of Bill? I'd exhausted myself over recent weeks trying to understand what on earth was going on, doing my best to appreciate Cam's opposite reality and take more notice of how I came across. Well, this time I wasn't going to stand for it. He'd taken me for a fool, and I'd had enough.

I couldn't bear the thought of hearing his voice, so I texted him: 'It's over, Cam. I know all about you and Vicky. I am divorcing you. Do not come home.'

Less than a minute later, the phone calls started. Cross at first, and accusing me of making things up, he then turned to begging and pleading as he realised I had the evidence in front of me. I have never before felt such blind fury! Shaking from head to foot, I yelled down the phone for all my worth.

'How could you?' I screamed. 'Don't you dare think about coming back here! You lying, cheating bastard. What else have you been doing behind my back?'

He stayed quiet before pleading with me to listen and to understand. Telling me that I'd got it all wrong. That it was just some silly flirting from a girl he didn't know. That he loved me more than anything in the whole world and that surely I wanted us to work – didn't I?

'Of course I bloody well wanted us to work!' I yelled, holding the phone away from my mouth and slamming my fist on to the table. 'What the hell do you think the past few weeks have been about? You must think I'm some kind of stupid idiot! You've taken me for a fool – again! Well, sorry, mate, but this time it's over!'

Packing an overnight bag, I drove over to stay with Henry and Ruth, an older couple whom we'd 'adopted' some time ago as surrogate grandparents to Dylan and, therefore, surrogate parents to us. The mechanics might not have been quite accurate, but I certainly saw them as more like family than friends.

They soothed and supported me, giving me lots of love and kind words as well as space to cry and be cross in equal measures. We decided that I would stay there over Christmas. I had my friends arriving from Dubai just before New Year, so I would go back home then. In the meantime, we would take each day as it came.

Cam, of course, didn't do as I had asked him. He came back to the house the following morning while I was there collecting a few bits and bobs for the coming week with Ruth and Henry. I had some warning. Henry had driven back with me, as I didn't want to walk in alone. He left once I was settled inside but was back again within just a few minutes.

'He's up at the church,' said Henry, looking confused and concerned at the same time. 'He drove all night and is desperate to see you. I think you should listen, Mel.'

Almost as soon as Henry had finished his sentence, the car pulled into the driveway. Seeing Cam climb out, I quite literally flew over to him, screaming at the top of my voice. I think that is the one and only time in my life when I have totally lost it. I now know what is meant when people say they were overcome with fury!

Striding up to him, fists clenched and white-hot rage powering my body, I stopped just short from where he was and shouted at the top of my voice.

'Go away!' I screamed. 'Get out of here – NOW! This is MY home, this is MY house. You are NOT welcome here any more. Now LEAVE!'

But he stood his ground. He looked terrible, grey and exhausted, but his voice was steady.

'I am going in to get my passport and laptop, and you can't stop me,' he said, his calm defiance igniting my wrath even further. Blinded by the strength of my emotions, I screamed at him again, at the same time lunging towards him and slapping him across the face with all my might, the force knocking his glasses from his face.

It shocked him, but not half as much as it shocked me! That was the first (and last) time I have ever hit out at anybody.

Poor Henry didn't know what to do with himself at this stage and stayed a safe distance away from both of us.

That was when the expletives started. There were no tears, just more and more rage. My fury turned the air blue as I let rip with all the names under the sun. Not terribly grown-up, but boy did it feel good!

I knew he would need his passport and laptop to fulfil January's work commitments, but, hang on a minute, had he only come back here to get those things? What about the damage he'd caused to me? What about 'What happens next?' What about 'I'm sorry, can we talk?'

I refused to let him into the house and collected the two items myself. I can't tell you how tempted I was to just throw the computer on the floor at his feet. Oh, it was torturous! But I managed to hold myself back. Logic told me it wouldn't do any good. I was also hugely tempted to rip up his passport – that would mess things up for him! But, then again, it would mess things up for me as well. So I just gave it a bit of a scrunch as I passed it over to him.

'You stupid little bitch,' he spat at me as he ripped the passport from my hands.

'Thanks, Cam, nicely said. And you're not taking the Land Rover,' I replied, calmer by now. 'It's in my name and I need it for Dylan. You can take your precious BMW. Here are the keys. Now go. And don't come back!'

He went. And I walked back inside the house, followed by Henry.

Adrenalin does funny things to the body. I couldn't settle but neither could I pace the room. 'Sorry for the obscenities,' I said to Henry as I went to put the kettle on. 'I can't speak any more at the moment, I'm afraid. I do hope I didn't offend you.'

'It's all right, sweetheart. It's OK. It'll be all right. Two sugars in my tea, please!' and he gave my shoulders a squeeze. That was enough to threaten the walls of my emotional dam, which were already straining under the pressure. But I couldn't afford to dissolve into a trembling jelly – not just yet.And not while I was still experiencing so much anger.

'Still, that showed him, eh?' I said, trying to crack a smile. 'Don't think he knew I had that in me!'

'I don't think I did either!' Henry agreed, taking his tea from my shaking hand.

Henry left some time later. I said that I wanted some time on my own, to gather my thoughts and chat to a couple of trusted friends. Matt was the first person I spoke with, and then Jayne – both dear friends in the UK. How I wished they could be here with me.

This might sound weird, but the overwhelming feeling I had at that time was shame. Yes, I might have put on a great display of a rabid Tasmanian devil, but that was to mask my pain and the indignity I felt about the fact that my husband had once again been deceiving me and manipulating the situation to make it seem my fault. I felt humiliated that I'd once again bent over backwards to understand his 'pain' and was terrified about the horror of what was to come. What was going to happen? How would I tell Dylan? What was to become of us? But still I refused to crumble. I couldn't. If I did, I might never re-surface.

Unbeknown to me, Cam went straight to Ruth and Henry's house and spent the next hour or so chatting with them. He knew he couldn't hide, and he got it both barrels from them as well. Ruth called some time later to let me know that he was with them and asked if I wanted to come and chat.

'No thanks,' I said in a matter-of-fact way. 'I've got nothing to say to him. It's over, that's all there is to it.'

'I know you're hurt, Mel, of course I understand,' Ruth continued. 'But at some point you're going to need to talk with him – whatever happens. He's in a terrible mess. I think you owe it to yourself – and each other – to at least try to have a sensible conversation. You can do it here if you like, so you're safe. We'll stay out of your way, and you can chat for as long as you like.'

Twenty minutes later, I walked in to find him slouched against the wall in the room adjoining the kitchen and the entrance. This was the room where they smoked cigarettes, because it led outside to the garden.

'I see you've started smoking again,' was my greeting to him. I had stopped many months before, and Cam had been free for a couple of weeks.

'Well, what do you expect?' was his response – less cocky now, but still cold.

We talked. And I cried. He reasoned. And he confused me. He told me he was numb. That he'd shut down. That I'd become so much stronger and that he felt inadequate. It was the same old stuff regurgitated yet again. And I was tired of it. Tired of fighting. Tired of trying to understand. And tired of Cam's lies. And this time I wasn't taking anything he said lying down.

'You're upset because you think I've become stronger?' Picking up on the point he'd made earlier, I looked him straight in the eyes and held myself tall. 'Well, you'd better get used to it, because this is just the beginning, and I'm going to get even stronger. Just you watch!'

He told me that the flirting was nothing. 'It's just a symptom, Mel. The problem lies with us, nothing else. And I think we've lost ourselves through each other.'

'Well, then we'd better say goodbye. We'd better work out the best way through this and go our own separate ways.' And with that, the floodgates opened and tears coursed down my face. Saying those words out loud was too much for me, and my bravado dissolved. This was the man I loved with all my heart and all my soul. I couldn't understand how he could be so callous towards me. Again. After everything we'd been through.

He must have noticed. He looked confused. His head tilted.

His brows furrowed. 'But I don't understand. Why are you crying?'

'Why do you think? I'm losing the man I have loved as my soulmate. You. Campbell Deveraux. I don't know where it all went wrong. And my heart is breaking.'

We talked some more, but Cam kept his distance – no warmth, no cuddles, no reassurances. He said he didn't want to lose me but that he needed some space 'It's for the best,' he said, reaching out suddenly to stroke my face. 'I've got to find out who I am. I'm not helping you by sticking around here. I'm going to check into a hotel, but let's talk again tomorrow.'

So that's what happened. And that was how it continued over Christmas. We would talk in the day, and he would stay at the hotel in the evenings. It didn't make sense to me. Why would he want to do that? How could staying in a local hotel possibly be helping? Didn't he realise it was making me feel even more rejected? More confused? More isolated? But it didn't make any difference. That was what happened. Some days with him were good, other days he would turn cold and aggressive again. Every day was like walking on eggshells. It felt to me that I was in the company of a loose cannon, somebody with the ability to turn at the flick of a switch, regardless of what I did or didn't do. No matter what I did or didn't say.

His words at times made sense, although I was still confused about how we'd come to this position. 'We can get through this, Mel, but we have to find each other first. When we come back together it will be different – a different shape, a different colour; nothing will be as before. It can't be. We have been suffocating each other. When we find ourselves, just as Bill said, then we can work on each other' – but somehow I was in constant freefall.

Dylan came home just after Christmas, and our friends arrived the next day. Cam still refused to budge from his hotel. He also told me that after the New Year he was going to base himself at our Edinburgh flat, find some professional counselling and get his head sorted out. So I was left with no choice but to give an explanation.

I told Dylan that Cam and I had been arguing and that, although we still loved each other, we were giving each other a little bit of distance. I told my friends the truth. That I'd found flirty messages and that I didn't understand what was going on. That I was frightened and confused, as well as being angry and ashamed that Dylan had once again been put in a position of uncertainty. Sarah and Kevin were absolutely great. Sarah is more like a sister than a friend, and Kevin had been Cam's closest friend. Their children, Katherine and Toby, were great friends with Dylan, and I had been hugely excited about their visit.

To say it was awkward is putting it mildly! We played 'showtime' while Cam was at home, and the messages he gave me were confusing and frightening. He would hold me tight in the kitchen. He would rub my back and tell me I looked gorgeous and sexy. Then he would ignore me or tell me that I was doing his head in. I'd ask him an innocent question and he'd fly off the handle, leaving the house in a rage and leaving me to once again cry myself to sleep. It was a living nightmare.

16

Ultimate Torture – Ultimate Betrayal

Kevin, Sarah and the kids left on 2 January, and Cam left the following day. He refused my suggestion that he might want to spend a little time trying to work things out, instead insisting that the sooner he got to Edinburgh the better.

There was no further talk of divorce or separation; instead, the talk was about us having to find ourselves as individuals and then coming back to create something different and better as a couple. About him finding a strong counsellor and about me holding the home, Dylan and myself together.

It was daily torture. Only a couple of people knew what was happening. To the rest of the outside world I continued as if everything was normal. Cam was just working away, as normal, and I was working on home-based projects. We still had some contracts to complete, but there was no new stuff coming in and I was worried.

'Do you have any idea just how unhelpful that is to hear?' Cam's cold voice made me sit up straight. 'I'm here in the UK, doing all I can for the business – while I'm in the middle of the worst emotional meltdown I've ever experienced, by the way – and then you phone me to bring me down with your worries! Thanks, Mel. Thanks. That's really helpful.'

But my worries wouldn't subside. Cam was still running the finances, and while he assured me that everything was under control, he did confess that he was worried about the future. The first priority, though, he said, was getting himself well and both of us sorted out and back together. He said he wanted to find some effective counselling to get his head sorted out – to help him through his 'emotional meltdown'. He apparently tried one person who 'just didn't understand' and then found two specialist coaches who came highly recommended, worked as a team and charged a hefty £300 per one-hour session.

'Mel, it's hardly a lot to invest when it's going to help us, is it?' was Cam's justification when I balked at the amount of money. I wasn't comfortable, but I couldn't find a strong enough argument to protest. Professional fees aren't cheap and, well, if they were the best, then goodness knows we needed all the help we could possibly get!

On the last day of January, he emailed to tell me about his first coaching/counselling session. He seemed to be making progress, though he said it was tough. Further updates told me that he was doing some pretty deep emotional work. He'd discovered that he had a lot of hidden anger issues that he'd buried since childhood. The diagnosis made some sense to me, although, since we still hadn't seen each other or had any kind of decent conversation, I wasn't certain that he was actually doing anything concrete to make a positive difference in helping us heal as a couple. He still insisted on staying away, and I felt as though the void between us was getting wider. The days turned into weeks, and we got no further forward, despite Cam's assurances that he was making progress.

In one of his emails he told me that he'd realised during a session that he was scared of me and that he struggled to express his emotions. Apparently one of the counsellors had suggested that he make a list of songs that would help him to express his feelings more clearly. Would this be something I was interested in?

I, of course, said I would love to hear whatever music tracks he wanted to send – at least it would be something that would give me a clue about what he was feeling! So in his next email he attached a list of songs that he said he hoped I wouldn't view too negatively. What I got from these songs was a mish-mash of messages. Some songs seemed to be an expression of his defiance, saying that he wasn't going to change and out relationship was a mess. Others conveyed the message that he felt squashed and helpless. Others still seemed to suggest he was saying sorry and was asking me to wait while sorted his head out. I listened to them all, desperately trying to understand the meanings he felt were contained within them. One particular song, 'Light On' by David Cook had me in floods of tears, and I found myself nodding and saying to myself, *Of course I'll leave the light on so you can find your way home. I'm here for you and always will be.*

I responded to the list, as always, thanking him for opening up and continuing to offer my support and understanding. I was learning to use all my Louise Hay and coaching training with my husband. Although I was hurting, and even though I felt so alone, I decided I was strong enough to turn to my skills and help him through whatever emotional and psychological crisis he was facing. Whatever had gone wrong, he insisted he wanted to save us, and I wanted to save us – so I decided I'd do whatever it took. I used the same skills on myself at home and somehow managed to keep my sanity, but it was hard. He didn't call the following evening (this was becoming a regular pattern) but instead sent me an email.

From: Campbell Deveraux
Date: Thu, 19 Feb 2009 19.24.11 +0000
To: Mel Carnegie
Subject: Hey there
Hi
Hope your day has been good?!
Having a pretty 'bottom of the pit' day after a reflection session that

had me bawling my eyes out – feel sad. feel I have started to let go a bit though too. Can't I just sell the emotional stuff to the highest bidder on eBay!

Can we chat tomo if you are OK with that?

Need to eat and sleep now.

Lots of love xxxx

Me

From: Mel Carnegie

Date: Thu, 19 Feb 2009 19.53.13 +0000

To: Campbell Deveraux

Subject: Re: Hey there

Hey you

Big day eh? Well done . . . Not easy though! Keep at it . . .

Don't think emotions are saleable on eBay . . . !! Anyway, the bigger the nasties the bigger the goodies too . . . So they're all of great value to you . . . though it may not seem so right at this moment . . . !!

Letting go sounds such a simple thing to do eh? Pah!!!

Yes we can chat tomo . . .

whenever suits you. No worries lovely.

Have a good rest, you deserve it.

I'm very proud of you. I know how hard this must be for you . . .

I love you,

Mel xxxxxxxx

From: Campbell Deveraux

Date: Thu, 19 Feb 2009 20:06:40 +0000

To: Mel Carnegie

Subject: Re: Re: Hey there

Thank you! Pain has set in :-(

Chat tomo later in the day then. Have a good flight eh.

Love you too xxxx

It was absolutely excruciating! There was my husband, going

through emotional trauma, and there was absolutely nothing I could do. He was totally shutting me out, choosing instead to deal with it all on his own. It was coming up for two months now since we'd seen each other and the limbo state was quite literally tearing me apart. But he wouldn't talk about the way I felt.

'Mel, I can't even deal with what's happening for me! I'm sorry for being an unsupportive shit, but I'm afraid that's just the way it is. I understand I'm hurting you. I know that. I'm doing all I can to get us both through this. I can't do any more than I'm already doing!'

This to-ing and fro-ing went on for another two months. I saw him in the UK a couple of times, and we would talk/text and email practically every day, even though the conversations rarely went in to detail about 'us' – he just wouldn't go there. But each time I felt that I'd had enough and had been pushed to the limit, Cam would seem to make some kind of breakthrough. It was like being on a crazy emotional roller coaster that held no fun of the fair, just psychological turmoil. I was holding on for dear life – holding on to what, I didn't know – and it was exhausting.

Cam came over to France for ten days over Easter but had to fly back to Scotland over the Easter weekend because he was doing his best to make amends with his mother as part of his counselling process. Although I was bitterly upset that he was deserting a family gathering, I decided it was probably helpful in the long run. The times we were together, though, ended up being even more agonising than the long times apart.

When he was at home, I could touch his face and see his body. I heard his every familiar movement as he ambled about the house and noticed his smell every time he came near. But he was further away than ever and, despite hours and hours of talking, I just couldn't reach him. I couldn't make sense of the situation and felt stretched to beyond the end of my tether. I couldn't go on.

One afternoon, after a particularly upsetting exchange – me in floods of tears, him seeming cold and confused at what was happening – I decided it was time again to face the truth. 'So, we'd better just call it a day then, eh? We're clearly not making any progress here, and this is far too painful for me and unsettling for Dylan.'

'But, Mel, we've done a decade together! What are you saying? It would tear me apart if we split up! That just can't happen. We've just got to keep at this. I know it's painful, but hey, no pain no gain.'

Nothing seemed real. The sentences didn't add up, and, as far as I could see, the only person experiencing any real pain was me. It was excruciating. I bared my soul, I plumbed the depths of my fears, I shared my hopes and declared my love . . . but he remained a void. An empty shell who would sometimes say the right things or make the right noises but make no logical sense.

He left on Sunday, 19 April to deliver some training. Dylan and I were due to fly to the UK on the Thursday and meet up with him in London. He'd given Dylan a huge hug, ruffling his hair with his usual 'I love you, dude! See you Thursday!' I drove him to the airport, holding him close with tears in my eyes as I wished him a safe journey.

'Oh, don't be so soppy. There's no need to cry! You know I'm no good at that emotional stuff!' he'd teased me, trying to make light of a situation that was ripping my heart out. We'd made no progress. Each time I'd tried to push the situation to a logical conclusion it seemed to slip away from my grasp. Bewildered and exhausted, I had no fight left.

A couple of nights later, my friend Gemma came and spent the evening with me. We ended up drinking far too much wine – as usual – and sharing all manner of secrets. Until then I hadn't told anyone the details of what was happening between Cam and I – how could I? I couldn't even make sense of it myself! But with Gemma, I poured my heart out.

'Fucking hell, Mel! No wonder you're feeling so shit! God, if I was in your shoes I'd bloody brain him!'

'Believe me, I've been sorely tempted. The anguish he's putting me through is so selfish, but at the same time, what if he really is going through the biggest meltdown of his life? How can I just throw him out when he keeps telling me he needs me and he's making progress? Oh, please help me, Gemma. I'm losing my flaming sanity here!'

We talked, questioned, confided, laughed and cried throughout the night, finally going to bed at six o'clock the next morning. We hadn't come to any conclusions. No matter which way we looked at things, nothing made sense. Parts did, yes, but the whole story? No, there were gaping holes and mis-matches. Something just wasn't adding up. So by the time Gemma left the following afternoon, I had decided to take matters into my own hands. I had to find out what was going on.

It was Wednesday, 22 April, and in my hand I held the private password to Cam's email account. It was our business account, and we used the services of an IT consultant to deal with all email, server and password issues. We'd had a problem a few weeks earlier when our email had crashed and he'd had to re-set our passwords, so I had a good reason to call. Telling him that I was going through some logistical details, I asked him for both of our new email passwords to add to the office records.

As I sat in front of the computer, my heart raced and a lump came to my throat. I put in the password and pressed the send and receive button on Cam's email account. There were over 1,000 messages waiting to come through, but I was overcome with guilt and stopped the process after just a few seconds.

What are you doing, Mel? For goodness' sake, this is your husband! Surely you shouldn't be spying on him? Do you really want this to work? How can you have a relationship when the trust has gone? The questions carried on in my head as I prepared the evening meal for Dylan and myself. *Stop it, and stop it now. This can only lead to trouble. No good can possibly come of it. So leave it alone.*

But I couldn't. After I'd settled Dylan for the night and poured myself a large glass of wine, I restarted the download and waited.

And waited. It took forever, but once it was done I started going through the emails to see whether there was anything that would shed any light on what was going on.

There was. Lots. Tons in fact. And a set of email trails that led me to discover the horrifying truth that my husband, my Campbell, was not the person I had believed him to be. The expression about blood running cold was an understatement. Ragged shards of frozen ice crackled through my veins as the evidence surfaced. I discovered he'd been running up thousands of pounds worth of credit buying top-of-the-range mountain bikes and other trinkets on the company account. No wonder he hadn't wanted me to come and visit him in Edinburgh! He'd also been refusing to pay suppliers, putting them off with a stream of excuses and lies. He'd been meeting people for sex and goodness knows what else. I had proof of two such liaisons that dated back to the summer of 2008 – the time when we were just about to celebrate our ten-year anniversary together. He'd signed up for numerous porn channels – all on the company account – and had even set up his own pornographic website advertising his wares under the pseudonym Happyman 213. In his tasteful introduction, he described himself as: '. . . a fit 40 and happy guy! Would love to have some fun – meet some great people and never grow up – just grow hard! Which I am all the time! Get in touch – I like sexy women who know what they want!'

He was regularly online, liked to use a webcam and called himself 'Bi-curious' and also 'Bi-lingual English and French'. Well, he certainly wasn't the latter. His French was rubbish and his English language skills left a lot to be desired judging by his adverts and the tawdry messages he'd been exchanging with other members. As for being bi-curious? I felt sick to the stomach.

Well, that's shocking,' Gemma had said a few days later, putting on her best straight-face and nudging my arm. 'You mean he's not even bi-CERTAIN? I thought he was a man who could make decisions!'

That night, right in front of me, suddenly everything became clear and started to make sense. Well, not 'sense' exactly, because it was incomprehensible, but at last I knew what I had to do. The evidence was all there. There was no denying it. Cam had been leading me on a merry dance and ruining our business in the process. No wonder he'd been so keen to take over the finances!

After the initial almighty shockwave, I felt pretty numb as I read through tale after telling tale of his deliberate deceptions. His important visit to his mother in Edinburgh at Easter was also a blatant lie. He'd called us on Easter Sunday, saying he was outside the nursing home with his sisters. His emails confirmed that in actual fact he was camping with one of his lady friends – or maybe it was a male friend. Who knows? And actually, who cares?

I called Ruth and Henry as soon as I could find my voice. It had been nearly an hour since I'd first started reading.

'I can't explain what's happened on the phone, but please could you come over and would one of you be kind enough to stay the night? I really need your help.'

The emotion kicked in as soon as I put the phone down, but it wasn't tears. It was trembling. Confusion. Terror. And a smouldering rage as I stumbled into the kitchen and poured myself another large glass of wine. Before then I had maintained a business-like calm, forwarding some of the incriminating evidence to friends who had been concerned about me over recent months. I knew it would shock, but rather than try to explain I wanted people to see for themselves. Even to me, even with all the evidence in black and white in front of me, I still couldn't quite believe that this was the work of the man I called my soulmate. So how could I expect others to believe me if I couldn't show them at least part of what I was seeing?

One of the emails backfired when a well-meaning friend responded to me. I had mistakenly forwarded an email while still logged in to Cam's account, and my friend had replied to Cam's email address. Which meant he would know that I was on to him. That was OK. I hoped that my discovery would shock him to the core.

It would appear that it did. He'd been booked into a hotel to run a very important training course the next day, Thursday, 23 April. He must have woken early in the morning to prepare himself for the meeting and discovered the email I had sent to my friend, and the response he had given. The huge team-building training session had taken months to organise, but the shock of realising that I'd uncovered his murky secrets must have rocked his world – and not in the way of the sex sites he loved so dearly! Even then, though, the lies came thick and fast as he emailed our trusting clients, who had travelled miles to be there, to tell them that he'd been called away to the hospital bedside of his seriously ill daughter. He apologised for the inconvenience, particularly as it had been so difficult to find a date that suited everyone, but said he was sure they would understand in these most difficult of circumstances.

Back in France, Ruth arrived at the house on her own. She must have known it was to do with Cam and figured that some motherly love and advice was in order, or perhaps it was because I'd terrified poor Henry last time I had a 'problem' and he'd decided it was safer to stay where he was!

It was only once she was there and I'd showed her some of the stuff I'd found that the tears started to fall and the full weight of shame, guilt and pain started to hit home.

'I've been so goddamned STUPID! How could I have been so blind? What made me fall for his lies? How could I have allowed him to torture me for so many months? He must have been laughing in my face while I fell to pieces in front of him! How could he have been so cruel? Where did I go wrong? What did I do to deserve this?'

Ruth stayed right there with me, quietly and patiently giving me space to cry, to swear, to question and to crumble. She was brilliant. I don't know what I would have done without her.

Of course, there were no answers. It was a night of broken sleep but strangely more peaceful than I could remember in a long while.

At least I now knew the truth, but boy was it going to be difficult to tell Dylan.

The following morning, true to form, was absolutely excruciating. Ruth was still there, and while Dylan was surprised to see her, he accepted her presence and asked no questions. We all sat down together at the table outside the kitchen. I had made him some toast for breakfast and waited until he'd finished before bracing myself for the inevitable – the news that I knew would break my son's heart. It took every ounce of strength to hold myself together and explain gently that Cam was not the person we had both believed him to be, and that he would not be coming home ever again. I made it perfectly clear that Dylan had played no part in Cam's bad behaviour, that we had all been duped – friends as well as the both of us, and that there was nothing to feel guilty about. I reassured him that we would come through this together, that we had plenty of people who love us, and that, although it would be tough, I would be there for him every step of the way.

I waited for his response, and my heart was once again ripped in two to see my 13-year-old son break down with the shock of the news. Never again do I want to witness so much pain and anguish on the face of someone I love with all my heart and all my soul. His little face crumpled in front of my eyes, and I remembered my own pain when my mother had to tell me that my daddy had died. It was heartbreaking, and I would have done everything within my power to take the hurt away, but of course I couldn't.

'I'm never going to see him again, am I, Mummy?' he wailed, the tears once again welling in his eyes.

'No, my darling. Neither of us are. I am so sorry. So very, very sorry for the hurt this is causing you,' and my own tears fell as well.

So I let him cry, and I held him tight. I gave him the headlines about the information I had discovered and why, therefore, I would never let that man back into our lives. I told him that when people do bad things, it's not our fault, but it is our choice and responsibility to bolt the door and never let them hurt us again. I also invited him to ask me any questions about what I was telling him – at the same time letting him know he didn't have to ask anything if he didn't want to. It came as no surprise that he wanted to know everything, so I listened to his probing questions. How had I found out? How long had it been going on? What would it mean to us? How were we going to live? I didn't have answers to everything, telling him quite honestly whenever that was the case.

After what seemed like hours (it was probably only a few minutes), his sobbing subsided and he sat up straight. His face had changed.

'I'm angry now,' he announced. 'I want to smash something – something of his.'

I offered clothes to cut up or burn, but he was insistent that smashing and fury was what he wanted to achieve.

'I've got an idea!' I said, responding to his obvious need to create some damage. 'Come on, let's get busy and make a huge mess!'

So, empty bucket in hand, we went up to the bedroom I'd shared with Cam for the past six years and collected all his bottles of aftershave. Bottle after bottle of Gucci, Chanel, Paco Rabanne, Tom Ford, Armani and goodness knows how many other top-name brands went into the bucket, filling it to the brim.

We then marched down to the bottom of the garden, climbed over the low wall and jumped down into the field, where there was a huge dry-stone wall that ran along the left-hand perimeter. It was the outside wall to our neighbour's garage – high, wide, and a perfect target. Putting the bucket by our feet, I told Dylan my plan.

'These perfume bottles are all made of glass,' I explained, 'and smashing glass makes an incredible sound. And, more importantly, Cam loved his aftershaves, so he'd be furious if he knew what we were going to do!'

Dylan nodded, his face still set firm but the beginning of a twinkle in his eyes starting to show.

'So, we're going to take every single one of these bloody bottles and throw them with all our might against that wall. I want you to use all your strength and all of your anger. Let it out with every single explosion. What do you think, will that help?'

He nodded, the faintest hint of a smile beginning to appear. I advised him to shout and scream, and gave him permission to use whatever swear words he wanted as well. All rules of decorum were thrown out of the window for the moment!

His smile widened as he picked up the first bottle and hurled it at the wall. As it smashed into tiny pieces, the air filled with the heavy sticky smell of very expensive aftershave. Dylan shouted and jumped, kicking his feet and punching his fists in the air, his face purple with anger, and, goodness me, I discovered that his earlier training in swear words had increased beyond my imagination! The air turned blue as Dylan shouted out all manner of obscenities about Cam, and I decided it was time to join in. After asking if I could help, we then spent the next few minutes shouting, screaming, swearing and smashing glass bottles against the wall together. Boy it felt good!

When the last bottle had been thrown, we stood there in silence, holding onto each other in an emotional embrace.

'I'm so proud of you,' I said. 'And I promise I will never let anyone hurt you like this again. I am so sorry.'

'You have nothing to be sorry about, Mum,' he replied, squeezing me tighter. 'It's not your fault. You didn't know.'

The tears slid down my cheeks and the sobs returned. I had no idea what the future held, what we were going to do or how on earth we were going to get through this. But I knew I would do everything within my power to keep my son safe, to stick by him and to love him even more than I ever had before.

'Anyway,' I said, smiling through my tears, 'at least the village is going to smell pretty good for the next few hours!' He smiled back and we walked arm in arm back towards the house together. Something had shifted, and we were now united in our determined battle to pull through.

The last piece of communication I ever received from my husband arrived not long after I had told Dylan the news.

From: Campbell Deveraux

Date: Thu, 23 Apr 2009 09:22:56 +0100

To: Mel Carnegie

Subject: Talk

I am not working today as you probably know – I can't!

I am not having affairs nor have I.

I am in the process of selling stuff – bike for a profit even!

I am not meeting up with anyone probably though you don't believe me.

I am not Internet dating – I am NOT!

I would like to talk when you want but don't if you feel you can't!

Lots of love

Cam x x

I responded with just seven words – 'Lies, lies, lies, lies, lies, lies, lies' – and shut the laptop before turning my back and heading upstairs to pack for our trip to the UK.

17

The Bitter End

The next few days saw me become the efficient survivor. I knew I was in trouble. Even if at that stage I had no comprehension of the sheer magnitude of the mess that surrounded me, I knew darned well that this was serious. The betrayal of my husband was one thing – and God only knows my heart had once again broken into tiny pieces – but I knew I couldn't afford to dwell on my emotions. I had to fight. I had to pull on all my previous experiences and prepare myself for battle. I was prepared to take this one to the death if needs be. To be blatantly honest, I'm pretty sure it was anger that drove me through those early hours and days. Focusing on what Cam had done gave me the determination to keep going – his deliberate torture, his callous lies and his ongoing cat-and-mouse treatment of me and, to top it all, for taking and breaking the innocent trust of a little boy who loved him, my little boy.

Melanie, this is not the time to fall to pieces. Come on, girl, you have got to be strong! Staring at myself in the mirror, I pulled myself up and locked eyes with my reflection. Steely determination stared back at me; I was poised to do whatever was necessary. Gritting my teeth, I nodded with satisfaction. *Deep breath, shoulders back, head up, stay strong – BE strong – you ARE strong! You can do this – you KNOW you can. Good . . . well done, now let's get to it!*

Dylan and I flew straight to the UK that very same morning as previously planned, and we met with my sister and Paul, Dylan's dad, both of whom were, of course, incredibly supportive and also incredulous about my story. It didn't matter. The most important thing was that Dylan felt supported and loved. Cam had been his stepfather since he'd been a toddler, and his world had been destroyed in just a few short hours. He was going to need all the patience, kindness and understanding that he could get. So did I, but my focus for the time being was Dylan. It was only after he'd gone off with his father that I let a few tears fall, but not too many. Just a few, just to stop me exploding.

The next day, Friday, 24th April, I called our company accountant and our bank manager. I told the accountant that I had evidence to prove that the accounts had been mismanaged and, on that basis, was certain that the company was insolvent. It is illegal to knowingly continue trade while insolvent, so I instructed him to call in a firm of liquidators. I further warned him that Cam may or may not decide to call him, but that he was to take anything he said with a pinch of salt.

'It may well be that I need to get the police involved here. So we all need to tread very carefully from this moment on. I must be sure that every single step I take is legal, above board and done to the very best of my ability as a company director.'

I instructed our bank manager to freeze the company account and also the associated credit cards. There was a good few thousand in the account at the time and a further wedge of income due in from outstanding invoices. Even though I had clearly been duped about the management of the company finances, I always knew what sales invoices were outstanding because I was the one who raised them. After a good deal of toing and froing, the manager ensured that nothing could leave the account but that income could be received until the final invoices were paid. Good. That meant I'd ring-fenced as much cash as possible so that suppliers and other company creditors could be paid.

It felt good to know that I'd kept my wits about me well enough to put those two things into action. I might have been blinded as a co-director of a company, and I would doubtless be accused of being incapable at some point in the future, but I was pleased that as soon as I found out the truth I had taken every possible measure to do the right thing.

I phoned around a number of solicitors and arranged a meeting for Monday. Even with the scantest of details about my situation – a company in liquidation, joint ownership of properties in UK, Scotland and France, debts and deception and no form of income – I was warned that my case would be complicated. Many solicitors refused point-blank to see me, but I managed to find one who was at least willing to meet with me.

I then went with my sister to an STD clinic. I had to get myself checked for all manner of potential sexual diseases that my promiscuous husband might have exposed me to – herpes, HPV, Chlamydia and a whole range of other STDs I hadn't heard of – as well as taking a dreaded HIV test. That was when it hit me. That was when I shrank and imagined Alice falling down the rabbit hole. I was lost, frightened and all of a sudden terribly, terribly small. I had loved that man with all my heart and all my soul, and since the first moment I laid eyes on him he had been the only one for me. How could he have let this happen to me?

Abigail stayed with me every step of the way, and I remember lying with my legs akimbo while a very kind nurse asked me all manner of questions and poked about between my thighs.

'When did you last have sexual intercourse? When was your last period? Did you have oral sex? Sexual aids? Anal sex? Drugs? When do you suspect your husband first started his affairs? Have you ever been unfaithful?' They were all questions that needed to be answered, of course, but it seemed that I was on trial. Feeling shameful enough for having been conned so completely and over such a prolonged period of time, I now felt guilty about answering intimate questions about my love life. Because that's what it had always been to me – a love life, not a sex life. Private demonstrations of affection shared with my husband, my soulmate, the man I believed I was going to grow old and die with. It was never meant to be like this.

With the main 'tasks' dealt with, the rest of my time in London was a bit of a blur aided, I confess, by copious amounts of wine and also the revival of my smoking habit. The agony was almost too much to bear and no matter how hard I tried I could not blot out the ache, so severe that it threatened to stop me from breathing. Sometimes I thought it would be better to stop breathing for ever, but then I thought of Dylan, and I also thought of Cam.

No way – no how, no way! He's not getting that pleasure! I have to come through this. I must find a way. Come on, Mel, remember 'this too will pass . . . this too will pass'. That was one of Mum's sayings, and I remember repeating it over and over in my head, willing myself to take one more breath, one more step, to face one more hour and one more day.

I received a text from Cam on the following Tuesday, six days after I'd discovered his lies. It was direct and to the point: 'Let's talk. We need to talk. We have got to sort this out.'

It was no coincidence that the text had been sent at the exact time I knew he would have landed at Stansted airport and tried to use the company card to buy a train ticket. *So now he decides he wants to talk? Now he's discovered that his cash supply has been cut off? Tough.*

'The only talking will be through my solicitor, who you'll be hearing from in due course,' was my reply. It was the very last direct communication I ever sent him.

Back in France, the reality of my perilous position hit home. I had arranged a post re-direction service from Edinburgh, and as soon the letters started to arrive it became clear that the situation was even more severe than I had appreciated. Final demands, court orders, notices of repossession – the financial catastrophe was beyond comprehension. How on earth had he hidden this mess for so long?

What had possessed him to ignore all these bills? What did he think was going to happen?

I had found a solicitor through a recommendation from our accountant. She was Scottish and believed that we would have to follow Scottish law since Cam was living there. The solicitor I had previously visited in London proved to be no help whatsoever, apart from helping me to appreciate that my situation was so dire that I'd be lucky to find anyone who would deal with it. Oh, and it would also cost thousands of pounds.

'But I don't have thousands of pounds!' I'd cried at one point, boiling with frustration and humiliation. 'Haven't you been listening? I've been conned! I have nothing! I just need to find out what I can do now. Please help me!'

My Scottish solicitor made contact with the mortgage companies and discovered the extent of the problem. It was disastrous. Our buy-to-let property was in the process of being repossessed and the tenants had given notice as a result. The mortgage on the Edinburgh property had only been paid twice over the last eight-month period and had suffered a number of bounced cheques in the meantime.

I had a small amount of money in my personal account, but nothing near the amount that was needed to clear the arrears. And, anyway, what was Cam going to do about it since he was living in our apartment in Edinburgh?

'That doesn't matter, Mrs Deveraux. The mortgages are in joint names, meaning that the debt is joint and several. They can come after either of you for payment,' my solicitor explained as tears of despair rolled down my face. 'You must deal with them, since, going by previous evidence, your husband is unlikely to do anything about it himself.'

Property prices had fallen dramatically in the 18 months since we'd bought the places, and with the mounting arrears both were now in negative equity. So I didn't even have the option to sell, and if I just handed back the keys the mortgage companies would sell them at a rock-bottom rate and still come after me for the debt.

This was just the beginning of the nightmare. The days turned into weeks, and more and more evidence of Cam's irresponsibility came to light. Hit by wave after wave of new evidence, each day found me reeling from yet another blow. Crying out as yet another blade of cruel betrayal pierced my heart. Never having the time to take a breath let alone recover from the sheer exhaustion of everyday existence.

By the beginning of July 2009 the outlook was still bleak and it took every ounce of strength to keep going. The company had long since been closed and, although I had been touting for work on my own, nothing had been forthcoming. To be honest I really don't think I would have been capable of running any training or coaching sessions, so it was probably a blessing in disguise! But it meant I had no income. And, of course, no savings.

I had discovered more evidence of Cam's unquenchable thirst for spending. I already knew he had a soft spot for training shoes, but when I looked through all the cupboards I found no less than 50 pairs of shoes, all of them expensive, some of them still with the label on. That also went for clothes, belts, aftershaves (already disposed of!) and an array of electrical equipment. Who, in their right mind, needs eight mobile phones and three Blackberries? And as for the IT equipment, much of it still in boxes, what on earth was he thinking – and how could I not have noticed? How had I been so oblivious to what had been happening right underneath my nose?

I remembered one of his more recent returns from the UK. He had come home wearing another new leather jacket with a very smart briefcase bag slung over his shoulder.

'That's nice,' I'd said, worried about the cost but not wanting to upset him.

'Yeah, I saved us £100!' he replied. 'This bag was down to £400, so I decided to buy this as well,' he added, opening it up and brandishing a top-of-the-range Macbook Air laptop. My face must have said it all.

'Why on earth did you buy that? We've just leased two new Macbook Pro computers. We don't need it!'

'Oh, stop making such a fuss. We're professionals and we really do need to look the part. We've got to up our game. Added to which it'll be so much easier on me when I'm travelling around, and, anyway, it's less than a day's training fees! It's a no-brainer!' he'd retorted. 'Don't go and spoil it. I thought you'd be pleased!'

There had been many similar occasions when I worried about his extravagance. After the purchase of his seventh guitar, I pointed out that perhaps we could sell a few, as he was never going to need them.

'You know how much I love my guitars,' he'd said, sulking like a schoolboy. 'And each one of them makes a completely different sound. I love them all, and you love it when I play them too! We'd get nothing for them if we sold them anyway.'

And so it would go on. My concerns constantly pushed aside with his reassurance that 'it's less than a day's training fees', and I couldn't argue. He was in charge of the finances, and I believed he knew what he was doing. I had always been careful with money, but his motto was always the same: 'It's no point buying anything on the cheap. Expensive equals quality, and quality lasts.' Yes, it's true, quality lasts, but how did that equate to the sheer quantity of unopened and unused toys gadgets and gizmos that I found after he'd gone?

In a desperate attempt to raise some money, Dylan and I collected everything we could find and took it to a local car boot sale (*brocante*, as it's known here). Books, DVDs, CDs, shoes, belts and clothing – not the big stuff, but things we no longer needed and, more importantly, things of his that we no longer wanted in the house. We didn't make a lot of money – I think we came away with just over a hundred euro in the end – but it made me laugh when a bunch of gypsies came and started haggling over his shirts. There were ones by Polo Ralph Lauren, Burberry, Lanvin, Gucci and many more, all hanging on a makeshift rail and blowing in the breeze. It was the end of the car boot sale and we really didn't want to take them home with us.

'You can have the lot for 30 euro,' said Dylan. 'Each one cost more than £100, so you've got a good bargain there,' he added, in full sales flow. They haggled him down to 25 euro, and we giggled at the thought of local farmers and labourers strutting around in Cam's designer shirts. He'd have been mortified if he knew!

I sold larger stuff on a local website, including a second-hand sports car he'd 'had to have', together with a fridge, freezer, canoe, sports equipment and all the IT equipment. None of it came to much, but every little helped, and I was absolutely desperate for money. As I said, I had expected to land some private coaching work, but it proved more difficult than I had first thought. Perhaps it was also that I wasn't in the right frame of mind.

How can I possibly go in and coach people now I've made such a mess of my life? Who on earth is going to take me seriously? My confidence was at an all-time low, and there were many mornings when I could hardly drag myself out of bed – and many afternoons when I the only thing I could do was to retreat back under my duvet. This was a new world filled with emptiness and confusion, and I didn't know how to live in it.

On the other hand, I would often wake to find anonymous gifts of fruit, vegetables, bread or flowers left on the table outside my kitchen, and I became a dab hand at make do and mend, and finding the cheapest food options. I'd done it before in my 20s, but the situation had never been this bad. But then it's amazing how far you can spread a few euro when you need to!

The worst thing was the aching in my soul and in my belly. I missed Cam so much it hurt, and the battle between my heart and my head was ferocious.

How can you be so stupid, Mel? I'd ask, finding myself picking up the phone and starting to dial his number. *He's nothing but a con man, leave well alone!* But the pain was indescribable. I still couldn't understand what I'd done so wrong to make him treat me so badly. Had it ever been real for him? Or had I done something so bad that he'd fallen out of love with me? Was he thinking about me? Was he sorry? Did he miss me?

18

Life's Little Lettuces

A few weeks after the fateful evening of my discoveries, I happened to meet a lady who subsequently turned in to a staunch ally and soul sister. She, it appeared, had been through a similar set of circumstances – betrayal, deliberate deception and mountains of debt – with a husband she'd escaped some 20 years earlier. Her name is Anna and she is 20 years older than me, and, like me, she understood the importance of emotional support as she'd trained and worked for many years as a counsellor. We met under the strangest of circumstances, at a ladies lunch that I had agreed to go to just for some light relief from the daily drudgery of survival. I am convinced it was one of those pre-ordained meetings, and it was Anna who encouraged me to 'write it all out, Mel – just write it all out'.

This was an approach I was already familiar with, as I had kept a daily diary from the age of 15 through to my mid 20s, but rather than write by hand, this time I decided my laptop was the better option. Starting just with the odd document on Word, I soon found Google's Blogger site and set myself up with an online diary. I wrote for myself. I wrote about myself. I started exploring my inner thoughts and questioning my previously held beliefs. I pretended that I was explaining what was happening to somebody who was listening to me. And I started feeling better.

Gradually I invited friends to take a look at what I was writing. As it was online, it meant it could be read from anywhere, and their comments encouraged me to open it up to a wider audience. That audience grew through word of mouth, attracting readers from around the world. The messages of encouragement continued, with both friends and strangers telling me that the deeply personal accounts of my struggles along my journey to healing were helpful to them.

The stories themselves do not give the day-to-day details of what was happening to me – shutting the business, calling in the liquidators, uncovering more and more debts, sobbing on the shoulders of friends as yet more evidence of my husband's true character came to light. No, my blog tells of my inner emotions and my determined fight to make it through.

Now, for the first time, I can tell my story in more detail, spurred on by the messages of encouragement and thanks I received as a result of the blog. I hope this will give more understanding to a wider audience. I hope that my experiences will resonate with more people. If, as a result, I can help just one person to either get out of an existing abusive relationship, or heal from an old one, well, then it's all been worthwhile.

One of my earliest posts – 'Life's Little Lettuces', which eventually became the title of the blog – was written at a time when my days were full of darkness and my nights were full of torture. There was no escape. My dream had turned into a living nightmare, and it hurt like hell.

'It's OK,' my dear friend Vera had said. 'I always thought there was something odd about him. I guess he's just a typical bloke – and a stupid one at that! How could he just walk away from so much love? You'll come through. I know it hurts, but we're all here for you.'

But it wasn't OK. Not in the slightest. No matter what anyone said, or how much they tried to understand, I was not OK, and I couldn't believe that I was ever going to be OK again. Yes, it's true,

I was 'functioning' on a daily basis, mainly for the sake of my son, but 'functioning' was all I was able to muster – and that was on a good day! It had been only a matter of weeks since the evening I had discovered the ghastly truth, and it was only now that the full horror of my situation was really sinking in.

The divorce proceedings with the Scottish lawyer had started making some level of progress, but since I had so far failed to secure any work I had no money to pay the bill and of course they had to stop the work. Just before the work stopped, she had helped me to discover the huge arrears on the buy-to-let mortgage and the fact that it was about to be repossessed. The ensuing conversations with the arrears advisor highlighted the grim reality of my financial situation. I realised, with growing humiliation, just how stupid my circumstances must have seemed.

'You're saying that didn't know what was going on? Didn't you check what your husband was doing? Didn't you think you should ask to see the accounts for yourself, Mrs Devereaux?' The accusations stung, and I fought back the tears and bit my tongue. The points were perfectly reasonable and impossible to counter.

Lost, defeated, and not knowing where to turn, that night I fell to the floor and sobbed until I could sob no more. The pain was excruciating, made all the more worse by my hatred of myself. The next day I wrote this post:

FRIDAY, 3 JULY 2009
Life's Little Lettuces

Having had great success growing my own herbs, and experimenting with the odd runner bean sown quietly among my container pots, I decided this year that I'd take the next few tentative steps to 'growing my own'.

I already have tomatoes, beans, peas and a good crop of rocket, and a few days ago I bought a punnet of 24 baby lettuces from a market stall to add to my collection.

They are lollo rosso variety – a beautiful, vibrant mauve colour with pretty curly leaves. I'd been told that you can pick just a few leaves at a time and they'll continue to produce all through the summer – fantastic!

They had been grown individually in little 'cubes' of soil that were joined together. So I carefully broke off each one and eased them gently in to their places in my garden. I watered them in, welcoming to their new home, and thought no more of it.

The following day I went down to check on my latest additions and found they had all wilted and shrivelled – every single one of them. I was gutted! Still, I reasoned, they've just come to a new home and, even though I've done my very best to give them care and attention so they can settle in, it must still have been a stressful move. To be uprooted from the place you grew up, separated from your friends, and placed in a new place that must seem huge, empty and hostile – they'd probably never been out of their greenhouse before! Even then I couldn't help but chuckle at the very obvious links to my own childhood experiences.

So I continued to water and tend them – propping them up and talking to them as well (oh yes I did!). But the days passed and they didn't seem to make much progress. Four of them completely shrivelled (like lettuce that's been left in a fridge too long? Watery and floppy) two of them seemed to be picking up a bit, and the rest of them just looked generally wilted. They simply didn't seem to have the energy to do anything at all, even though the sun had been shining every day, the soil was good, and I continued to nurture them.

It was just a few days later when we had the most almighty of storms. It started, as usual, with a sudden drop in air pressure. The birds went silent, sensing the impending changes, and the brooding skies started to unfurl their rumbling cloaks as the sunlight became overshadowed by the gathering storm clouds. A warning crack of thunder split the air, and then came the rain. Sparse at first, but steadily gathering momentum as the ferocity intensified, turning the gentle thrumming in to relentless heavy pounding, bouncing off every hard surface and intensifying the sounds even more.

I imagined my poor little lettuces – being beaten, battered and drowned, and I felt sad at my unforeseen role in hastening their untimely deaths. They'd seemed so happy and full of promise at the market stand, and I'd thought that I could give them more. But I was wrong. The storm was too mighty, they were no longer together, and they couldn't fight alone.

I noticed again the similarities in my own life and the battles I'm facing on a daily basis as I try to make sense of the past two months. Now I am unable to pay my bills, there is still no work booked, and my estranged husband is doing nothing to move forward with the divorce proceedings. I feel alone, helpless and vulnerable – and some days I wonder how to keep going.

With my own storm clouds gathering above me, I've been using every nerve cell and fibre of my being to stay positive, strong and determined for both myself and my son, even in the face of continued adversity. It's like a slow, relentless monster moving towards me. I can't always see or hear it, and I can sometimes pretend it's not there, but it's always getting closer and I cannot escape no matter what I do.

Yesterday I received two bits of unfavourable news, which, for me, announced the thunder and lightening of my own personal storm. That was it for me. I had no fight left, no more solutions to create, nowhere to turn and I felt I simply couldn't carry on. I was totally drained – emotionally, physically and spiritually. I was all washed up, and I sank slowly to the floor and let myself go as the hot tears of frustration, hopelessness and exhaustion coursed down my face, blurring my vision as my body shuddered with hard rasping sobs.

Finally exhausted, I dragged myself to bed, to face yet another night of vivid and disturbed dreams as I continue to try and make sense of this ongoing living nightmare.

This morning, it's another beautiful sunny day. I decided I'd spend my first couple of hours tending my garden and assess what damage had been left by the storm. The earth was once again dry – too dry in fact, so I switched on the well-pump and went about watering the beds.

It was about 11 a.m. by the time I got down to my vegetable patch. Absent-mindedly sprinkling the water spray over my beans and peas, I suddenly noticed out of the corner of my eye a little flash of mauve in the next bed. I shook my head and blinked, surely it couldn't be? I edged closer and more purple tinged leaves came in to view, as I saw that every single one of my lettuces had not only survived the storm but were now actually standing upright and strong, and waving in the breeze! Even the two that I had previously thought were completely dead had sprouted small, determined new leaves right at the centre of the 'blob' that was left of them.

And I found myself laughing – quietly chuckling on the inside at first, and then growing to shoulder-shaking guffaws as I continued to take in the lessons on every single level of my being.

'The darkest hour is the one before dawn' is one of my favourite sayings, and these little plants had taught me some invaluable lessons. About how difficult it can be to settle into a new routine after change. About how no amount of external nurturing can make you 'come back to life'. About how the biggest storm that to most people would appear a killer, had actually washed them clean, nourished them and made them strong.

Nature is truly wonderful. And nature's little lettuces of life have given me hope and inspiration today.

Perhaps I'm not alone, though. Perhaps other people have learned from lettuces before me. And perhaps that's why one variety was named Little Gem . . .

19

A Deal with Hannibal Lecter

It was six short days after this post that I was to make a discovery that shocked me to the core and was to change my life forever. Rather than explain the discovery, I would rather simply share my blog entry for that day.

It was nearing midnight on Thursday, 9 July 2009. A typically warm summer's night that found me in my bed at home in France, distractedly checking through my emails on the iPhone for the umpteenth time. Anything to try and quieten my mind and bring me back to normality. I was mentally and physically exhausted, but my tortured mind and aching soul refused to let me sleep. No matter how much I tried to rationalise the past ten weeks, or how much I attempted to make sense of the situation, I simply couldn't find any answers. Peace seemed a very distant memory as I continued to search for clues. What had happened? Where had I gone wrong? What had prompted my beloved husband of ten years to lie to me for so long? Why did he need to create so many other lives?

What had I done to make him stop loving me? How had I missed the signs? What could I have done differently?

The questions circled, round and round my head like the mythological embittered Harpies – snatching at my rising fears, cackling at my confusion, their cruel wings fanning the flames of despair that threatened to engulf my soul.

And then I saw it. It was an email from my dear friend Mary, which pricked my interest. She had worked with us in the business, so knew both Cam and I very well. It was a kind and thoughtful message of support, the contents of which seemed harmless, but it was this very email that had me shaking to the core just a short while later.

'. . . *Interestingly, you may or may not know that I am doing my masters degree in forensic psychology at the moment, and recently have done loads of work on sociopaths. Lets put it this way – Cam shows all the signs – in retrospect of course! So in fairness, he was highly skilled at fooling everyone. In fact, not just skilled, it was natural to him. Therefore, who would have known? He has no conscience. And before long, he will find another place for himself, and will never feel any remorse, because he doesn't know how to . . .*'

Sociopath was a term I had not come across before, but after a quick scan for more information on the Internet I discovered that a sociopath is also known as a psychopath. My brows furrowed as disbelief and comprehension entered my head at the same time. So I asked the question out loud to see if it made a difference:

You mean to tell me that my husband, my Cam, is actually a PSYCHOPATH? Chills ran through my body, my mouth went dry, and the Harpies were suddenly very still and very quiet.

Random images of famous psychopaths came flooding into my head – Norman Bates from *Psycho*, Peter Sutcliffe the Yorkshire Ripper, America's Ted Bundy and Heath Ledger as The Joker – the absurdity of the idea prompting nervous laughter to erupt from deep within me. And then silence again as I truly began to consider the enormity of this new information. The room was still. My mind was quiet. My heart started thumping loudly in my chest. Holding the iPhone in my left hand, cradling my mouth and chin with my right hand, I read another 'checklist' for sociopathy and realised with absolute clarity that Cam's behaviours actually ticked just about every one of the boxes. I shuddered, forcing myself to breathe, and blinked wildly, hoping that I had somehow misinterpreted the information.

I was in a state of shock, and that was the precise moment when the archetypal psychopath Dr Hannibal Lecter made his sudden and unwelcome appearance in my mind – crystal clear and standing just a few feet away from me in the corner of my bedroom. Sucking air through his teeth and smacking his lips, he held me hypnotised with his ice-cold beguiling stare, clearly enjoying my confusion as I quietly considered the overwhelming evidence that my estranged husband, the man I had loved with all my heart and soul, was in fact a textbook psychopath.

But surely I'd know if I was in the company of someone like that? I reasoned to myself, the dank smell of Hannibal's cell now beginning to permeate my senses, his chains rattling my imagination.

But I'm an executive business coach! I've been working in the field of personal development for over 13 years! I'm wise to the ways of different personalities and what makes people tick! I tried to rationalise, becoming more aware that my bewilderment was arousing the curiosity of my uninvited imaginary guest.

Hooked, I had to find out more. And as I read further, uncovering facts, examples of typical traits and stories from other victims of a sociopathic relationship, I was gradually coming to the shocking realisation that my friend's diagnosis was correct. In equal measures of horror and relief, I also began to understand that I was not alone. That there were literally thousands of women with stories just like mine. I allowed the weirdly reassuring feeling that I was not the only one to grow within me, gratefully confirming to myself that there were hundreds, thousands – perhaps millions – of other people just like me. Intelligent, professional and successful women who had willingly succumbed, fallen in love, followed their dreams and been thwarted by the malevolent charms of the skilled and charismatic sociopath. Chillingly, I read that as much as 4 per cent of the population (widely reported but not proven that 25 per cent of which are female and 75 per cent are male) are afflicted, yet remain undiagnosed, with what mental health officials refer to as 'antisocial personality disorder' – or, to you and me, these are psychopaths who live, breathe and feed among us. If you think (as I did) that this kind of thing could never happen to you, then think again.

While there are plenty of psychopathic women who live and breathe among us, most of the stories I found online have been written by female victims like me who have been targeted by a charismatic male sociopath. Men who are charming, witty and the life and soul of the party. Men who can sweep you off your feet, make you believe that you are the most precious person in the world. Men who let you dare to dream that all your dreams have come true and convince you that you've found your true soulmate. Men who make you feel that anything is possible and encourage you to live life to the full. Men who slowly and deliberately bleed you dry, suck out your soul and leave you for dead, without even a backwards glance, but by the time you realise this, of course, it's too late. Much too late.

Suddenly I began to see things from a different angle. Suddenly things started to make sense. Dr Lecter, for now, faded safely back into the darkness of my imagination as I began to replace his image with strangely comforting feelings of relief. The deeper truth was dawning that the experience I was living, my own personal living nightmare, was not something I could have foretold. So I was not to blame for what had happened – there was nothing more I could have done. In fact, I'd had a lucky escape.

This was the beginning of my understanding about what had happened to me. How I'd found myself in such an unimaginable mess. After three long months, the hurricane of discovery that had all but broken me in its relentless force to destroy all that I had believed in was gradually beginning to loosen its grip in light of this new information.

I realised, with frightening clarity, that in order to truly understand what had happened, to come to terms with how I had come to find myself in such a nightmare situation, I was going to have to embark on a journey of self-discovery. I would need to find out more about what had happened to other people. Understand the true meaning behind the word sociopath, or psychopath. Recognise the traits within myself that allowed me to be the perfect target. Dig deeply into my own psyche and explore my own choices in life. Examine how I'd got here, what I'd believed about myself and others and my own deeply held personal values. And, most importantly, to find my strength and finally heal.

My years of experience in personal development told me it was not going to be an easy journey. Some of the deeply buried feelings and experiences of my past would need to be re-examined. I would need to dredge through parts of my life I thought I'd already dealt with. Old scars I thought I'd healed would need to be re-opened and treated anew. It would be painful. And I would also need to venture into the depths of this new murky world I was beginning to discover. Stand in the shoes of these soulless people I now knew existed for real and who live and work among us. People who have no conscience. Sham human beings who exist purely to win, who see other people merely as tools to be used and abused – and discarded once they are no longer of any value.

I was alerted to the sounds of Dr Lecter shuffling around in the back of my mind, his interest clearly intensified by my growing fear at what lay ahead. And I heard a barely perceptible laugh – or was it a cackle? – coming from the darkest corners of my imagination. The unpalatable solution hit me like a steam train, and I understood at that moment that he would need to become an ally in my journey; for who better than the archetypal sociopath, Dr Hannibal Lecter himself, to help me understand the twisted workings in the mind of a psychopath?

'If I help you, Melanie, it will be "turns" with us too. Quid pro quo. I tell you things, you tell me things. About yourself. Quid pro quo. Yes or no?' his perfect and calculated logic slithered towards me, the words and the consequences of what I was about to do sending shivers through my body. I would need to let Hannibal Lecter inside my head if ever I was going to become free.

It was the only way to regain my sanity and claim my life back. And surely this couldn't be any worse than the real-life experiences I had already survived? So I nodded my silent agreement and the deal was done. I would allow the spectre of Hannibal to steer me as I unravelled the past and made sense of my pain.

Hannibal fixed me with his steely eyes and held tightly to the bars in his cell. 'Clearly this new assignment is not your choice,' he hissed. 'Rather, I suppose, it is a part of the bargain, but you accepted it, Melanie. Your job is ultimately to craft my doom. So I am not sure how well I should wish you, but I'm sure we'll have a lot of fun. So let's start at the beginning – tell me everything you know.'

With that, his image once again faded away, and I truly felt that I had just made a deal with the devil. But at the same time, I knew that my journey to freedom had begun.

20
Sociopathy - A Whole New World

The discovery of sociopathy became my bridge between disaster and healing. While it shocked me at the time, it became my stepping stone to emotional freedom. Now I had something else to help me make sense of the incomprehensible set of circumstances in which I had found myself. Now I could come to understand some of my husband's seemingly cold behaviour, if he was indeed a person who had no empathy, no conscience, no remorse. To me, it now appeared that everything he had said and done had been nothing but a sham. In my opinion, the man I had been married to was a textbook sociopath.

Over the weeks following my discovery, I scoured the Internet and read books on the subject, doing my best to understand the condition. One of the very first was called *A Dance with the Devil* by Barbara Bentley – the story of a woman whose 'soulmate' not only swindled her but tried to murder her as well. I emailed her to thank her for her book and tell her my suspicions about my estranged husband. 'You are lucky,' she said, 'many don't make it out at all.' I felt inspired and grateful, and continued my research in earnest.

One particular site called lovefraud.com was of particular help to me. It was there that I found story after story from people who had suffered a similar fate. People who described intense shock, emptiness, humiliation and the difficulty they found in explaining their situation to others – the same feelings that I was experiencing.

The website was founded by Donna Andersen, a lady who herself had unknowingly married a man she now considers to be a sociopath, and her quest is to educate people and help them to heal. It's a remarkable resource and for me was the first time I stopped feeling alone. There were other people out there just like me. Women (and men) who had given their heart and soul to somebody who bled them dry, sapping their confidence and money before moving on without a backwards glance. Psychopathic relationships, of course, aren't limited to romantic partnerships. Far from it. Dysfunctional and damaging relationships can happen with parents, siblings, family members, friends, colleagues – the list is endless. Sociopathy exists in all walks of life.

These are Donna's opening words on her website:

Experts estimate that 1% to 4% of the population are sociopaths, depending upon whom you ask. That means there may be 3 million to 12 million sociopaths in the United States, and 68 million to 272 million sociopaths worldwide. What's worse, as adults, sociopathic men and women cannot be rehabilitated. Once a sociopath, always a sociopath.

Sociopaths have no heart, no conscience and no remorse. They don't worry about paying bills. They think nothing of lying, cheating and stealing. In extreme cases, sociopaths can be serial rapists and serial killers.

Think you can spot a sociopath? Think again. Sociopaths often blend easily into society. They're entertaining and fun at parties. They appear to be intelligent, charming, well-adjusted and likable. The key word is 'appear.' Because for sociopaths it's all an illusion, designed to convince you to give them what they want.

> Sociopaths are masters of manipulation. So before you give away your love, your money or your life, read this website and the Lovefraud Blog.

Scouring the blog, I read story after heartbreaking story of people who had been betrayed. People who were suffering the same pain and confusion that I was, people who felt that their closest friends and relatives just didn't get it. And, whilst I was saddened by the number of people who were suffering, I also gained comfort from the idea that I was among friends, people who had been there, seen it and got the T-shirt.

Cam's betrayals had cut me deeper than any of my previous experiences of trauma. The death of both parents and the painful experiences with my guardians paled into insignificance compared with the devastation I experienced on discovering the truth about my soulmate, compounded by the fact that I'd worked so hard to forgive him the first time the mask had slipped. This time, you see, I had been an adult. I had walked into the relationship with my eyes and heart wide open – not once, but twice. Now I realise that, in return, Cam's deception although perhaps subconscious, appeared relentless and without mercy. For my part, I had completely believed everything he had told and shown me, and I had never before felt so loved, so special and so safe. How could I have been stupid enough not to spot the signs before? How could I have been so gullible to take him back after his first betrayal? What was it about me that made me so goddamned stupid to trust a con man not only with my love but also with that of my precious son? I knew I had really messed up, and although friends and family were supportive, I continued to berate myself for my stupidity. I was embarrassed and ashamed. I had totally fallen for his charms, but to all intents and purposes it was as if he never felt anything for me at all. He seemed to me as if he was indeed a cold and calculating predator.

And, try as I might, people didn't seem able to grasp what I was

238

telling them. Even faced with mountains of black-and-white evidence, they wanted to make excuses for his behaviour.

'Perhaps he was just having a breakdown', 'People do go off the rails sometimes, you know', 'Well, sometimes we just don't notice when relationships are breaking down', 'Even the best marriages fail, you know' – all words designed to show empathy and understanding, I know that. But the fact was that they just made me feel worse, particularly in the early weeks before I discovered the existence of sociopathy. During those early times, believe me, I was berating myself more than you can imagine. Trying to find out where I had gone wrong. Desperately wanting to understand how I could have turned my once loving husband into such a distant stranger. Hugely tempted to look through old photographs and listen to old songs because I missed him so badly that the pain was physical. But, thank goodness, even in those early days I knew I had to keep clear – no matter how great the agony of missing him. I'd get over that someday, I knew it.

The reason, as I've since understood, why neither my friends nor I could make sense of what had happened – and why their best-intentioned attempts at explaining away Cam's change of character as something that 'normal' people could possibly do under intense pressure – is because the fact is that 'normal' people cannot possibly begin to comprehend the workings of a person with no apparent conscience. It's physically impossible. There's a proverb that says 'We see things not as they are, but as *we* are.' These are wise and, as I was beginning to realise, true and valid words. How can we comprehend, really understand, something that is so alien to how we are?

We reason, we justify, we go through all manner of possibilities, but we can only work on scenarios or 'what ifs' based on our own imagination, experiences and beliefs. We assume, quite naturally, that everyone else has emotions. Values. Empathy. They feel things like we do – of course we do! How could we possibly imagine that what appears as a perfectly functioning, charming, charismatic, articulate, well-presented person is actually somebody who has no real sense of feelings whatsoever? That the person who seems so intent on listening to our every word is in fact only processing information in order to mirror back our words and actions so that we feel at ease with them?

The Lovefraud website highlights symptoms of sociopathic behaviour (compiled by Dr Robert Hare) and recommends that anyone suspicious or troubled by their partner's behaviour should read. The more I read and the more I learned, the more I started to believe that the charms I had fallen for in Cam were likely only luring devices evident of sociopathic behaviour. It seemed to me that his approach had been textbook, just like so many of the other stories I read. So he hadn't even been special, no imagination whatsoever! That, at least, raised a wry smile.

Sociopaths, apparently, are renowned for making super-fast connections with their chosen target. Of course they can. They are experts at mirroring back even the tiniest nuances of a normal person's behaviour. They will confess to falling head over heels in love, tell the target that 'you are the one I've been waiting for' and ask for commitment very early on in the relationship. I had actually believed that my magical set of circumstances was unique, and for many years I had no reason to look any further. But once I discovered the truth and started exploring sociopathic relationships, well . . . there were countless other stories of couples who had fallen in love almost overnight. It's what a sociopath does. It's how they entrap their prey.

And as for the pity-play? Well, I can testify that Cam was adept at that. Someone was always to blame – a classic sociopath trait.

Cam's impeccable manners were something else that was notable in helping to charm me. These were small things, but they all added up – bringing me a coat, pulling out my chair for me, filling my glass first, opening the car door for me and always making sure he stood on the outside when we walked along the pavement. As a normal person, I just thought he was extremely caring and polite. It turns out this is also a typical trait in a sociopath. They study in minute detail all the tiny things that create a positive reaction in 'normal' people and add them to their repertoire of mechanical behaviours. They approach their target with absolute surgical precision – nothing must go wrong, and their only goal is to get them under their spell.

Of course I can't prove that Cam had no feelings for me, no feelings for anyone, but reading the profile of a sociopath unnerved me. There were too many overlaps in personality traits. I couldn't help but feel as if I'd been a target.

21

Breaking the Silence

Hold on a minute, though. It was all very well getting to know and understand the traits of a sociopath, but what had my role been in this whole process? I knew instinctively that if I was going to get over this experience I would also need to understand the factors that made me a target. I had to explore which personality traits had shown up in me – and from what stage in my life, because I was now convinced that living with Cam was certainly not the first time that I'd endured emotional abuse. I knew that it wouldn't be easy, but then again, how much more difficult could life be? So along with sociopathy, I studied the traits of typical targets, the signs of abuse, and the personality traits of people who partnered abusers.

These are some of the lists I used to help me with my quest.

PERSONALITY TRAITS IN VICTIMS (from sociopathicstyle.com)
This list is not exhaustive. A person possessing the traits listed below is a prime target for victimization by a person desiring a Sociopathic Style™ relationship.

A belief that if you love enough the person will change
A belief that if you love enough the relationship will succeed

Difficulty establishing and maintaining boundaries

Not being able to say no

Being easily influenced by others

Wanting to be rescued from your life situation

Wanting to rescue others from their distress

Being over-nurturing particularly when not asked

Feelings of shame and self-doubt

Low self-esteem

A lack of memories about childhood or periods of adulthood

Shyness

Difficulty communicating

A lack of self-confidence

Wanting to please

A lack of motivation from within and being motivated by what others want

THE SIGNS OF VICTIMIZATION

The signs listed below are typical but in and of themselves are not symptoms of victimization. If you or anyone you know have these signs, please see a qualified professional for evaluation. These are the primary signs but the list is not exhaustive of the signs.

Depression

Anxiety

Fear of relationships

Numbing of feelings

Irritability

Difficulty falling asleep

Fear of being alone

Severe mood swings

Loss of energy

Loss of interest in life

Suicidal thoughts or actions

The classical symptoms of Post Traumatic Stress Disorder

One of the many books I read over the coming months was called *The Bigamist* by Mary Turner Thompson. She, like me, had worked as a motivational trainer. She lived in Edinburgh and had been duped by a man who led her to believe he worked for the CIA. A serial bigamist, fraudster, paedophile and father to countless children by different women, her world fell apart when she received a phone call from his 'other' wife.

Mary's story provided the inspiration for Jon Ronson's book *The Psychopath Test*, in which he includes the 20-point checklist based on the findings of Dr Robert Hare that I've detailed above. He interviewed her in what ended up being an award-winning programme, and as a result he became fascinated by the subject and went on to explore it further. I was particularly attracted to her story because there were a number of similarities and her words resonated with my own feelings. I contacted her by email and was surprised and delighted when she called me on my home phone just a couple of days later. We chatted like old friends and I arranged to go and see her.

It was November 2009 and it was my first time in Edinburgh without Cam. Mary and I drove and strolled around the city, Mary constantly encouraging me to keep opening my eyes

'Reclaim your spaces, Mel. This was your home too once – you've every right to feel attached. Now see it with new eyes, wipe away your old memories and salvage the good feelings you once had about the place,' she said as we pulled up in George Street for a coffee at Waterstones. She was right, I had been scared to revisit any places that I used to go with Cam and that bookshop was one of them. There had been many days we'd spend time there looking at business books together, enjoying a coffee and sandwich in the cafe afterwards.

Chatting with this strong, sassy woman and hearing more details behind the story in her book, I knew I had found a friend. Somebody who understood. Somebody who had pulled through despite all the odds. Somebody who had found the courage to speak out. And through understanding more about Mary, I knew that I could heal.

Our meeting and subsequent chats caused me to think back on some of my earlier experiences – not only with Cam but also with my guardian. Another charismatic charmer. Another businessman who could be the life and soul of the party. Another person who treated those closest to him with disdain and contempt. Could it be that he had also been a sociopath?

I remembered one particular evening, not long after Abigail and I had started living with them. I must have been coming up for 17 years old – a tricky time for anyone, let alone someone who had recently been orphaned and was trying to fit in to a new family – and I'd had a particularly tough day at school. I was sitting on the breakfast bar in the kitchen, swinging my legs and most likely with a sulky look on my face. I felt isolated, not only in my new home but also at school. I was different. I was the girl with problems, and everybody, it seemed, knew the details. So when I was struggling with something, I rarely asked for help. I didn't want people to pity me or to link any perfectly normal tussles in my education with anything to do with 'my problems'.

'I just can't do it!' I'd moaned, fighting back the tears. 'I'm trying so hard, but for some reason I just can't do it!'

'Well, you're obviously not trying hard enough!' came Eddie's cold response. He was sitting at the table with a glass of something alcoholic 'It's about time you pulled yourself together and stopped making a fuss!'

It felt as though I'd been thumped in the stomach. My legs went still and I fought even harder to contain my rising emotions, blinking hard to hold back the tears that were pricking at my eyes.

'What do you mean?' I'd asked, squaring up to him. 'Don't you think I am trying? Don't you realise how difficult it is for me at the moment? I'm trying to fit in here, look out for my sister and also complete my A-Levels. Just how much pressure do you expect me to deal with?' As I spoke, the fury inside me rose, and I knew my face was turning red.

'Don't you dare speak to me like that, young lady!' he'd replied, standing up and coming to face me.

'Why not?' I countered, anger now causing me to shake. 'Why can't I express my emotions? What's so wrong with that? I feel like shit and you're not helping!'

With that, Eddie slapped me across the face and ordered me out of the kitchen.

'And don't come back until you can be more civilised! Go away and snivel if you like, but I will not have that kind of behaviour in my house!'

I remember running up to my bedroom, slamming the door and throwing myself on my bed. Embarrassed by the scene I'd caused, and feeling guilty for rocking the boat, I cried out for my mother and my father, and I just wanted the world to open up and swallow me.

There were many other incidents along those lines and now, as I looked back, I came to the conclusion that the situation at my guardian's house was not just 'unpleasant'; it had, in fact, been abusive. The rest of my experiences with my family had not been much better. I had been the victim of emotional abuse! Yes, I said it out loud. I had been emotionally abused. Going back to the checklist, I realised that even as a child I had fitted just about every description of a victim of abuse: numbing of feelings, fear of relationships, suicidal thoughts, severe mood swings . . . the list goes on. Hindsight, of course, makes everything clear, but at that particular time in my life I had only managed to turn the fear and hatred upon myself.

It must be that I'm a bad girl. I must have done something to deserve this. And rather than speaking out about the bad things that happened, I kept silent, blaming myself for letting things fall apart.

I must try harder. I'll do it properly next time. I'll be a good girl. I can save the day. All self-talk messages that I used to get myself through.

All positive strokes for the aching heart of a confused and lonely young woman. All personality traits that helped me to succeed as a Louise Hay trainer – somebody who is strong on empathy, has a desire to understand, and cares about making things better – and each one of those a typical personality trait of somebody who is an attractive target for a sociopath. It's chilling, don't you think?

As I furthered my education about emotional abuse and sociopathy, I continued to explore my past experiences. The patterns were disturbingly similar. My overwhelming desire to please and to 'rescue' other people who were in trouble. My belief that if I showed enough love, or that if I nurtured this person or situation enough, it would get better. And, more to the point, my desire to understand where I had gone wrong when somebody behaved badly towards me. Ping! Crystal clear. So clear it was frightening.

Looking back over my marriage with the blinkers off, I realised that I had often chosen silence over confrontation. Like Eddie, Cam would sometimes snap for no reason and with no warning. Each time he hit out at me – verbally, never physically – the shock would be so great that I didn't know how to deal with it. It was so out of character and usually happened after he had been drinking. So I kept quiet.

I remember one particular evening in London. We had taken Dylan to Hard Rock Calling, an annual rock and pop concert in Hyde Park, and we'd had a wonderful day together.

When we got back to the hotel, it was not yet 11 p.m., so, after making sure Dylan was safely in bed and had a mobile with him, Cam and I decided to share a bottle of wine in the bar downstairs. It would be a perfect ending to a perfect day. I ordered some crisps as well, and then the barman announced that the bar would be shutting in a short while.

'Shall we?' Cam suggested, looking at the nearly empty bottle. I would have been quite happy to go straight to bed, but on the other hand here I was enjoying the company of my husband on an evening that didn't involve work. So I agreed with him.

'Go on then!' I said.

'No, you go on then,' he countered, draining his glass. 'You order it – go on. Stand up for yourself. It's a woman's right to go to the bar these days!' I never quite understood why he would do this, but it happened every time we were in a bar or restaurant. Cam would instruct me to go to the bar to order drinks, and on the odd occasion he went he'd make a point of getting me to thank him and acknowledge what he'd done. I thought it was a silly game of one-upmanship, but on this occasion I was actually quite happy to go, as I needed the toilet as well. So I ordered another bottle and brought it over to the table before heading out to reception and down the stairs to the ladies' toilets.

When I got back, Cam had already finished the first bottle and filled both our glasses from the second. He was swirling his glass in his hands, his head down and staring into the bottom. I sat down and picked up my glass.

'Cheers, my darling!' I said happily, holding my glass out in invitation to his. But the response I got back shook me to the core.

He stopped swirling his drink and put the glass down heavily on the table. It made a loud noise and the barman briefly looked up from polishing the pumps. Lifting his head to meet my gaze, Cam's eyes were cold and dark, his expression hard, his lips pulled thin and tight across his teeth as he spat out the next few words.

'I hate you calling me darling. It's so patronising,' he hissed venomously, 'and if you don't get over this mistrust of me, well, then our marriage is on the rocks. Take it or leave it, Mel. I can't keep going in this marriage if you can't get over what happened.'

Still holding my wineglass in the air waiting for the return to my cheers, I was utterly speechless. This was a total left-fielder and I felt as though the wind had been knocked out of me. My mouth started opening and closing, but no words came out as the questions flew around in my head. What on earth had happened to make him say these things? We were having such a lovely evening! We'd all had a lovely day together! What had changed? And from where had he got this ridiculous idea? What had I done to make him change his mood so suddenly?

I knew it must have been the drink talking, but I simply couldn't make any sense of what had caused this outburst. I thought we were having a great conversation, and I had been feeling really close to him. So I really didn't know how to respond. I knew I didn't want to anger him, and I also knew there was no sense in countering his accusation – that would just give credence to something that was so far from reality it didn't warrant a response. But at the same time I couldn't just ignore it. So I had to tread carefully. Painting a smile on my face and softening my eyes, I carefully put my glass down and tried to soothe him with a quiet but firm tone of voice.

'Whatever do you mean?' I said steadily, desperately scanning his face for any sign that this was some kind of sick joke. 'There's nothing I need to get over, Cam. What are you saying? I thought we were having a really nice time. What's happened?'

'So now you deny it – that's rich!' he snapped back, taking another swig of his drink. 'Well, so who do you think you're kidding now, Mel? We're struggling here in this marriage, and you just won't see how much I've been trying to hold us together, to make everything better. I've been wanting to talk to you about this for ages, but because I'm working so damned hard to keep the business going there's just never been the opportunity. Well, so here it is. Deal with it, because it ain't gonna just disappear!' Draining his glass, he slammed it back on the table and refilled it from the half-empty bottle of wine in front of us.

Well, I hadn't expected that. As I tried to make sense of what he was saying, images flew in and out of my mind. Perhaps I had been a little bit harsh recently, certainly in my questioning about his financial dealings. And, yes, our sex life hadn't been as active as normal, but then hadn't we both been through the most enormous stresses over the past few months? Yes, Cam had indeed now taken over the finances of the business, but in what other ways had he been trying to 'hold us together' and how, exactly, did he think we'd been falling apart?

'But why didn't you say something earlier?' I continued steadily. 'How, exactly, do you think I'm not trusting you or in some way holding onto anything from all those years ago? It's just not true. Help me understand here, will you?'

But try as I might, I couldn't get to the bottom of it. I just ended up feeling deflated, defeated and shameful. Perhaps my marriage was indeed falling apart. Perhaps it did indeed have something to do with Cam feeling that I didn't trust him. Perhaps, yes, I had noticed that things weren't perfect between us. But show me a perfect marriage for goodness' sake! I reckoned we were doing pretty well under the circumstances. But the fact was, if this was how my husband was feeling and I hadn't even noticed it, then, yes, he was right, our marriage was in trouble. And, yes, perhaps as he suggested just before falling asleep as far across the other side of the bed as possible, perhaps we should consider marriage counselling.

Silent tears fell down my cheeks. How could such a perfect day turn so suddenly into such a horrid evening? Had I been just as blind about today as I'd clearly been about our marriage for the past few months? Perhaps it was true. Perhaps I did live in cloud-cuckoo land, as Cam had said to me on many occasions. Because I always wanted to see the good and always wanted to make things better, perhaps I just couldn't see what was right there beneath my nose. But this wasn't the way things were meant to be. This wasn't the fairytale ending I'd had in mind! This wasn't in the plan!

Exhausted, I fell into a fitful sleep, berating myself for being so blind, for failing, yet again, to see that I'd been living in a marriage that had a whole heap of issues. For putting my son's happiness at risk yet again. And for becoming, as I had been told so many times before, a useless orphan who'd never come to anything or be able to sustain a lasting relationship.

That episode had taken place in the summer of 2008, but as I remembered the exact words and my feelings at the time, more and more examples of abusive and manipulative behaviour swam into my memory. Not just with Cam but also with my guardians, together with many of the cruel things my family had said and done after the death of my mother. I now knew for certain that I had allowed myself to be abused – not physically but certainly mentally and emotionally.

The blinkers slid from my eyes and I realised to my horror that I had played a part in the abuse. Unwittingly, I had allowed the abuse to continue. Because I'd remained silent and kept things to myself, because I hadn't found a way to share my fears with friends – let alone to confront the perpetrators – I had simply turned all the shame and anger in on myself, keeping the smile on my face and repeating to myself that 'all is well'. But it wasn't. And I wasn't. And, daft as it may seem, it was a complete revelation to me.

That night I wrote my feelings out, but it wasn't until a year later, spurred on by a conversation with my friend Beatrix, that I actually had the courage to post the article on my blog. I feel it's appropriate to include it at this time. Here it is.

FRIDAY, 3 DECEMBER 2010

Breaking The Silence

Today I have been thinking about the 'code of silence' that I have found exists among so many of us who have experienced abuse in one form or another.

Let's not beat about the bush here – escaping from a controlling or abusive relationship is difficult enough. Accepting the truth that you've been treated so badly is even harder. But having to explain to other people what happened is excruciatingly humiliating. Particularly when they will often need to question your version of what happened because they have only known the public mask:

'What are you talking about? He/she has always been such a lovely person! Surely there's some mistake!' That one's a double whammy, because if they decide to believe your story then they also have to realise that they have been duped as well . . . it's tough going!

Then comes the underlying implication that you must have been extremely gullible – stupid even – not to notice the signs.

'If what you're telling me is true, then they must surely have been so obvious – how could you possibly not have known? Surely you must have realised something was wrong?' And so it goes on . . . It's exhausting, and each time becomes a public tar and feathering as you are forced over and over again to explain exactly how you were so stupid to let somebody else put you in this position.

I remember one particular evening, sitting at home with my head in my hands after a well-intentioned but hurtful telephone call with a distant relative.

During the conversation, I found myself justifying and explaining my situation, doing my best to overcome her blatant disbelief that I could find myself in such a dire predicament – almost as if I'd done it on purpose and certainly implying that it was clearly my own stupid fault! Rather than find out how I was doing and whether I needed any help, she challenged me over and over again with the question 'Surely, an intelligent woman with your positivity and get-up-and-go should have been able to see the signs?' And each time I countered that yes, with hindsight and a good understanding of what I had been dealing with, then, yes indeed, those signs were there. Well disguised but there nonetheless, and yet I had been totally blind to them because his deception was deliberate. I told her time and time again that a sociopath employs ruthlessly surgical precision to trap and bleed their targets dry. That there are many more women – much more intelligent and much more successful than I – who have also fallen prey to these creatures and who have been left in even more serious financial and emotional situations than where I found myself!

And each time I have had to explain the story, to do my best to convince people of the facts, I felt I was once again reliving the horror and crazy emotions I lived with for the decade I was in the cold grip of my sociopath. The same emotions that mirrored my childhood feelings when we lived with our guardian. And on both occasions I was equally astounded and horrified by the number of times I found myself in the situation where I needed to justify what happened. You see, people just didn't believe me – either because they couldn't accept that such people exist or because it would mean they'd have to admit they'd also been totally conned. So I listened to their objections, I keep my calm, and I answered their questions truthfully and in full. But let me tell you, at times I just wanted to bang my fists on the table and scream in their faces

'Why can't you see? It's ME and my SON who are the victims here! Why don't you believe me? Stop making it worse!'

This is why, I believe, there is an unspoken code of silence among the vast majority of people who have suffered through any kind of abusive relationship. Whether at the hands of a partner, parents, siblings, friends, bosses, colleagues – the list is endless, as are the stories and perceived seriousness of the abusers' misdemeanours. Different accounts, different histories, different responses. But the pervasively malignant feelings of disgust and self-hatred that become lodged deep within the victims seem to be the same. A universal sense of shame that permeates to the core, no matter the circumstances.

Not long after I made my discovery, I re-connected with an old friend I hadn't seen for many years – to protect her privacy I'll call her Beatrix. Our children had grown up together. We shared similar professional interests. We shared a healthy caring friendship. It also turns out that we shared a particular bond that only came to light as we continued talking. She had also been married to a charming sociopath – in her case it had been for 20 years, double my own sentence.

Our husbands had got to know each other while we were still in the UK, and they did their level best to break our strong bond of friendship. They succeeded for a few years, but now we are closer than ever. Ironically it is the behaviour of our respective husbands that have made it possible. Since we found each other again, we have been able to share our stories. Compare our experiences. Help each other through the dark days. Encourage each other to notice some of the deeply ingrained responses we sometimes fall back into as a habit following years of deliberate conditioning. We know what it's like. We understand the pain and indignity. We can identify on levels that people who haven't been through such an experience couldn't possibly understand. We share the common bond of survivors of abuse, and at first we thought that very few people would ever be able to empathise. We were wrong.

The meeting with Mary Turner Thompson was a massive eye-opener. Inspiring, bonding, validating and hugely valuable. Mary and I have since become firm friends. We call ourselves 'soul sisters' because we know what it's like to be deliberately targeted, deceived, manipulated and controlled. Soul sisters who know how it feels to realise that what you thought was true and lasting love was nothing more than a sham. Soul sisters who understand the shame and indignity of having to face the truth – and the difficulty in convincing well-meaning friends and family that you haven't lost the plot.

Beatrix and I talk about this regularly – as do Mary and I, together with many other survivors I've met along the way, men as well as women. As a result I'm convinced that there IS a code of silence. And along with the silence is the instinctive yet unspoken point of recognition whenever one survivor meets another. After just a few words, the nod of acknowledgement passes between us – sometimes without the need for any further discussion or admittance. We just know. And judging by the number of survivors I've met in my daily life since I became free, there must be millions of people who walk around in silent pain still bound by chains of humiliation and self-loathing.

Control and manipulation tactics are common strategies employed by abusers. Basic yet exceptionally powerful, this form of power play isolates people from those who support them and undermines their confidence to the point where they can no longer think or act effectively. Believing they are the underdog, the target is then no longer in control of their own life. The tactics used by abusers will vary depending on their experiences, their level of skill, their targets and their focus. A corporate sociopath, for example, will typically be exceptionally well versed in smooth language, subtle body gestures and impeccable manners. A street thug is much more likely to use physical violence. Encounters with the latter may well leave you with physical bruises and perhaps broken bones. Encounters with either of them will leave you with a broken spirit and emotional scars that may never heal again.

When I was working as a Louise L. Hay trainer in 1997/1998, I was always deeply touched by the intensity of guilt and shame regularly expressed by workshop members as they bravely shared their stories of mistreatment, stories that, in some cases, had been kept secret and buried for decades. Having the opportunity to finally tell their version about what had happened to them was a huge relief. As it turns out, it was also the easy bit – the hard bit was gently helping them to accept and forgive themselves for what had happened. Yes, you read right – the most difficult part would be helping them to find a way to forgive *themselves*. Not the other person or people, or even the situation, but themselves. To rid themselves of the shame and self-loathing for allowing such a thing to happen to them in the first place.

Back to my friend Beatrix for a moment. She is now reclaiming her life, but it's a long road. Last year was her first Christmas of freedom from a man who, to the outside world, appeared charming, charismatic and witty – the life and soul of the party. A familiar story perhaps? Since escaping, Beatrix has forfeited a number of her friends who simply refuse to believe that this charming man could possibly be guilty of the monstrous things she has accused him of doing.

Abusers, as I've said, can be very skilled communicators. Although there may be no visible external injuries, the damage to self-esteem and self-belief can be severe, life threatening – or even worse in some cases. Beatrix told me what an important time Christmas had always been for her. How for more than 20 years she'd religiously do everything within her power to make the most of the festive season and how, every year, her husband would equally religiously take great delight in destroying her. He'd criticise her for spending too much or too little. Complain about the tree being too big or too small. Whine about the fact that there were too many or too few parties and house visits organised that year. Consistent, deliberate verbal abuse, the psychological blows always accompanied by a Judas kiss or squeeze on the shoulder together with the words 'But you know I love you!'

Abuse of any kind is a killer. The resulting silence is perhaps even more of a killer. It strangles people. This is why I'm so passionate about speaking out. Self-loathing eats away at confidence. It is malignant, oppressive and relentless – and in some cases it claims lives.

The decision to break the silence through blogging was, for me, a massive step up in my own healing. The frustration I experienced when trying to explain what had happened to well-meaning friends was always surprisingly difficult and at times frustrating to the extreme. Each time I found myself once again thrown into the old humiliating pattern of seeking approval and acceptance – a ridiculous state of affairs since I had done nothing wrong. And neither, by the way, had they. It was just that they couldn't understand – exactly like Beatrix's friends who decided she must be insane.

Yes, breaking the silence is a powerful step to take. For me, I decided to write about my journey in a very public way when I started my blog. Fed up with trying to make myself heard by friends, I gradually found the confidence to express my inner thoughts and feelings to a growing audience of like-minded people. A process I found to be extremely cathartic.

Don't get me wrong – I'm not asking people to speak out or share their stories in such a public arena as the manner I chose. I'm simply inviting any of the silent people who have been there too – or who are still there – to know that you are not alone. I'm inviting you to reach out to the constantly rising number of people who understand. I realise that some may still choose to stay silent. And that's OK. As I said earlier, the code of recognition is often a silent one, but at the very least it IS recognition, and that's all it takes. It's the relief of knowing that at least one other person understands and is on your side. And if you've kept things hidden away and just to yourself until that point, well, surely by finding just one like-minded person you'll have doubled your team in one fell swoop.

As I write this, I am reminded of the Latin roots of the word 'person' that was shared with me by a fellow member of Lovefraud website. The word literally translates as 'through sound', which means 'can be heard'. So I started thinking – each one of us who have survived abuse are human beings, people who can and should be heard. We are people who have something to say. We are the very people who can break this unspoken code of silence.

One small step, that's all it takes. One by one we'll find each other. One by one we can join hands until we reach around the world – maybe further. Together we can stand strong and put an end to this destructive cycle of abuse and shame.

I, for one, am determined to keep banging my drum and inviting others to join the crusade – because I know that together we can speak out. We can link our different stories and our unique voices together and become a choir. And together we can produce the sweetest sounds as our voices sing out around the world!

22

Boy George, Handbags and Crutches

It was the third week in July. I was still struggling to make sense of what had happened, and struggling even harder to pay my bills. The French equivalent of Ebay was my only source of income as I put more and more stuff up for sale. It wasn't much, but by this time I had become a dab hand at eking out the few euros I was able to put into my account. The odd €50 here or €60 there – every little helps, I kept reminding myself, slapping my back pocket in parody of the advertisement for two of the UK's larger supermarkets.

More and more debts were appearing as redirected post arrived from Edinburgh – bills I had been told were taken care of months ago, all of them, of course, in my name.

Soldiering on, I used the mantra 'everything I need is within me' to force me through the ever-threatening feelings of darkness and doubt. Yes, I may well have come through difficult situations before, but this was different. This was worse than anything I had experienced before. This time it wasn't just me I had to look after, it was my beloved son as well. I had responsibilities – a roof to keep over our heads, food to put on the table and, most importantly, I had to provide reassurance and a sense of safety for a 13-year-old boy who had experienced his world being ripped apart.

I am lucky enough to have some wonderful friends, and they all continued to rally round as much as they could. You remember Sarah and Kevin, who had been with us over the last New Year? Well, Sarah and the kids had once again come over from Dubai to stay, partly as a holiday and partly to spend time with me in my hour of need. Sarah is like a sister to me. She is one of those super-capable, super-practical people who just manage to get things done. Making herself at home, she was an incredibly calming influence for me and a dab hand at keeping the house clean and tidy, even with three teenagers making their usual messes!

But even with Sarah I found it hard to accept help and support. I'd learned to cope in my own way from a very young age. Looking back I realise there was really no other choice left open to me – I simply *had* to cope. That was all there was to it.

I remember when my mother died. It was a Friday evening in February. Our house was full, as Nan, her sister (Daisy), my aunt (Rose) and her two children (Jane and Jenny) had all been staying with us for the past few days. They knew that Mum was coming to the end of her fight, and they'd wanted to be there. Abigail and I found it all a bit intrusive. Our home was being disrupted by people who didn't seem to understand what was going on. After all, it had only been the two of us who had been in on the whole story.

On the Saturday morning, Abigail and I woke early. I had hardly slept, spending the night with my arms hugged tightly around my body, stifling the tears and rocking away the frightening thoughts about what was going to happen to us now Mum was gone. I desperately wanted to lock away every single memory of Mum – the sound of her voice as she called for us to wake up in the mornings, the smell of her clothes, the feel of her cuddles and the look of her beautifully radiant smile that always made the world right. I knew from experience of losing my dad that these memories would fade in time, so this time I was determined to catalogue every nuance, every tiny sense of who my mother was and what she meant to me.

When we got up, I took the lead. I knew the feelings that Abigail was bound to be experiencing – I'd had them before when Dad died. And I knew that she'd need every ounce of strength to keep going. I was not going to let her down. I wanted to keep us busy, so she and I made cups of tea and toast for everyone in the house. It was our alone time in the kitchen. We were claiming our space and allowing ourselves to be 'normal' – something that seemed to be impossible in the company of others. We were both acutely aware that we were being scrutinised, and the whispers had been going on for what seemed like for ever, although it had only been a couple of weeks since Mum had gone in to hospital.

'Those poor girls,' I had overheard Nan saying to her sister, just a couple of days earlier, 'whatever is going to become of them? Oh dear, poor things . . .' In hindsight I find that a peculiar comment to make. Nan was in the ideal position to start planning our future, but instead her focus was mainly on her own loss. 'When my mother died,' she'd continued, sniffing into one of her lacy handkerchiefs, 'my whole world fell apart. But losing my daughter is far worse than that. I really don't think I can go on!'

Knowing that the rest of the family were finding it difficult to deal with the shock of Mum's death (they'd only discovered the truth about her illness a week or so before she died, whereas Abigail and I had at least had nearly a month to get used to the idea), my sister and I decided that we would take responsibility for letting other people know that our mother had died. We were both keen to behave in a way that we believed would have made Mum proud. Stiff upper lip and all that crap.

So, bizarre as it seems now, first of all we took breakfast in bed to all our wailing relatives

'I can't face it!' Nan had sobbed as we placed her tea and toast next to her bed – Mum's bed. 'I really can't get up, girls. It's all too much!' Her obvious distress made me pull myself up even stronger, sitting next to her on the bed and stroking her shoulders.

'It's OK,' I said, as she snuffled into yet another lacy

handkerchief. 'Abigail and I will take care of things.' *After all,* I reasoned to myself, *it's what Mum would have wanted. She'd be proud of us both right now.*

Less than an hour later, Abigail and I left the house together with our two cousins. Nan, Auntie Daisy and Auntie Rose, couldn't bring themselves to get out of bed. Their grief was too much to bear.

It was a crisp, clear day. There was a low mist gently swirling over the river, and the sun's white winter light created a maze of bobbing shadows as it shone through the trees. It has to be said that it was a beautiful day. One of those days that, just a few weeks earlier, would have seen Mum eager to make the most of the sunshine, the three of us enjoying an enthusiastic hike along the banks of the river. But those days were gone and today we had a different mission to fulfil. Today we were taking over where Mum left off, and we had no intention of letting her down. Heads held high and shoulders back, we all marched off together, united in determination and grief, preparing to deliver the devastating news to everyone in the surrounding villages.

Looking back, that whole episode was absolute madness! Firstly, how could 'responsible adults' leave two frightened, grieving girls to prepare breakfast and care for the grown-ups? Why hadn't they been there to look after us? What had stopped them from reassuring us that things would be OK? Where was the love and concern that should have come from them at this heartbreaking time?

Secondly, what on earth possessed them to allow us to go out into the village on the morning after the death of our mother to break the news to the people who had been our friends? To this day I remain bewildered and incredulous at the lack of care and consideration demonstrated by the very people who were meant to be looking after us. It was the total opposite from the love we had experienced with Mum, and their ongoing responses and treatment of both Abigail and me taught me many valuable lessons about how not to behave towards others.

At the time, I felt I had no option other than to stay strong and in control. Remembering what I had learned from Mum's example, I did everything in my power to remain calm and resolute in the face of adversity. That was how I managed to explain to countless friends who had loved our mother that she had passed away the night before. To most of them it came as a complete shock. Now I understand that their shock must have been twofold. First because they had no idea of the severity of Mum's illness, and second they must have been surprised to be told the news by her two daughters the very next day after her death – two orphaned children, with no adults accompanying them.

Each time the response was the same. A sharp intake of breath. Hands to the mouth. Tears in the eyes. Shock and bewilderment and a few hesitant words.

'Oh, my dear, but I had no idea!' 'Oh, you poor things. I don't know what to say.' And in some cases, 'This is too much for me to take on board, I will have to call you once the news has settled in.'

It was when we finally reached my friend John's house that the reality hit me. John, you'll remember, was the one person I had confided in when we first found out about the cancer. I had sworn him to secrecy, and he had shuffled off home swearing to keep my secret. So when his mother Stella answered the door to us that afternoon and I told her the news, she must have felt absolutely devastated.

'But I don't understand,' she stammered, frowning and holding her hands to her face, shaking her head in disbelief. 'John told me that your mum was going into hospital for an in-growing toenail!'

That was when I burst into tears – when I realised that my dearest friend had stayed true to his word. And as I saw John coming towards the front door and standing behind his mother, his was the very first look of concern and understanding that I had received since hearing of my mother's death. I dissolved on the doorstep, allowing myself to be held both by John and his mother, Abigail and my cousins joining in with what became a silent group hug punctuated only by sniffles and sobs.

As we sat in their living room nursing hot cups of sweet tea, Stella listened incredulously as Abigail and I told her what had happened. How we'd discovered Mum's illness. How we'd kept it quiet and how John was the only person I'd told.

'But why are you two girls coming round to tell people?' pressed Stella. 'You should be at home. You've had a huge shock and you should be being looked after! What are the grown-ups doing?'

'They're too upset,' I replied, aware how ridiculous my words sounded, stirring my tea for the hundredth time. 'And anyway, people have to know. Mum would want people to know. So we thought we'd do it.'

Stella is a no-nonsense sort of a person. She always has been. She'd known our family since I had been three years old. Her disbelief and disgust was clear to see, but she swallowed whatever thoughts were running around her head.

'Well, Dee would certainly be proud of you both today,' she continued. 'But I just wish I had known. I could have helped. Oh how I wish I could have helped.'

She drove us back home some time later, dropping us off outside the house, but not before holding me with her warm smile and determined stare. 'I won't come in now, but mark my words I will be having strong words with your grandmother. Now is not the time. Now you just need to get in there and look after yourselves. Your mother had a huge amount of friends, and we are all here now for you two girls.'

I locked eyes with her. No words came out, but I nodded, silently thanking her for her support.

We wandered into the house to find Nan, Auntie Daisy and Auntie Rose red-eyed and whimpering, huddled around the dining room table – our dining room table, where Mum, Abigail and I had shared our last few emotional and deeply sacred conversations. This was our space, and once again I felt invaded. They'd clearly been busy while we'd been gone. Pictures had disappeared from the wall, along with ornaments and other bits and pieces that Mum kept on shelves, sideboards and other nooks and crannies.

'What on earth have you been doing?' I asked, open-mouthed as my confusion turned to anger. 'Where are the pictures? What's happened to Mum's things?'

'Well, dear,' said Auntie Rose, shifting uncomfortably in her seat, looking at me with apologetic eyes. 'We have to start packing things away. You know it's got to happen. So we thought we'd make a start.'

'But this is our home!' I replied, forcing down the rising anger, determined to maintain my composure. 'And it's been less than 24 hours since Mum died!'

'I know, dear,' continued Auntie Rose, now unable to meet my steely stare and accusatory tone. 'But we're only here for a few days. We'd like to help while we can.'

I was speechless. The rug was being pulled from right under my feet and there was nothing I could do. I glanced at Abigail who looked like a rabbit caught in headlights. Instinctively I moved closer towards her. I decided that this was not the time to fight. Biting my tongue, I moved us both out of the dining room, my head swimming with questions. What was going on? How could they do this?

As we reached the hallway, Auntie Rose called out to us with a few more words of meaningless and utterly thoughtless wisdom. 'There's a programme on television tomorrow night about the latest cures for cancer,' she twittered as Abigail and I marched steadily away, desperate to find our own space. 'I thought we could watch it together. It's my birthday, after all, and I don't want us to be sad!'

No wonder Mum had been so concerned about keeping her illness secret! She must have known that her family was like this. For me, it had come as a total shock. They say that people show their true colours when faced with death. True colours or not, the Nan, Auntie Daisy and Auntie Rose who shared our home at that particular time were certainly not the people I had grown up with, people I loved and who I thought loved me back. Instead they had become strangers. At the time I put their peculiar behaviour down to intense shock and grief. I also reasoned that it was highly likely I was seeing things from a skewed perspective. But over the next few weeks, months and years, I came to realise that this was not just a passing phase. Their detachment was reality. It had been Mum's ebullience and wealth of positive energy that had held our family together. She had been the glue in what I now understand to be a dysfunctional set-up. Without her influence, they were nothing but hollow shells.

I sometimes ask myself which came first. Was it the coldness of my family during that emotionally charged and hugely impressionable time that made me so independent and resilient? Or had it happened before? I still don't know the answer to that one, but I do know now that for years I had found it very difficult if not impossible to ask for help and even more difficult to accept it.

This was made crystal clear to me during the first few weeks after my devastating discovery about my husband. My learned fallback position was to strengthen my resolve, pull myself together and carry on regardless. Yes, it was lovely having my friends around, but I realise now that they must have had a pretty tough time actually doing anything for me. I see myself as an easy-going person and, on the whole I think I am. In a crisis, however, I reckon I'm a time bomb waiting to explode.

And one particular evening, my time bomb detonated in a way that was absolutely devastating for me at the time. In another way, however (as has proved to be the case with every single one of all these extraordinarily tough experiences), this particular explosion brought with it a hugely valuable gift. Because through it, I finally learned how to accept the love and support I'd been subconsciously pushing away for so many years.

This time it was not an emotional disaster that rocked my world. No, this time it was a split-second accident that caused me some serious physical damage. This is the post I wrote immediately after it had happened.

MONDAY, 20 JULY 2009
Boy George, handbags and crutches

Or how this particular '80s chick has redefined the meaning of 'mind-altering joints'.

It was Friday night/Saturday morning, and the three of us (Sarah, Vera and myself) were in full throttle. Wooden spoons for microphones, handbags on the floor for something to dance around ('Well, it won't be a proper disco if we don't have our handbags in the middle!' Sarah had announced a few tracks earlier) and all of us gyrating and singing along to Culture Club's hypnotic 'Do you Really Want to Hurt Me?', the song and the music still as beguiling as it was the first time Boy George appeared on *Top of the Pops*.

The evening had gone well. All the children had already started their own party while we finished off our meal in the kitchen. It was well past midnight before we finished the main course, and we'd moved out to the back terrace to enjoy the evening and a few shots of the special vodka that Sarah had brought over from Dubai.

We decided some time later – buoyed up with more vodka and a couple of glasses of wine – that another 'sister', Gemma, should also be included in our party, even though she was not with us in person. So we hit upon the idea to call her so she could join in the festivities. Not, as it turned out, the best idea. She and her husband were both fast asleep, but, with typical grace and good humour, she quickly got into the groove with us. Vera was clearly enjoying the telephone conversation, her eyes sparking and cheeks flushed. 'It's so much harder to say she said than I said!' she trilled to a bemused Gemma, as Sarah and I cackled in the background. This all made perfect sense to us, of course, and Gemma simply commented that she was glad she was able to safely enjoy the humour without any risk of a headache in the morning . . . it was an omen.

Shrieking with laughter and boosted by Gemma's comments (and more Russian vodka) we made the fateful decision to start the disco.

Neither a graceful nor a confident dancer, I soon found myself throwing inhibitions out of the window and joining in with increasingly over-the-top gyrations. I had just completed a rather impressive 'how low can you go' routine with Katherine (Sarah's very beautiful and extremely lithe 15-year-old daughter – I did pretty well actually . . . considering!) when we decided to return once again to Culture Club.

I'd cheered loudly as 'I'll Tumble For Ya' started to play and the memories flooded in – another omen. Halfway through one of my rather more enthusiastic and ungainly moves, my knee twisted and made a popping sound in a way that nature never intended. I fell straight to the floor in surprise and agony.

I'm one of those lucky people who have never had a serious accident and am rarely ill. So when my body suddenly disobeyed my instructions, I was dumbfounded – and scared. I sat there, open-mouthed, unable to take in what had happened. But I couldn't get up. Try as I might, I couldn't put any weight on my leg – it just wouldn't hold me. I knew I'd done some serious damage.

This all happened just a few days ago. The past few months have already left me feeling out of control as, on a daily basis, I continue to deal with the never-ending nightmare that has been left for me to clear up. All I relied on has crumbled around me. And now, with my knee severely injured, I cannot even depend on my usually strong body to carry me forward.

I'm helpless and now totally in the hands of others until my knee is healed. Nothing done by half, it appears I have torn my cruciate ligament, meaning weeks in a brace, followed by 20 physiotherapy sessions before I can even have an MRI scan to confirm. And then, likely, an operation to mend the damage. Then months of bed rest and recuperation. And there I'd been a few days earlier thinking things couldn't get any worse!

Done in a fraction of a second, the twisting of my knee joint has forced me to adapt my approach even further. Just when I thought I was getting used to the emotional and financial challenges, just when I thought I was finally getting stronger again, I'm having to learn a whole new coping strategy.

Fiercely independent since childhood, I've always prided myself on my ability to look after myself as well as others. Now that particular skill, for the time being at least, seems to have gone as well. I am absolutely in surrender, and faith is now my crutch. I'm surrounded by great friends and a huge wave of support. But there is nothing more I can do for myself. My plans to secure work in September are now scuppered, and I simply don't know how I'm going to make ends meet.

Over just a few weeks everything has changed. I've lost my husband, my business, my 'reality' and now my physical independence. I'm wondering now just how much lower I'll need to fall before I can start to rebuild. The way things are going, I may well need to consider selling my beautiful home, as I just don't know where the money is going to come from now.

So much has changed. So much has shifted. I simply don't know what I can hold on to any more, but hold on I know I must. For my own sake as well as for the sake of Dylan.

And yet, in some very strange and subtle way, as I have no choice but to let go of my control, I am beginning to feel safe. I feel secure. And I know that things are working behind the scenes – they have to be.

Is this what people mean when they talk about faith I wonder? Whatever it's called, this feeling is what's keeping me going. Because as I look into the faces of my wonderful friends, and I feel the love that's supporting me, I just know that somehow I'm OK. For the first time in my life, I have reached surrender. I am, quite literally on my knees. But at the same time, I know that in one way or another I am now being nudged into the position where I can trust life to throw me the lifeline I've been searching for since childhood. I'm ready.

Just a couple of weeks after writing that post, another experience brought the message home with the most almighty thump. This time it was the actions of my son, Dylan, which taught me the lesson. This is what happened.

For years and years I've believed that I'm strong, tough and safe. Operating under those guidelines, I had felt that I did not require any help or support, that there were others more in need than myself, that I could cope, no matter what. I prided myself in my ability to survive and flourish even in the face of the most extreme of experiences.

Over the past few weeks, however, I've also been asking myself how much more I needed to be tested to prove this. What were the lessons that I was refusing to learn? Was I being stubborn? Deluded? Or could it be that in all innocence, and despite my best efforts, I honestly could not see . . .

I was about to find out.

It was late on Sunday afternoon and it had been raining cats and dogs. Dylan had cycled out some time earlier to feed our friends' horses while they were away. All of a sudden I heard our courtyard gates open and close with a slam and saw him coming towards the house. There was something wrong. His T-shirt was rolled up, as was one of his trouser legs. And he was hobbling.

It turned out that he'd slipped on one of the pedals on his bike. The wheels had jammed and he'd flipped headfirst over the handlebars and into a ditch about 1.5 km away from the house. There was nobody around, so he'd had to pick himself up and hobble home alone, pushing his damaged bike in the pouring rain. Blood was pouring from his foot and shoulder, and he was covered in cuts and grazes. His T-shirt was ripped and he was white as a sheet. It was a shocking sight, and Sarah and I went automatically into nursing mode.

A cup of hot sweet tea later, with his wounds bathed and bandaged, Dylan was clearly still in pain and needed to rest. Here's where his actions gave me the biggest 'ah-ha moment' perhaps of my entire life. Despite being surrounded by people who wanted to help, and despite being urged to stay where he was and put his foot up, he was absolutely determined to do things for himself. Hauling himself up and onto my crutches, he hobbled out of the kitchen and towards the sofa, picking up a cushion along the way. Moving away games and DVDs that had been left lying around, he settled himself down and swung his legs up on to the sofa. He was completely ignoring every offer of assistance, determined instead to do things by himself.

I felt wracked by frustration and helplessness because he wouldn't let me help him. When I turned round and noticed the same frustration on the faces of everybody else it was as if a light bulb exploded in my head. I laughed out loud and enquired of Sarah, 'That's exactly what I do as well, isn't it?' The expression on her face told me all I needed to know, and all of a sudden I recognised the lesson I had been failing to learn up until now. If I was to fully heal – on all levels – then I had to learn to start trusting others to look after me, to accept support graciously and to stop trying to be so strong.

It struck me that in my efforts to look after myself I've inadvertently pushed away many offers of caring and support. Yet, paradoxically, it's been care and support for which I've always yearned.

And now so many things are falling in to place as I ponder that simple yet profound realisation. I could not see it in myself, yet my beautiful and brave son played it out so clearly in front of me that I couldn't help but learn. As always, Dylan has touched my soul and has once again enriched my life in a way he probably doesn't even realise.

23
Something Inside So Strong

My injury forced me to take things more slowly – I had no choice. Unable to drive, pretty rubbish at getting around at all, and incapable of moving even a couple of steps without my full leg-brace and crutches, life was now physically as well as emotionally draining.

'Honestly, Sarah, just look at me, would you?' It was a beautiful evening in August. We were sitting at the table outside and talking about nothing in particular. One of those beautifully relaxed conversations that can only be enjoyed with a real friend. I recognised it as a valuable gift and felt deeply grateful for the everyday riches I was noticing in my life. 'If this was to go on TV as a storyline in a soap opera, nobody would believe it. It's all far too far fetched for reality!'

'There's nowt stranger than reality, I'll give you that,' agreed Sarah, nodding sagely before I broke the mood with a burst of hysterical laughter.

'Can you honestly imagine anyone in their right mind asking me to coach them now? Come on, picture the scene . . . "So, Mel, tell us how you've made such a success of your life then?" as I hobble on to the stage, dressed in old rags and smelling like something the cat threw up!'

But somehow, since the accident, I'd reached a new level of calm. My focused exploration of sociopathy together with the ongoing soul-searching and review of my past seemed to be working at last. Don't get me wrong, to all intents and purposes my situation hadn't really changed that much – at least not on the outside. But on the inside, I was certainly beginning to feel better about myself and about my chances.

Yes, I was continuing to have a number of run-ins as I battled to move forward. My latest battle was to find a way to progress with the divorce. With no work and no possible way of securing an income, I'd decided the only option was to sell my car. It was a Land Rover Defender that we'd bought new when we first came over to France. Car prices in France are, on the whole, greatly inflated compared to the UK, certainly within the second-hand market. I'd been researching Defenders of similar age and condition, and had realised that I would likely be able to sell mine for somewhere in the region of 15,000 euros.

'That'd be an absolute godsend and a massive relief! If I can actually achieve that price, it would be a lifesaver. Can you imagine? After surviving on bugger-all, I'm certain I could make €15,000 last for months on end!' I'd enthused to the Brightmans, who had been over for most of the summer.

In actual fact, they had arrived the day after I had my accident. I had been due to collect them from the airport, which, of course, was impossible. At the time I thought it was just a bad sprain, so I'd put myself on the sofa while Henry had gone up to collect them. Jayne and John had taken one look at me and told me I had to get to hospital. They are both no-nonsense people. Jayne, in particular, is somebody you just don't argue with. She may be small – pulling herself up to just over five feet tall when she's really cross – but her formidable 'Brightman-stare' and stern voice let people know they'd better not mess with her!

'Well, it's up to you' she'd said, but it wasn't of course. Her tone of voice told me that I had no choice in the matter whatsoever. 'But I think you should get to hospital, and I'll drive you.'

Tom insisted I use his wheelchair to get out of the house, across the courtyard and next to the Land Rover (a huge gesture of kindness and generosity that still warms my heart and will stay with me to the end of my days), and Sarah and Jayne hoiked me up into the passenger seat. Sarah had piled into the back before Jayne yanked the driver's seat forward and we'd set off like Thelma-and-Louise-plus-one on our perilous journey to the hospital.

'Down for second gear! Harder on the clutch – left hand down!' Doing my best to help, I couldn't help chuckle each time the gearbox emitted a new grinding sound, despite my pain and despite the seriousness of the situation. I'd driven the Defender for years, but I remembered it could be pretty tricky the first time around.

'I'm fine, I'm fine!' Jayne had retorted, stalling for the second time before we'd even left the village. 'Now stop making me nervous. Do something useful, like plan exactly how you're going to explain what happened to that knee of yours without the doctors laughing at you!' I love Jayne so much. She's got the cheek of the devil, the strength of Atlas, and one of the biggest hearts I have ever come across.

Over the many subsequent trips to various hospitals, pharmacies and knee specialists, Jayne had eventually bonded with the Defender. 'Oh, that's a shame, and just I was just getting used to her!' she teased when I told her my plan to sell it, before handing me a steaming cup of coffee. 'Now get that down you, you look like you could do with it!'

I found a buyer remarkably quickly – a ruddy-cheeked cheese merchant who had been looking for a Land Rover for his delivery business. After he'd 'hmmmd' and 'aahhhhd' his way around the vehicle, kicking tyres and feeling the quality of the seat fabric (why do people kick tyres when buying a car?), he sat at my table sipping his coffee before engaging in some serious French haggling. Sarah and I sat on one side, the cheese-maker and his equally ruddy-cheeked wife the other. I wasn't budging on the price. It might have been a game of male machismo to him, but for me this was my lifeline. The sale of my Land Rover would guarantee me safety at least for a few months. Finally I was swayed by his Gallic charm and his promise of 'some of the best cheese you will ever have tasted, I promise you. *Delicieux, Madame . . . formidable!*' Kissing his finger and thumb together, he winked and beamed his best brown-toothed smile at me, his eyes twinkling against his weather-beaten skin. Well, what else could a girl do under the circumstances? I agreed to knock 150 euros off the price on the condition that he doubled his cheese offer and came back to pay and collect the car within a week. It was agreed. Spitting on palms, we shook hands on it. The cheese farmers trundled off with smiles on their faces, actually patting the Land Rover as they walked past it, and Sarah and I cracked open a bottle of one-euro fizzy wine that tastes very much like champagne (well, with a good amount of imagination and artistic licence in any case!) To me, it was perfect, and I grinned from ear to ear as Sarah and I raised our glasses to a very successful sale.

'Can you believe I've just sold it for £2,000 more than I bought it for brand new six years ago? It's unbelievable! No wonder the French keep their cars for years – they're so expensive! Still, chin chin, eh? Here's to some financial stability for a change!'

I still had to arrange the paperwork of course. The vehicle had an English registration plate, as I had given up on the process of changing it a couple of years earlier after no less than five failed attempts to complete the task. Paperwork is the very lifeblood of French bureaucracy. Everything has to be stamped, copied, signed, re-copied and stamped yet again. It's the law, I'm sure of it. Along with the same law that states lunch must be taken between the hours of noon and 2 p.m., not a minute before and certainly not a minute after. A German friend, Wilf, often jokes, 'You know we only managed to invade France because we came in at lunch time!'

This time, though, I had to see the task through to the bitter end. There was no other option. The sale couldn't be completed unless the Defender was registered in France and I could provide all the official paperwork to demonstrate its provenance. So, with Jayne back in the driving seat, we completed our visits: to the tax office to collect the stamped certificate stating there was no import tax to pay, to the Controle Technique to make sure it was roadworthy, and finally to the Prefecture, clutching our fistful of signed and stamped documentation to collect the all-important Carte Gris. This was the last piece of French certification that would allow the sale of my Land Rover and finally bring me some desperately needed financial respite.

I held my breath and Jayne and I put on our very best winning smiles as the bespectacled red-lipsticked lady behind the desk checked and re-checked every piece of paperwork. She was clearly in no hurry and was not going to be influenced by any amount of our smiles or thoughts willing her to get a move on and get it done. Nope, this lady was going to check everything, running over every last square millimetre of each piece of carefully collected paper with her expertly manicured hands. I'm quite sure she took some macabre enjoyment out of the process; her top lip curled in pleasure on more than one occasion.

All of a sudden she gave a loud harrumph, looked up and told me that everything was in order. Breathing a huge sigh of relief, I noticed that my shoulders dropped a good few inches; they must have been up around my ears while we were waiting for the verdict! Less nervous but still alert, I waited for the next instructions. She handed me a piece of paper that looked like a bill.

'You just need to pay €350 to the gentleman at the next counter and then we can print your Carte Gris, madame. Just over there, if you please!'

I stared blankly ahead as the blood drained to my feet. I wished the floor would just open up and swallow me there and then. Get it over with. Stop this torture. I give in. Enough already!

So near and yet so far. It had been such a struggle to even get to this point, and I was within a hair's breadth of finally being able to support myself for the foreseeable future. But this was an impossible request. I didn't have a penny to my name. Perhaps a couple of euros in my purse, but that was all. My face reddened and silent tears ran down my cheeks as I felt my careful planning unravel at the final hurdle.

'Come on, give it here,' instructed Jayne, tugging at the piece of paper and holding me firmly by the arm. 'Come on. Come with me. It's OK.' Her no-nonsense yet kindly voice jolted me back in to reality.

My darling friend stepped in straight away to cover my embarrassment and paid the unexpected fee, but it was yet another reminder of just how vulnerable a predicament I was in at that moment in time. Precarious was an understatement, and there was no safety net. One false move, one tiny piece of the plan not quite in place and I would slip. There was absolutely no room for error or misjudgement of any kind. I had to stay poised, like an athlete, fully alert and prepared for every eventuality at every step of every plan I made.

The weird thing was that through this process I also had to learn to let go. There was so very little that I could actually influence myself, so much information I had to collect, process and deal with, so many overwhelming obstacles to overcome, that I had to let go. If I had kept worrying myself about things that were beyond my control, I would have driven myself crazy! Yes, there were mounting piles of brown envelopes collecting from the re-directed post from Edinburgh. I knew what they all were – notices from the bailiff, threats of county court judgements, nagging, pleading and menacing letters, all from a series of creditors churning out automated communication designed to intimidate. They worked. I did feel intimidated. I also felt furious that I was the only one being chased because, of course, the bills had all been in my name. The only debts that had been in joint names had been those that belonged to the business – supplier invoices, VAT, Inland Revenue and suchlike. All of those, of course, had been written off when I put the company into liquidation. In addition to those sorts of transactions usually associated with running a business, there was also the matter of the company credit cards that were intended to cover genuine business expenses. Instead of which, the spoils of his spending sprees (gadgets, bikes, furniture and other stuff) had all been paid for on these cards, and remained at the flat. Nobody seemed interested in trying to reclaim these – although I argued that surely they held some value and should be sold to help repay the company debts.

But the fact was, nobody could kill me. It might seem drastic, but that was what I kept reminding myself. Yes, I was in a terrible position, but I was in another country and even if the bailiffs came to find me, the worst they could do was try to take some furniture from the house in France, which I thought unlikely. They could write as many threatening letters as they liked, but there was absolutely nothing I could do about it, and until I could, well, they couldn't kill me.

So, bizarre as it may seem, I learned how to let go. I began to learn to accept the simple joys in life, like appreciating a warm summer's night outside in the company of my precious friend Sarah. I learned to appreciate the friendly smile of a neighbour. The laughter of my son and his friends. The affection from my pets. The changing floral displays as different flowers bloomed in my garden. The colour of the skies. The smell of the grass. The sound of the river as it burbled along next to the winding road at the bottom of the village. Gratitude now flowed from me as a natural way of being, and I started to feel safe, probably for the first time in my life.

When I felt helpless, vulnerable and often very lost, I decided I had a choice. I could either focus on the things that were too big to handle (How was I going to earn an income? How would I look after Dylan? Would I lose our home? Where were we going to live?), or I could let it all go and focus instead on what I already had that I could be grateful for. At the beginning it was difficult, and it also felt false. It seemed as if I was deceiving myself or perhaps just burying my head in the sand. But the fact was that my head was well and truly above the parapet. I was ready to stand up and fight, to do what I could, whenever I needed to, in order to secure a future for both of us.

Perhaps this was part of what I'd been doing wrong all my life. For as long as I could remember, I'd been fighting. Fighting to stay strong. Fighting to survive. Fighting for my little sister. Fighting for justice. I'd also been doing everything within my power to find acceptance. I'd been trying to please, trying to prove that I was good enough. Trying to achieve love and safety. But in the process of working so hard to achieve that feeling, I'd pushed so much away in the process. I'd never learned how to accept the good that was already around me. The beautiful things – like friendships, sharing, early mornings, sunsets, and all the wonders of nature. Things that had always and always would be surrounding me all the time. Simple things that I was finally learning held the highest value – and I'd had them all the time. I just didn't know it.

It's true. I was actually enjoying life. I had learned to put myself in the eye of the storm and remain calm even though all around me was a chaotic mess. What an amazing lesson to have finally learned! How to feel good when everything around me continued to throw unquestionable proof that I should, by all rights, be feeling pretty rotten to say the least. But I didn't. OK, it's true that I can't say that I was on top of the world, well, at least not all day everyday in any case. There were some days where staying in bed was the best option. So I did. No pressure, no guilt. I just did as my body requested. For once I listened to what was good for me and stopped the push. Stopped cracking the whip, stopped berating myself. Instead, I did the only thing that was left open to me – I let myself be.

Perhaps this is what is meant when stories are recounted about prisoners-of-war who refused to let their surroundings imprison their minds. Perhaps this is what is meant when survivors come home and share their vivid daydreams of visiting new countries, practising their golf swing and spending time with loved ones. Is this what is meant when people talk about freeing their minds even though their captors did all they could to keep them locked in prison and often in darkness? Perhaps this is what is meant by true survival instinct – the real one. The healthy one. The one that carries people through tough times. That certain something inside of us, something so strong that it ensures people escape, get out, survive and, more than that, actually go on to thrive. It felt to me as though I had uncovered another vital missing link. That somehow I'd made yet another connection that was bringing me back to wholeness. I was glad.

The sale of the Land Rover went through without any further hitches. With the money, I opened a new bank account in my own name and paid off an outstanding balance of €2,000 on Cam's French credit card, which had been on the joint account. How on earth had he managed to spend so much money? And on what? It baffled me, but there was no point trying to understand. I just had to pay the debt. It was the only way that I could close the account. I also agreed a payment plan to bring the mortgage on the buy-to-let up to date. And I moved forward with finding a new solicitor. Further investigations and a deeper understanding of my options taught me that I could file for divorce under English law. At the beginning, I had been told that this would be impossible. Just one of the many bits of conflicting professional advice I was to be given as the months progressed. So I contacted my old advocate James Getting. At last I was advancing. I may well have been in the trenches, and progress might have been pitifully slow and excruciatingly dangerous, but with each new day I learned more and more about the situation, and my steps gradually became more confident.

THURSDAY, 27 AUGUST 2009

Life is good . . .

'Forgive me father for I have sinned . . .' well, I haven't actually, but since my blog often feels like a confessional, it seemed appropriate to start this post with those familiar words!

Since I last wrote, just ten days ago, life is continuing to improve and expand in the most surprising and wonderful ways as I continue to find myself and stay open to possibilities. People are asking me whether this 'new me' is real, checking to make sure that I'm not putting on an act. And I find that really very refreshing.

In my 'old life' I was known for being positive, optimistic, energetic and always on top of my game. I was expected to be bouncy, full of fun and always have something on the go. No questions asked, no checking, because this was the reality of Mel. And in many ways it was, although, as I've discovered, there was much of myself and my life that I was denying in the process.

Over the past few months, my friends and family have seen me at absolute rock bottom. Unable to pick myself up and unwilling to put on a pretence. Uncomfortable at first in asking for help and support, I have become more receptive as the days and weeks have gone past. My friends will tell you it's been a battle, since I'm stubborn as a mule! And I have to agree.

Today, I'm sitting at the table outside my kitchen. The weather is perfect, and I am waiting for my son to arrive back from England with his father. All is well.

And now, when I look back at what has happened over the past few weeks – couple of years, in fact – I can only smile and feel grateful, right to the very depths of my being. It has been a journey that at times I feared I would not survive. With my promise to fully feel emotions, and conscious of the fact that many of these would involve past experiences the roots of which were deeply buried in my psyche, it's taken every ounce of courage and energy to go there. To explore the places I feared would engulf me with the intensity of hidden pain I'd chosen to lock away over the years. The small hurts and the life-changing shocks that threatened to destroy me – all had left their mark.

And, I must be honest, given half the chance I would quite

willingly have left them there, never to have surfaced again. Little did I realise that the catalyst for these seismic shifts would be my beloved husband. The person to whom I'd freely given my love and my life, and who I worshipped more than anything else. This same person who would then cut me down, betray me and abandon me, all with such callous precision that I had to make a real choice.

Would I choose to blame him? Would I fall and crumble? Or would I instead take responsibility, accept my own part in my predicament, and find the courage to change within myself so that I could heal and secure my escape and freedom. Of course, I chose the latter.

I honestly believe that this is the route I've always chosen – certainly in consciousness since I started studying self-improvement as a serious way of life. And I honestly thought I had it sussed. No, honestly, I really did! I truly believed that I had cleared out all my old blocked emotions and had truthfully dealt with the painful issues of my past. And I had – as far as was possible for me at the time.

One of my great teachers, Dr Patricia Crane, once said that the spiritual journey is like peeling back the layers of an onion. Just as you think you're there, there's another layer to discover and more tears to shed. It was 1997, and I was on the Louise Hay Teacher Training Programme, and, boy, I'd shed enough tears that week to float a battleship! That particular experience put me in good stead and, I believe, has kept me rock solid for more than a decade.

But this latest 'gift' of betrayal by Cam has allowed me to remove and explore more layers. To shed more tears. To open my heart more than I knew was possible. To remove the blinkers of habit and reassess my life. On my own terms.

And this time, I know I've gone deeper than before. It's been excruciatingly painful and more terrifying than any of the nightmares that would often haunt my dreams, and I accept there are still plenty more battles to fight and win. But now I know that I have my own army with me and within me. Not just the bouncy, noisy, laughing soul-army of previous times; now I have the added battalions of peace, measured wisdom and a gentle inner knowing that is now part of my everyday life.

I've pulled, poked and prodded at the old scars – opening them up one by one, scraping out the hurt and betrayal, facing my deepest fears – and through that process I've found myself. More of myself than I ever realised existed before. Yes, I've grown. And, like the sunflowers that surround the village, my face and soul now turns automatically towards the sun without me having to think about it. Many scars have healed, leaving marks of experience in place of my old battle wounds. Scars I'm now proud to show, proud to know are a part of me. They're proof of my journey of love, innocence and courage to find myself. A rite of passage that I now choose to wear with pride.

Daily, now, I automatically notice the gifts in every situation and accept the good in my life with gratitude and a sense of excitement. And the surprises are coming along thick and fast. Opportunities are showing themselves in the most unexpected of places, and I'm enjoying life more than I ever have before. At last I've discovered what it means to be truly authentic. To say when I'm feeling lost or sad, and to accept the love and support that surrounds me every day.

Life *is* good, and I celebrate the gifts that have ultimately been bestowed upon me through the absolute betrayal of the person I trusted most in the whole world. Was that person Cam? Or was that person me? That's an added gift to ponder. It keeps me chuckling, my soul basking in the warm feeling of acceptance that is deeply engrained in my being.

So I'll finish this post with thanks. Thanks to Cam for his treatment of me, thanks to my friends for rallying around and showing me the richness of my relationships, and thanks to myself for having the courage to face the impossible and come out victorious.

24
Life Is A Roller coaster

As a result of my blogging, I decided I'd write a book about my experiences, highlighting the skills of a sociopath and warning people against falling into the same trap. I researched how to write a proposal and approached just one literary agent. He signed me immediately. Can you imagine my surprise!

It was Thursday, 10 September – a significant date for me as it was the birthday of my best friend since childhood, Tanya. She had died way before her time, just a few years earlier, but I always marked that date as a special day. I still do. It also happened to be the day when I married my first husband, Adam. The marriage might not have lasted, but I still knew that he had loved me with all his heart and soul. I was just incapable of reciprocating at the time.

This year, 10 September 2009, I was in London and had just finished the meeting with the literary agent. Holding a copy of the newly signed contract in my hand, I was fizzing with excitement and about to pop with the sheer madness of it all.

'I've done it! I've done it! I've bloody well done it!' I screeched into my mobile 'Bloody hell! Can you believe it! OH MY GOD! OH MY GOD!!!'

Matt, as usual, was calm and comforting. 'Of course you have,

Mel. It's like I've always said. It's a good story and you tell it well. He knows talent when he sees it – that's his job – so of course he signed you!'

My next port of call was to hook up with an old client I hadn't seen in a long while. Stephanie was a lottery millionaire who had subsequently set up her own successful advertising agency. She was the same age as me but with masses of long auburn hair extensions and a figure to die for – and she knew it. Dressed top to toe in the most expensive figure-flaunting designer clothing and dripping with garishly over-the-top accessories, she certainly knew how to make an entrance. Heads would turn wherever she went, and she attracted barely concealed whispers and in some cases giggles. She and I had connected during a particularly gruelling workshop some years earlier when she'd gone through a series of painful yet enlightening personal discoveries. It had been a difficult process, and I had been with her every step of the way – coaching and supporting her as she slowly came to terms with the life changes she determined to put into place as a direct consequence. The way I saw it, that particular episode resulted in a bond of mutual respect between two strong women, so I was looking forward to seeing her.

'Come to my hotel, honey. Meet me in reception. I can't wait to hear all about it. We've got some celebrating to do, darlin! Can't keep a powerful woman down for long, eh? People like us, you know. We just get up and get going again, eh, darlin?' she'd trilled, giving me the Sloane Square address for the taxi.

I was still in a knee brace at this time, although it was a much smaller one and I could just fit it under my jeans. The London visit was the first time I had been in the UK since I'd discovered Cam's email trail, and it felt really odd to be back on my old stomping ground. It was also odd to be dressed in 'business clothes' rather than the shorts and T-shirts that had been my uniform over the summer. It had clearly worked with the agent, and now, to top it all, I was also sporting a smile that would give the Cheshire cat a run for his money! The taxi ride was a luxury for me, but I decided that spending £4.50 to arrive in style was worth it. After all, I'd just agreed a deal that was likely to change my life.

'Honey, you look stunning. What a difference! You've shed tons of weight and you look amazing!'

Well, that was an enthusiastic greeting I wasn't expecting, and my confidence levels eased up another notch.

'Wow, thanks, Steffi. I must admit, I'm feeling pretty chuffed with myself!' I grinned, as we headed out of the hotel and into another waiting taxi.

It was mid-afternoon and Steffi made sure we started as she meant to go on, with champagne at the exclusive bar in an upmarket clothing-store I would never have dreamed of entering had I been on my own. We were ushered to the polished brass bar by a man dressed in full butler's uniform, who pulled out two stools for us and assured us there were no journalists or photographers allowed in before sliding us a list of the most outrageously priced drinks I had ever seen.

'Just two glasses of your best champagne to start, please, my darling, and we'll let you know if we need anything else!' Steffi waved him off with a huge toothpaste-ad smile, a wink and then a sultry-toned 'Thank you' that made him turn around again and blush every so slightly.

'That's the way to do it you see, Mel. Let them know who's boss, but always allow them to think they're in with a chance. They're not, of course, but, hey, nothing wrong with a bit of flirting if it gets the right results!' Flicking her fake chestnut tresses behind her shoulders, she raised her glass to mine. 'Here's to us, honey. Strong powerful women who know what they want and know how to get it. Cheers!'

Of course, I couldn't afford to pay for this kind of extravagance, so I let Steffi know I was only going to stay a short while.

'Nonsense!' she snorted. 'This afternoon is on me! This is our treat! I'm going to show you what it's like to live the high life. After all, you'll be one of us soon, making millions of your own. You've got a lot to learn, so now I shall be your teacher for a change!'

Well, she certainly opened my eyes to a few things as the afternoon and evening went on, I can assure you! We moved on to another exclusive and dimly lit bar. There were more butler-clad gentlemen at the entrance, but this time I was sure they were acting as bouncers. I saw them politely turn away a couple of long-legged scantily clad young women, who, although they looked like they'd stepped out of the pages of *Vogue*, had clearly enjoyed one too many glasses of champagne with their caviar.

'It's all a matter of control and class, you see,' observed Steffi, nodding her head towards the amusing scene outside. 'You've got to know your limits and how to behave in public. Those two silly women out there, they just let themselves down!'

I confess, I forgot all about my own limits as Steffi ordered glass after glass of pink champagne. We ate the most delicious meal – nicely prepared and presented, but ridiculously overpriced for what it actually was. I knew could get something just as good in France for a quarter of the price. But it didn't matter. We were paying for the atmosphere. For rubbing shoulders with the rich and privileged. For being part of a pseudo-elite group who absolutely believed they were above the vast majority of people. People who wouldn't think to question whether the prices were a rip-off because it gave them more opportunities to flash the cash and impress their guests. And for me, as a keen observer of human behaviour, the quality of entertainment was absolutely priceless.

At one stage we were joined by an immaculately groomed, dark-suited young lady who had spotted Steffi from outside. Sashaying towards us, she extended her hand before air-kissing my companion and sitting herself down at our table.

'Do excuse me, but I simply had to come and say hello!' she gushed, before raising a perfectly shaped eyebrow in my direction – perhaps I didn't quite fit the bill?

'How are you?' she beamed at Steffi. 'It's been simply an age! You really must come in and view the new collection. It's just divine and there are some gorgeous pieces that you simply must have! No, seriously, they're this season's must-have items. They are absolute darlings and I know you'll love them. We have a private viewing this afternoon, but of course you can come. It wouldn't be the same without you!'

Well, this was certainly an education. An invitation to a pre-launch private viewing of exclusive designer clothing. Steffi was right, I did have a lot to learn! I stifled a snigger with another sip of champagne.

'Thank you very much, Lauren, but I'm cutting back these days. Business isn't what it was, and I'm afraid designer collections are out of the window for now. But I'll be back as soon as we're back on track, mark my words! Thanks for the invitation and give my best to Bertie, won't you?'

Lauren glided back out of the bar, but not before leaving an embossed business card for both of us. 'Of course, I understand. Whenever you're ready. I shall look forward to it!'

Drinks continued to flow and tongues became looser, with the language less controlled as well! Steffi can swear like a fishwife and, while I have a good few colourful words under my belt myself, I admit I was no match for her.

'I never fookin did like him, Mel, if truth be told. We were travelling in a taxi once, but I felt right fookin uncomfortable sitting next to him. I never did know why. Now I realise that was my female instinct telling me something. Of course it was – I knew it!'

The conversation had naturally returned to Cam. She was horrified to hear all the gory details (the champagne meant I probably shared far too much of the detail if truth be told, but, hey, it was all going to come out in the book, so I didn't care!) and promised me she'd do everything she could to help.

'Us girls have got to stick together, you know, honey. And anyway, now you're going to be a world-famous fookin author, I reckon we should team up! I've got a few stories to tell and all, you know!'

I was staying at the Brightmans, and I finally tottered in just after 11 p.m. I'd been out all day, and drinking champagne with Steffi since mid-afternoon.

'You know what?' I giggled, as Jayne passed me a huge cup of coffee. 'I think everything's going to be all right. I've got the contract, Steffi's going to help me, and it's Tanya's birthday. Things are on the up!'

For a good while it certainly seemed as though that was the case. Steffi and I agreed to re-launch an old business idea of mine that I had let fall by the wayside. She was as excited about it as I was.

'You see, only some people actually "get it", don't they, Mel? I do, and you do too, of course, but there aren't many others who really do – get it, I mean.' She was talking about intuition and personal development. Since working with her, I had introduced her to many of the books that had inspired me over the years, and she loved to talk about her own special interest in that field. She revelled in sharing inspirational books, poems and sayings with her team, knowing how important it was to stay motivated during tough times.

'I've been through it myself, you see! Just like you, I've been through the tough times, and now I feel it's my duty to share what I know with others.' She was right. She'd built up her business from nothing and had taken some hard knocks along the way. They were currently experiencing some particularly rough financial challenges, but Steffi was a tough cookie, a fighter, and she refused to let anyone or anything stand in her way. But underneath it all I felt that she had a soft streak. I believed that she wanted to do right by people, and I was happy that she wanted to get involved and resurrect my idea that was based around giving and receiving positive messages of support.

'You've got the idea, and I've got the know-how,' she smiled, toasting our agreement with her favourite champagne after we'd completed the meeting with her accountant.

We spent over two months working together on the project. I

spent much of my time in the UK at Steffi's house and at one point there was talk about me taking over one of her apartments and potentially bringing Dylan over as well. I wasn't keen on that idea, as our home was in France, but, as Steffi pointed out, 'When this goes worldwide, Mel, we'll all be drinking champagne on our own fooking yacht somewhere in the Caribbean, and Dylan will be taking lessons with a private tutor!'

She seemed keen to at least involve Dylan in what was going on, so I agreed to bring him over for a weekend during the school holidays. She had bought tickets to see a Michael McIntyre show, and Dylan and I had a whale of a time. We were in the VIP area during the interval and were once again rubbing shoulders with the well-heeled, extravagantly groomed and loudly spoken.

'It's all a bit over the top, isn't it, Mum?' Dylan had confided in me as we walked from the venue back to a waiting taxi. I had to agree with him. I know Steffi was trying to educate me, but it didn't seem real to me. I was much more comfortable in my house in France, making chutney and sharing simple food in the company of good friends. I wondered whether it was just because I was feeling shy, but as time went on my discomfort didn't diminish. Quite the opposite in actual fact.

While in Steffi's company, I met important person after important person. She was incredibly well connected, and I spent much of my time wide-eyed and pinching myself to check it was real. After so many months of struggle and hardship, it was hard to take on board the idea that things had changed so dramatically. I remember one particular evening when we had been out for dinner at an exclusive restaurant with a highly connected politician. I couldn't believe the amount of name dropping and fawning this man did, both at the table and with people who came to say hello. I found it incredibly embarrassing and, as a friend of mine would say, 'a perfect example of oily toadying at its best'.

Now, maybe it's my own inverted snobbery, but over the previous months I had been learning that authenticity, for me, was the only way I wanted to move forward. I found this gentleman's approach towards Steffi to be inappropriate and somewhat aggressive, and his treatment of those around him equally dismissive. While he said he was interested in our business idea, I really didn't feel he was the right person to have on board, and I told Steffi as much as soon as we left. I may have been looking a gift-horse in the mouth, but I wasn't about to be pushed around or have my ideas tainted by somebody who had displayed such a warped set of values in such a short period of time. We were still sitting in the bar when a bunch of footballers arrived and made themselves comfortable in the corner. They were well mannered and unassuming, but Steffi was up and off her stool in an instant.

'How was the game? Did you score tonight, Frank?' She had marched straight over to the group and directed her comment at Frank Lampard. He smiled politely and shook his head. 'What? Well you'd better try harder then, pet, don't you think?' she teased, before sashaying back to the bar, flicking her hair as she perched back on her stool and raised her glass to the group.

'She's got some chutzpah!' I thought, admiring her cheek. 'Give her credit, she certainly knows how to get herself noticed!'

We had agreed that Steffi would fund the business and that I would take a minimal monthly salary to cover my basic living expenses. You have no idea what that meant to me. The fact that I knew I could pay my bills was such a huge relief that, to be honest, I felt I was the richest person in the world!

Steffi also knew somebody who could help me with my credit issues. By that time, another enormous debt had shown itself. It was another one of those bills that I had believed Cam had taken care of and one that I would never be able to repay in a million years. Over the weeks, Steffi's contacts taught me that there is always a solution when it comes to money, and, without going into details here, I learned some of the reasons why the rich stay rich and the poor stay poor. Oh yes, I was getting an education indeed. Steffi had been right about that!

But then, during the second week of November, she suddenly went quiet. She wasn't responding to texts or emails, nor did she reply to the messages I left on her mobile. I knew she had some minor health issues to deal with, but I realised that something else was seriously wrong. Feeling that somehow I was the underdog (after all, as she'd said so many times, I was new in her world and I had a lot to learn), I was unwilling to push too hard. But the old familiar feeling of dread once again appeared in my stomach like a lead weight.

The email came just before the end of the month. Steffi told me that she had taken some time to step back from the project and after giving it serious thought she no longer felt able to continue. She felt she wouldn't have enough time to fulfil her role as a partner, but hoped that the many people she had introduced me to and the meetings she'd set up would be of benefit to me.

She then went on to say that she wouldn't seek to be reimbursed for the expenses she had incurred in the way of flights and subsistence, but she did request repayment of £1,500 she had loaned me. The email ended with her wishing me luck and hoping that we could remain friends.

Remain friends?! Or, as Steffi would say, 'Fooking remain fucking friends?! You're having a fooking laugh!' And as for the 'friendship loan' of £1,500 – well, that had been only a small portion of the salary we had agreed to cover my living costs while I devoted time and energy to the project – and, more to the point, freely shared the details of all my ideas! That was no loan. That was payment. And it wasn't even the correct level of payment that had been agreed for what amounted to nearly three months' input! I was furious and hurt, and, more to the point, thrown right back into a place of fear and despair.

Because I had dedicated myself to the project, I had, of course, not been focusing on any coaching work, or any other kind of employment in actual fact. So here I was, a few weeks before Christmas, with no money, no income, no prospects and a worse financial situation than I had been in just a few weeks before.

Back to hell. Back to bedlam. Back to pain. And back right up against the wall, this time only a few seconds away from the firing squad. I sank, hard, fast and deep. But I refused to be beaten.

A few weeks later, I took to my blog once again. It was the morning of my birthday, and I had just experienced an almighty revelation.

FRIDAY, 18 DECEMBER 2009

I'm back!

It's been a while, I know, so what's prompted my return? Many things. And I'm not sure where to start. The big thing, I guess, is that it's my birthday.

Yup, Friday, 18 December 2009 is a huge day for me in so many ways. I'm 45 (which means I've now officially out-lived both my parents), it's my first birthday in over a decade when I can finally say I'm out of Cam's clutches, the day is Friday (my day of birth) and, to top it all, it's snowing! For the first time I can remember since I was very small!

So what's been happening since my last post? Well, to start with, I took the blog down for a while after a major move forward. In response to all the messages and encouragement I'd been receiving, I wrote a book proposal, which was accepted by the very first literary agent I approached – very exciting! So that was why I stopped. Added to which I had reason to believe that it had been noticed by my estranged husband. But the book itself is now coming along very nicely, and I have decided that now is a good time to re-start my personal blogging, it being my birthday and all that . . .

I'm in a very different place now from the space I was in on my last entry. Lots has happened – many more challenges than I could have begun to anticipate – and I must say there have been times when I've been absolutely on the floor. But now, somehow, I've found my 'mojo' and believe I have the strength to come through everything that has happened and anything else that is now going to be thrown at me.

My latest and most profound 'ah-ha' moment happened just a few days ago, last weekend in fact. Too many things have happened over the past few months for me to attempt to explain here and now, suffice it to say that at that point I had hit rock bottom after a series of disappointments despite my best efforts to keep strong. Try as I might, even after throwing myself into new opportunities with all my heart, it seemed that the tables were well and truly turned against me. I found myself sinking even further down than I had ever been before, and, to top it all, I'd suffered an ear infection that, had I still been scuba-diving, would have prevented me from plummeting the physical depths, and in the meantime prevented me from exploring the emotional descent I had to achieve to in order to purge myself – the irony is not lost on me.

And yet, and yet . . . out of those depths that I could only imagine, I seem somehow to have found a new strength, a new lust for life (to quote one of my favourite tracks). This is how I found it.

Last Saturday night, 13th December, I'd gone to bed with the now-familiar ache in my heart and blind panic in my mind that I'd grown used to over the previous few weeks. My financial situation was at an all time low. I had nothing left to sell. The business project to which I'd dedicated the previous two months plus, and which had promised so much, had suddenly fallen by the wayside, and finding work this close to Christmas was proving to be an uphill battle for which I was not sufficiently equipped. But that didn't stop the bills. Electricity, telephone, oil, my son's school fees, mortgage – all reasonable bills that I had no way of honouring, and from which I had no place (or desire) to hide. I was embarrassed, frightened, overwhelmed and exhausted from the fight.

That night, I started reading a book that had just been returned to me. It's an old favourite entitled *You Cannot Afford the Luxury of a Negative Thought* and is a book I've given out to numerous friends and colleagues over the years. That night, though, it had come back to me, returned by Henry and Ruth. It's often said that the teacher or book you require turns up at exactly the right time, and this was most certainly the case for me.

I was physically shattered. I'd spent the evening putting on my best smile, but I knew I was fooling nobody with my jolliness – least of all myself. My grey pallor, eyes sunken into black sockets, skin itching and sensitive, I'd gingerly manoeuvred myself into my bed, taking care not to jolt my cruciate-less knee. Once I'd settled as best I could, I picked up the book and opened its well-thumbed and yellowing pages.

The words instantly took me to a place of familiarity – a 'home' that I'd temporarily forgotten about. No wonder I had recommended it so wholeheartedly to so many people! The book was (and is) a godsend. It's designed for people who are suffering from a life-threatening illness – including, as it so wisely states, 'life itself' – and I realised that I had indeed been combating a life-threatening situation myself. I might not have had the physical symptoms of an illness, *per se,* but the emotional depths to which I had allowed myself to sink were certainly life-threatening nonetheless. And that was brought home to me by a simple question that was posed in the early chapters of the book.

This is the question. 'You have a decision to make. A question you need to ask yourself. For until you are clear, you cannot move forward. The question is this – ask yourself from deep within in your soul, do you want to live or do you want to die?'

It's a simple enough and straightforward question. And you'd think that the answer is obvious. But at that moment, when I read those words, it hit me like a ton of bricks. I could NOT answer the question. In my heart of hearts, from the deepest core of my being, I simply didn't know the answer. And that realisation absolutely rocked me – more than any of the experiences over the past few months.

My blood ran cold, and I recognised that I'd been in a place so dark, so soulless, that I was no longer sure that my life was worth living any more. I've had multiple experiences of suicides – my best friend, two of my mother's friends, friends of friends, my neighbour when I lived in the flat in Eastbourne, and perhaps (although not proven) my father. It shook me to the core to think that I had allowed myself to sink so low that I was no longer certain whether I wanted to live or die. And the shocking truth that I hadn't even recognised it for myself was absolutely mind-blowing.

At that moment, the breath went from my body, my mind went blank, and I felt myself on the brink of the black and bottomless pit that was beckoning my soul. And I found with frightening clarity that until now I had almost been willing to accept the invitation. And that was the point when I made my choice. I made my commitment to live – more consciously and with more certainty than I can ever remember. And as I made that choice, I could easily have reprimanded myself for being so selfish as to allow myself to sink so low. But instead I had the strange and comforting experience of holding myself in my arms, of singing a lullaby to myself, of forgiving myself for falling so far and so deeply.

So is this what the past few months have all been about? Has my lesson been to find a way to forgive myself? I've spent so long finding ways to forgive and accept the people and situations that have caused hurt to me and to Dylan, but perhaps the person I really needed to forgive and accept had been myself all along? I don't yet have the answers for sure, although I sense that this is indeed the case, but I do know for sure that now I am alive.

Now I choose to live. Not just to survive, not just to be strong and tough and soldier through, but now – possibly for the first time ever – to actually live. To live with joy. With excitement, with passion and energy, and to truly thrive. This is my God-given right, and I have been denying myself this right for more years than I care to remember. So now, in the early hours of my 45th birthday (it's never too late to learn!), I am finally embracing my life with arms wide open. With a heart that is now pumping with joy and a new-found determination to thrive, not just to survive. For I am sick of that – and, indeed, I have been sick, life-threateningly sick, to the pit of my stomach and the depths of my soul.

Now I believe I am truly on the way to living with peace of mind. Yes, there are still battles to be fought and won, but somehow they've lost their hold over me. They've shrunk. The battle cries are quieter and the scent of fear has all but disappeared. Now I'm here to live. Now I am on my side. Now I understand myself better than before. And now, finally, I don't need the approval of anyone else.

For now I finally love and approve of myself exactly as I am. And I'm grateful for my life. So now, on my 45th birthday, I feel I've been lucky enough to be born again, and this time I'll take nothing for granted and will look after the one person who can help me. The one person who has been with me all the time. The one person I chose to ignore. Myself.

Happy Birthday, Mel. Life has now begun.

25

Bring Me My Soapbox!

The challenges, though, didn't stop there. Not only was I stuck for income, I also still had the small matter of the debts to deal with, as well as still trying to find my way around the legal quagmire that was my divorce, or lack of it in actual fact. There had been no further move forward since my conversation with James in the summer. He had told me that I could indeed divorce under British law, but in order to do that I would need to have been registered at a UK address for more than six months. So I had registered immediately at my sister's London address. It was coming up for six months since then so, although I had no way of paying, I knew it was right to start preparing for proceedings.

The debts were my highest priority. I wanted to be able to go to James with a full and frank explanation of the situation. So I spent hours researching my options with countless debt-advisory bodies, and the differing advice I received was absolutely astonishing. It would appear that there is no such thing as one law. I discovered that the law is there to be interpreted depending on the understanding and motivation of the person who is handing out the advice. By my third call, to the third advisory board, I found I was able to pick them up on some of the points they were making. I could question from a point of knowledge. And I could argue the case when I felt they were giving me incorrect guidance. The bottom line was that I was losing faith in the professional systems that are meant to be there to guide people in times of hardship.

Even more interesting, though, was the wealth of information I had been gathering in the process. Any discussions about finance details, interest rates, credit agreements, mortgage contracts and the like had previously had the automatic effect of flicking the 'off switch' in my brain. I used to find all that stuff more boring than watching paint drying. Although I knew that it was important for me to understand, I could never quite find the time or the inclination to learn the nuances or, if truth be told, even move beyond the basics.

But after hours and hours of trawling the Internet, talking with advisors, providing information, checking back in with advisors – both from the Scottish and English legal viewpoint – I was becoming quite the expert. That information, coupled with the information I had learned while in the brief partnership with Steffi, meant I was finally growing in confidence that I would be able to find a way out of my difficulties. Although not, it would appear, before somebody did their level best to give me a nasty birthday surprise.

It was late morning and I'd just finished the third phone call with a person who said she had found a solution for me. The same person who had painstakingly listened to my story and taken down the details a few days earlier. The same person for whom I had also spent hours collecting every last scrap of paperwork and evidence she had requested. The very same person who then decided it was her duty to deliver the bad news. This is what happened.

FRIDAY, 18 DECEMBER 2009

Bring me my soapbox!

And the UK is meant to be a 'developed' country, one where human rights and justice form the backbone of our society? Well, this latest turn is enough to make your teeth curl.

OK, so, as a direct result of my husband's deliberate deception, misappropriation of company funds and fraudulent actions, I have discovered that I'm left with a whole mountain of personal debt running into tens of thousands of pounds. And he is getting away totally completely and utterly scot-free. Because he planned it that way.

He took sole charge of our finances in 2008 and assured me that everything was in order and that financial agreements were all being honoured. And I believed him – after all, we were not only happily married, we were business partners as well. Why would I doubt what he was telling me?

But in fact this was far from the truth. He had failed to pay the mortgage for nearly six months. He had refused to pay suppliers. He had failed to pay back even a single penny of the business overdraft that I had personally guaranteed. And behind my back he was funding another life and spending money like water – on gadgets and shiny things for himself. Mountain bikes, computers, holidays, jewellery, love trinkets, clothes, sports equipment – oh, and, of course, the countless sex sites and porn channels.

So, as you know, once I discovered the truth back in April this year, I immediately froze the business bank accounts and instructed an insolvency agency to put the company into liquidation. It was the best I could do, at least to safeguard some money to get our suppliers paid. And yet even though I personally called in the liquidators, they have still failed to give me details on exactly where we are with the process. Because, of course, they've met my ex in person and have only spoken to me by telephone and via email. No matter how many times I ask for an update, nothing is forthcoming.

I've also been pushed from pillar to post in trying to deal with the debts that have landed on my doorstep. I accept that my situation is perhaps out of the ordinary, and as a result I've spent hours on the phone to UK and Scottish debt advisors. The messages I've been receiving are really quite astonishing.

Firstly, nobody, but NOBODY, seems to be in the slightest bit interested in my ex's mismanagement of funds and deliberate deception. They are not interested that he has deserted the marriage and fled to safety in our home in Scotland where he stored all his gadgets and trinkets that have cost me so dearly. They are unwilling to seize any of these goods, despite the fact that they are worth tens of thousands of pounds. And why not, you may ask.

'Because, madam, the debts you have are in your name. They are nothing to do with your husband.' And that is as far as anybody is willing to look.

But I've done everything in my power to bring the truth out into the open, and to put things right! I didn't need to freeze the company accounts as I did; I could have chosen to take the money out for myself! I've passed over every scrap of evidence to support my claims that his actions have been reckless. But no. None of that seems to matter. All that matters is that the debts are in my personal name and, therefore, it's me personally who has full liability. It's me who is the baddie – not him. Full stop. No argument. That is the law.

The latest advice I have received is just unbelievable – and grossly unfair to the extreme. I have been exploring the route of obtaining a Protected Trust Deed through Scottish law, because I am still registered as living in Edinburgh. Because of the equity I hold in my share of the family home here in France, this deed would mean that I have to pay back every penny of debt that I owe, plus interest. Fair enough, you might say – and, yes, I'm perfectly willing to pay back money that I rightfully owe.

But now, here's the rub. Despite the fact that my husband deceived and abandoned me (and my son), and despite the fact that as a result I've been placed in a perilous financial predicament, the courts deem it just and fair that he has a claim over 50 per cent of the family home. Despite the fact that he is currently living the life of riley in our place in Edinburgh. So this is the course of action I've been told I must take.

I have to sell my home, even though I have a child, my son,

living with me full time. The proceeds of the sale will be split 50:50, and my estranged husband will receive his lump-sum amount in cash. My 50 per cent share on the other hand, will go immediately to the Trustees, who will in turn pay my creditors. I will then be expected to make arrangements to pay the outstanding balance.

So, my son and I will be left homeless, penniless and still in debt, while my ex gets to keep the place in Edinburgh and also benefits from a nice bundle of cash from the sale of the house.

Is this justice? Is this fair? Is THIS what we call a civilised and fair society?

No, it is not. And, needless to say, I will NOT be taking their advice. I'm now seeking other ways to deal with the problem, but it's hard work. And it's wrong. I've been the victim in all this, and yet I'm the one left holding the baby and being treated like a criminal.

I have a lot to learn, and as I move forward with this I realise that there ARE other options I can explore. And explore them I will, for I will NOT lose any more to that conniving, soulless shell of a man I once called my husband and soulmate.

And once I've found another way, I'm going to shout from the rooftops and find a way to bring this injustice out into the open. Watch this space.

26

Debt, Divorce and Discovery

And I did start finding another way. I secured James's services, with the help of an unexpected loan from a friend here in France. You know who you are, and to the end of my days I will remember that day you witnessed me at my wits' end sobbing at my kitchen table. Thank you for coming to my rescue, I am forever grateful.

James and I and together worked out a way we could weave the debts into the divorce settlement, and at last I began to believe that there might be some light at the end of the tunnel. As my knowledge and confidence grew, so did my determination that I would attack my financial situation with vigour and courage. I had nothing to lose, which meant I was dangerous. No longer was I going to cower and be one of the 'little people' who don't have a voice. I'd done that for far too long! Ever since I can remember, I'd been the one who would do everything to smooth over any awkward situation. To be understanding, caring, supportive. The one who would avoid conflict at any cost. The only thing was, the cost (as I had been realising over the past couple of months) had been *myself*. I was the collateral damage. And that was far too high a price to pay.

I remember a particular occasion when I'd slunk away from a situation where anybody in their right mind would have hit the roof.

We were living with Eddie and Gilly, and it was just before my seventeenth birthday, so somewhere around nine months since we'd first moved in. While Abigail and I had done a good job at settling as best we could, I always felt under pressure to fit in, to be, as I've said before, 'the good girl'. For me, fulfilling that role seemed to manifest itself in shutting up and putting up. In hindsight, it was probably a pretty good survival tool given the circumstances we were in, but ultimately it turned into a habit that I now believe, meant I allowed people to take advantage of me in far too many ways.

That particular evening there was a party for one of Eddie and Gilly's best friends, a couple called Steve and Tiggy. It was Steve's birthday and, since I'd shown my talent for creating and decorating unusual cakes (years of helping Mum ice cakes for numerous family occasions had taught me some pretty nifty icing skills!), Eddie had thought it would be a terrific joke if I could create a booby cake for the occasion. Quite literally, a cake made to look like a pair of women's breasts.

'Steve's such an old letch, this will turn the tables on him and serve him right. Go on Mel-The-Pel [my nick-name when Eddie wanted me to do something]. I'll bet you can make something suitable!'

Reluctantly, I agreed. Well, it's what a good girl should do . . . isn't it?

We were all gathered in the kitchen when the time came to present the birthday cake. As usual, everyone was in high spirits. Eddie's friends seemed to have an insatiable appetite for alcohol and risqué party games.

The lights were turned down among a drunken sea of slurred 'shushes' and giggles as Eddie tapped his glass with a knife and made the announcement: 'For my dear friend Steve. A cake we thought both fitting and appropriate for his advancing years and reputation for indiscriminate fondling of our female friends. A one-off birthday cake made by the fair hands of Mel-The-Pel . . . A huge round of applause please for the birthday boy!'

The cake looked absolutely revolting, and I was desperate to hide myself away in the corner. Two flesh-coloured mounds were presented to Steve, each chocolate nipple sporting a lit sparkler. The room erupted with laughter, but Steve was clearly uncomfortable. It was only for a split second, but I noticed a look pass between him and Eddie that seemed far from friendly. But it quickly turned into a broad smile as Steve made his acceptance speech.

'Thanks, Eddie. Thanks, everyone. Glad to realise that you all know me so well! And Mel-The-Pel? Thanks for making this for me – looks like you might have fashioned them from a pair pretty close to home, eh?' His eyes scanned the room for me, but I had now shrunk even further back into the corner of the kitchen behind the fridge. I wished the ground would swallow me up there and then.

Later on that evening, Steve and Eddie were talking together at the breakfast bar, the remains of the booby cake sitting just a few feet away. It was late and I was tired, so I had come to make my excuses and say goodnight, like a good girl.

'Not so fast, young lady, not so fast!' Steve was a little less steady on his feet than earlier, and he grabbed me by the arm. 'I've got a game to play with you. Are you up for it?'

Looking to Eddie for a reaction, he motioned for me to continue. Taking a deep breath, I pulled myself up taller.

'OK then. I'm up for it.'

Steve then said he'd bet me all the money he had in his pockets that he could make my boobs wobble without touching them.

'After all, you made me the cake. Boobs seem to be a bit of a thing with you, eh?'

I wasn't sure. Frowning, I checked my understanding of the challenge he'd set and decided it wasn't possible. I knew I had to go through with it. If I said I wouldn't take the bet, he'd call me a sissy, and Eddie would be disappointed. So, back straight and arms by my side, I said, 'No, I don't think you can do it.'

Steve looked me in the eye and smirked. Reaching out towards me, he grabbed my breasts with both hands, squeezing and wobbling them and laughing out loud.

'Oops! I lost the bet!' he said, taking his hands away and emptying his pockets of the bits of small change he had on him. 'Nearly a whole £2 there. Still, it was worth it. I don't mind!'

All I remember is the deafening laughter as red-hot shame rose up my neck and over my face. I noticed that Eddie was joining in the fun and clapping at the cleverness of his friend. I could only keep my gaze to the ground, moving as quickly as possible through the crowd of jeering onlookers before fleeing up to my bedroom. I could not cry. I would not cry. But the shame was unbearable. I felt so stupid. I'd fallen for a trick. I'd tried to join in with their games, and they'd mocked me. I'd played by their rules, but I'd been burned. I went to sleep that night feeling even smaller than I had the day before. I was a tiny fish in a huge pond filled with cold-eyed predators. I had to hide away or one day they might get me.

There have been many other times during my life when I've chosen to walk away or stay silent in the face of something so obviously wrong or unhealthy. At the time I thought that particular response showed strength – and in many ways I still believe that's the case. I am full of admiration for people who can stand up to the bully in a peaceful way. I believe in turning the other cheek. And I also believe that good will always win in the end. What I hadn't appreciated, though, was that by doing what I thought was the right thing, I was actually doing myself more damage than I could begin to understand, because I hadn't fully acknowledged my own hurt in the process. I'd just bottled it away so that it ate away silently from the inside out.

Fine, yes, walk away. Absolutely, use peace to diffuse attack. One hundred per cent offer the other cheek, but not, I repeat *not*, to the detriment of yourself! For so many years I had been *doing* the good stuff while still *being* hard on myself, thereby giving myself the double-whammy punishment. For example, I'd let Steve and Eddie make fun of me, walked away and then berated myself for being such an idiot to let it happen! Oh, Mel, how the truth finally comes out in the end.

'Well,' I said to my reflection one morning, 'I don't think so, Mel, not any more. It's time to change all that! No more Mrs Nice Guy!'

That was the attitude I took when my friend Julie offered to help me sort through the mounds of unopened nasty-looking envelopes I'd been collecting over the months. Now was the time to stand strong, face the contents and work out a plan. I was ready.

SUNDAY, 31 JANUARY 2010

Debt, Divorce and Discovery

This afternoon, Julie and I have been going through all the unopened letters that I've been keeping in a pile for the past few months. I knew what they were, you see. They were all re-directed from Edinburgh and relating to the debts that are all in my name. Until I found my solicitor, you'll remember, I'd been told that the only way to deal with them was to sell my house here in France. So, while I was exploring options – and seeking work – I decided the best route was to leave them unopened. There was nothing I could do to take any action. I knew what they were. So they would have to wait until I had a clear way forward.

Well, now I do. So today was the day that Julie very kindly came round and opened and sorted the letters to make it a more manageable task for me to deal with. I'd meant to get this job done since my return home last weekend. I'd already seen my solicitor and we'd agreed a way forward. But somehow I just couldn't bring myself to do it. I'm not known for procrastination – quite the opposite in fact – but this week I've been finding no-end of 'important and pressing' jobs that took precedence over facing that pile of letters.

Now that I have a solicitor who's prepared to fight with gloves off, I feel I'm finally moving forward. And, funnily enough, on a route that is totally unrecognisable from the 'only option' I was told was open to me just before Christmas. Persistence pays. Now the debts are 'under matrimonial jurisdiction' and, as such, will be contested and need to be included in the negotiations for the divorce settlement. No matter that they are in my sole name, the fact remains that I was unaware of their existence. The fact remains that my husband acted without my consent. The fact remains that I have been duped, because I was blinded by love and trust for the person I believed was my soulmate. No more. My emotions are now in check, and I see clearly the nature of the beast I am dealing with.

And the discoveries of this afternoon have made me even more grateful for my escape. And even more convinced of my innocence in the many financial hardships we faced over our marriage. For within the letters that have been forward were a few – just a handful – that were intended for him, so should never have reached me. Of course I didn't know the difference until I opened them. Having opened the letters, only I read them. OK, I accept, I should not have been privy to the contents, and technically I should really have re-sealed the envelopes the second I realised the letters were not intended for me, but hey, nobody's perfect, right?

The pile consisted purely of demands for payment – and this can only be a snapshot, for the majority of his intended letters must surely stay in Edinburgh. Debt collectors, solicitors, arrears departments all seem very keen to meet up and secure a relationship with my husband, threatening entry to the apartment by fair means or foul. But he appears to be ignoring them all – strange, because not so long ago didn't I find him advertising for 'new and exciting back-door encounters'? Perhaps he's had his fill.

Among the letters was a demand for £120 outstanding with Blockbuster – how on earth can anyone run up such a bill? There is a solicitor's letter chasing £780 from a mobile-phone supplier. An energy supplier threatening to cut off their services unless £87 is paid immediately. And BT suggesting very politely that perhaps non-payment of their bill for £73 has been an oversight on his behalf.

Now, OK, most of us are sometimes a little bit late paying a couple of bills. But this, surely, takes the biscuit? As I've said before,

I have earned nothing over the past year – and also suffered a serious knee injury which meant I couldn't move for a few weeks – and yet every single one of my current financial obligations has been met. I have a fantastic reputation with the bank and also with the mortgage company who were going to repossess while he was in charge of the finances! He, on the other hand, has had no such debts to deal with. He has had work with at least two of our unsuspecting clients. He has also been in full-time employment in a senior role since the beginning of September.

So what's it all about?

For me, it's about breathing an enormous sigh of relief that I discovered the truth. It's about realising that I was not to blame for our financial issues (although I hold my hand up to simply believing whatever he told me). It's about a new-found confidence in what I'm doing, and a renewed determination to fight against these financial institutions who think it's OK to threaten the 'little people' like me without care or concern about the effects it has on families who are struggling to cope.

Those who know me well can vouch for the fact that I will fight against any injustice. Well, after this afternoon, I've discovered that I have more fire in my belly than I had previously thought. And now I'm prepared to battle against the banks, credit card companies and other financial houses, for finally I believe in my own monetary skills.

Watch this space and mark my words – this is war.

27

Happy Anniversary!

Around Christmas time, a friend of mine whom I'd first met some nine years earlier when he was a client had given me a verbal shake by the scruff of the neck. To be fair, it had stared in the summer, but I hadn't taken any notice. By Christmas, though, I was much more willing to at least listen to what he had to say.

Greg is an HR specialist – one of the best in his field. Years of experience working with some of the largest brands in the world means that he has had contact with a whole raft of training providers. 'And you, lady, are absolutely one of the best I have ever come across! You find the real issues. You tell it like it is. You get to people. And you damned well give a shit. Good god, woman, it was you who changed my life all those years ago!'

I love Greg, and I must confess that I hadn't realised I'd had quite such a profound effect on him. Telling him as much, I backed away from his praise.

'Don't be so ridiculous, and stop being so self-effacing. It doesn't suit you, honey!' he chided me, as I giggled helplessly at his camped-up admonitions. 'You need to get out there, girl, and get yourself some work! You helped me more than you know, all those years ago, so now I'm going to open up my contact list for you. Cinderella, you shall go to the ball!'

True to his word, he did open up his contact list. He is incredibly well connected, and I was honoured that he was prepared to put me forward to some extremely senior people in a range of large companies. The heat was on. I would have to follow up, secure meetings and get out there to sell, sell, sell!

That was how the beginning of 2010 saw me suited and booted once more and ready for business. With each meeting, I found my confidence returning. I *could* speak their language. I *did* know my stuff, and I was still burning with passion for the professional path I'd followed for the past 12 years. Boy did that feel good!

There were many occasions when I couldn't help but laugh out lout at the absurdity of my circumstances. Here I was marching in to see some of London's most influential people who held hundreds of thousands of pounds worth of training budgets, and I was actually succeeding in talking their talk and making great connections. How funny it was then, that on many occasions I didn't even have enough money in my pocket to buy a cup of coffee, and usually no more than £3 at any one time on my Oyster card. One particular morning, a potential client who has since become a very dear friend suggested that we meet in the coffee shop around the corner from her offices. I don't remember the excuse I made, but I do remember re-experiencing the feelings I had had at the Prefecture just a few months earlier when faced with the bill for the Carte Gris. Even the idea of buying a cup of tea was terrifying. What if she asked for a piece of cake as well? How on earth would I get around that one?

'Oh yes, of course I can design and deliver a training programme for 250 of your top-level managers. Could you just stump up for the tea and scones, though? I appear to have forgotten my purse!'

As the meetings continued and my confidence grew, I really felt I was back in the saddle. In the January, Simon, another good friend of mine (and another person who originated as a client many years earlier), had booked me for a small piece of work with his team. On the insistence of Greg, together with the encouragement of Simon and my own growing sense of self-belief, I decided that I would deliver the day under the banner of the old company. The trademarked logo was registered to me, and by that time I understood that it would be in my best interests to resurrect a brand that still had such a brilliant reputation in the field of training and development.

For a long time I had refused to acknowledge it. For a long time I actually blamed the company for all the bad stuff. I got it into my head that the brand had become somehow dirty. That all the good things we'd done had been tarnished by Cam's behaviour – not just the recent stuff, but also the hangover from his misdemeanours the first time around. I had been afraid that if I resurrected the brand, I might stir up too many ghosts. But what I hadn't realised was just how many people still loved the brand and, more importantly, how many believed that I was the one who made the difference in the first place.

To be honest, I didn't believe it for a long time. I actually didn't *want* to believe it. Because if I did, then I'd be obliged to set it up all over again. I'd also have to come out of the shadows that had been my enforced 'home' and therefore become my comfort zone over the past few years.

Since the beginning of 2010, though, I had more and more proof of the strength of the brand. And gradually, bit by bit, I allowed myself to concede that perhaps I had always been the driving force behind it. I had chosen the name. I commissioned the logo design. I targeted clients. I took their calls. I met them all. I wrote the proposals. I designed the training. Goddamn it, there were even times when coached Cam on what he was to present and how he was to deliver! So how on earth I'd allowed myself to slink away into the shadows and to turn against the business, the brand that I had given so much to and that in turn had given so much to me – well, it's beyond comprehension. I take my hat off to Cam's skills of manipulation. He was very, *very* good.

As Greg had already been saying to me since the summer, and as so many people were saying to me now, to be recognised and admired just from a company name is a rare thing in this day and age. It's a diamond in these dull grey times where cash is king and reputation is everything. You know what they say about diamonds? They're a girl's best friend. And for many, many years the company had been everything to me, and it brought me riches in the way of experience, exposure, confidence, enjoyment, reputation, contacts and friends. So who was I to bury it for good?

The event with Simon was a huge success, and once more my confidence soared. I made a commitment to re-launch the brand even without my old team around me nor a proverbial pot to piss in. I found a simple-to-use website design programme and over the course of a weekend I mapped out a whole new image for the brand. I used words that came directly from my soul. Honest, straightforward and with none of the confusing corporate-babble that Cam seemed to love so much. I used old and new quotes, and re-contacted trusted clients to let them know what I was doing. I got new business cards printed and went back to all the new contacts I'd made over the past few weeks and told them my plans.

Then I went about contacting people – old and new – that I thought I could work with. A collection of professionals who all chose to work towards the same goal. People from different backgrounds and with different skill sets. People who could support one another outside he company, working with one another to promote their own businesses as well as working under my brand. Most importantly, people who walked the talk and brought only the truth to the table. Authenticity was the most critical component for any of the team. My mission statement? Quite simply 'To Create Raving Fans'.

I had absolutely no idea how this was going to pan out. I actually had no idea whether or not I'd be able to keep my nerve and deliver training once again. I certainly had no idea whether I'd be able to inspire people to want to be part of my team of professionals. To top it all, I still didn't even have two ha'pennies to rub together. But bugger me, I was absolutely determined to give it a damned good go!

By the third week in March, the date was booked, the people were booked and the venue was booked. My first ever day for a new team of people who I hoped would be able to shape the future with me.

SUNDAY, 21 MARCH 2010
Happy Anniversary

It's only just hit me. And hit me like a steam train. I simply hadn't noticed it. And the sudden realisation sent shivers down my spine, and a whooshing sensation I can honestly describe as being how I would imagine an out-of-body experience to be. It happened just a few minutes ago. I'm still in shock. I was sitting out in my garden, you see, soaking up the spring sunshine in the courtyard I'd been tidying earlier on in the day. Eager to finish the end of the novel I've been reading and thoroughly enjoying the chorus of birdsong that surely confirmed the end of a long cold winter, I'd settled down on the wooden lovers' seat next to the area where I grow my tomato plants. My dog, Hamish, was sitting happily in the other seat, and I was feeling pretty good about life. In the final chapters of the novel, the author raised the question whether, perhaps, things were just meant to be – that perhaps the characters in her story had been part of an intricate plan – call it fate or call it faith, wasn't it true that, in fact, everything always works out in the end? Her musing caused me to swiftly scan my life, so that I could gauge my response and perhaps add another opinion of my own.

And that's when it happened. I was smiling, finally feeling content and generally at one with the world. Last night I'd shared a wonderful evening of fun, friendship, food and plenty of laughter with some wonderful people who are really now more family than friends. And today the sun has been shining. I've been out on my bike for the first time since my accident last year, and this afternoon I've been tidying the garden and planting seeds so that I might enjoy a rich summer of colour and perfume. I allowed myself to bask in the fullness of my life and started to think about my new business and the wonderful future that I know is ahead of me. Absent-mindedly I was still scanning for any 'life coincidences' in response to the question posed in my book.

And then BANG! There it was. Clear as day, bold as brass, obvious for all to see. Except I hadn't. With a loud and deliberate 'Oh . . . my . . . goodness!' (or words to that effect) my hands fell to my lap, the book fell to the floor, and Hamish jumped from his chair.

How on earth had I missed it? The day last year when my life was changed for ever is a date I thought I would never forget – Wednesday, 22 April 2009. For that was the day when I discovered the truth about the man I loved and with whom I had shared my life for more than a decade. As well as being the day that my entire reality came crashing down around my ears, the day when everything I thought I could rely on as being real turned out to be nothing more than a sham, it was also, as you'll remember, the very day when I outlived my mother and, therefore, both of my parents. So it's a date that has been branded deeply into my consciousness. I confess, I'd been worrying about how to best celebrate the anniversary this year. Should I go wild? Party like there's no tomorrow? Or perhaps drown my sorrows with a couple of close friends? I hadn't decided, but I knew I had to mark the occasion.

Over the past week I have been working on pulling together the very first team event for my new business. The leadership team now stands at 15 people, not including the teams within the team, if that makes sense. Everyone has busy schedules and work commitments, so it has been interesting working out how best to organise such an event – what it should entail as well as where and when it should be held. We started off with five dates to choose from. And with 13 out of the 15 people able to make one particular date, we settled on it. Yup. You guessed it – Thursday, 22 April 2010.

In my focus on creating a team day, I had totally overlooked the significance of the date we have all chosen. So now, as it all falls into place, I am grinning like a Cheshire cat and feeling the sunshine in my soul absolutely matching the warmth of the early evening rays.

What an absolutely perfect way to mark the anniversary and finally wave goodbye to what has been the most testing year of my entire life. Yes, most testing, and at the same time most rewarding in so many ways. For I have discovered the richness of friendship. The strength in surrender. The peace in trust. And the comfort in the knowledge that no matter what happens, things always turn out well in the end.

So, on 22 April this year, with my new company up and running, instead of wondering as I was this time last year how on earth I was going to survive the shock and pain of betrayal, I shall be working and planning with my amazing team of trainers how to bring magic and delight into the lives of business leaders around the world.

What a difference a year makes, eh? Happy Anniversary!

28

I Know You're Out There

The team day turned out to be a huge success, although I confess to being absolutely terrified about how it would go before, during and even after the event. One of the things I hadn't quite worked out was how on earth I was going to be able to run a company in the light of what had happened over the past year. It was highly likely that I had been blacklisted as a director and my credit rating must be positively radioactive. I had no idea how the company closure was going, as the liquidators were still stonewalling me. I can only guess at the kind of stories Cam must have told them to make them stop communication, particularly since I was the person who'd called them in and it was my name on all the paperwork. Still, I had other things to focus my attention on. As long as they were doing their job – and they were legally bound to do so – I'd wait until much later on to give them a piece of my mind.

Over the year, ever since people started finding out about my situation, I had been consistently overwhelmed by the messages of support that continued to flood in via email, cards, telephone calls and Facebook, many from people I would never have expected to make contact. One of those extraordinarily touching surprises had come just a few days after I found Cam's email trail. It was a

Facebook message from another person I had met as a client. I had very fond memories of working with this lady, but I hadn't quite realised how much the training had impacted her life. This was the message I received:

Hello – not sure if you'll remember me . . .

Hi Mel!

I don't often get onto Facebook these days but have just logged on and would gather from the toing and froing that you are now flying solo – but then, I do often have 'blonde moments' these days and may have picked up entirely the wrong tack . . .

Either way, it has prompted me to drop you this mail and, really, the sentiment doesn't change, whatever your circumstances. It's just a shame that, like with most things in life, it takes perceived gloom to prompt something positive when you should have just done the positive thing anyway. But, I digress . . .

I just wanted to send you a message to say that you personally made a massive difference to my life and are largely to thank for the drastic change that I made in my own life. And, given your current possible situation, I think it is important that you know that you are, without doubt, one of the nicest, most supportive and positive people I have ever met and I am pleased that I met you – not only because of the change that you brought about in me but also because you are just a nice person to have come across in life.

Thinking of you and sending you big hugs – I am a firm believer in the 'this too will pass' edict – but sometimes it's not that easy to believe at the time. Rest assured, however, it will and you will be stronger for it.

If there's anything I can do, just shout!

Audrey xx

It arrived on the very day that I had endured a particularly snotty and po-faced estate agent poking around my house and telling me that it was worth close to bugger all, so there was no way I could sell it to pay off any debts. I had been on my knees, the left-field whack taking me so hard that I literally fell to the floor the second the odious woman had slithered out of the door. Ruth, as usual, had been with me and she instantly bundled me into the car and drove me to her house. It was during that car journey that Audrey's message had arrived. It was absolutely perfect timing, and I couldn't even speak when I read it.

'What's up my darling?' Ruth had asked, noticing my silent sobs. When I looked at her with tears streaming down my face, she was clearly reassured. 'Well, that's OK, then, so long as they're happy tears!'

Following that note, Audrey and I developed a strong friendship. She's feisty, full of energy, witty, intelligent and damned good company. I had liked her from the first minute I met her all those years ago – little did I know how important she was going to become in my life.

Audrey was part of the new team who met on 22 April. She and I shared a room at the B&B. She'd brought a picnic, a card, some books, presents and a bottle of wine, even though the last time I'd seen her had been on the training course so many years earlier. Deeply touched, I really didn't know how to respond, but I think she knew how much I appreciated her actions. She was incredibly supportive and inclusive during the event itself, and in the pub later that evening, she and I started talking. Really talking.

I decided to put a suggestion to her. I'd come to the conclusion that I would never be able to set up a company while I was still in such a pickle. I had no idea how long it was going to take to finalise my divorce, let along get myself square financially. But in the meantime I had to find a means of earning money. Working with top-notch clients meant I would have to have a limited company, together with all the necessary and relevant professional insurances. It was something I knew I would not be able to do myself. I had been considering whom I could ask to front the company for me, and all of a sudden it made perfect sense to ask Audrey. She agreed.

In the meantime, I was still hitting hiccups with the divorce. The solicitor I'd started with – not James, but one of his associates who also had a good understanding of French law – had moved on, and my case was being taken over by somebody else. I was concerned that my situation had not been fully understood and felt that they certainly didn't grasp the precarious situation I was in. Everything had to be taken one step at a time, and each move had to be made at absolutely the correct time and in the correct sequence. By then I understood exactly what kind of character I was dealing with, and I had a good idea about how to handle communication. The solicitor, on the other hand, did not.

I was constantly told that they would 'come down with the full force of the law – the legal system is on our side!' but would then find that when there was yet again no response to their latest set of letters it would cost me still more money to apply to yet another court for yet another piece of ridiculous information. So, once again, here I was paying for Cam's deliberate manipulation. How he must have loved all the power-play games! What fun! Ho ho, bloody ho! While I could do nothing but continue to run up legal bills with no means to pay them.

I had written to every one of my creditors, explaining that my lawyers were now dealing with all financial matters as part of the divorce proceedings and that they would be in touch as soon as we had any news. I explained that I was no longer living in Edinburgh, the only address they had for me, and that if they had any questions in the meantime they were to address them to my solicitor. Good. Dealt with as far as I possibly could.

In the meantime, another person who, really, I had only recently got to know had already proven herself to be another unexpected earth-angel for me. To some it had started to appear that I was getting nowhere with my efforts. There were many who couldn't understand why I hadn't just gone out and got a 'proper job' and also why I was still living in France. I couldn't seem to get them to understand that I had no other choice. I could not sell my house, and even if I could, the property market was so slow that houses could easily remain on the market for two years, sometimes more. I did not want to move Dylan, as he is, to all intents and purposes, French now. His friends are here, he's settled in school and French is his first language – it was critical to keep him stable. Added to which, I had started sending out my CV immediately, following the debacle with Steffi just before Christmas. I had not been picky, applying for over 100 jobs and getting my details out on every job site I could find. How many responses do you think I'd had? Correct. None. Nada. Zip. Zero. Not even any acknowledgements.

So, from my point of view, I was already doing everything within my power to rescue my life and create a new way forward. But still I was being castigated for having made what some saw as little or no progress. It was infuriating to say the least. I was having this very conversation early one morning in a cafe in central London. It was the beginning of the year and I had arranged to meet Kerry for coffee and a catch-up before heading off to another hugely important business meeting with another potential client. We had been introduced the previous summer, in France, by mutual friends, and we immediately hit it off. Kerry is a feisty lady who has fought and beaten breast cancer not once, but twice. She is stunningly beautiful and was in the process of starting up a health-based business. I had asked her to come along to the training day as I felt we could work together – me helping people with psychological health, while she focused on the physical side. I felt particularly stressed that day, and for some reason I had burst into tears while talking with her. As I struggled to regain my composure, Kerry then said something that shook me to the core.

'Let me lend you some money. How much do you need? Will £5,000 do?'

Oh . . . my . . . goodness . . . I could hardly believe my ears! I nodded silently and grabbed her hand across the table, the tears flowing again as I looked her in the eyes and thanked my lucky stars that someone was looking out for me. To this day, Kerry will always remain an angel to me. Thank you.

So, progress was being made, and I was finding the most amazing levels of support and love coming from the most unexpected of places. I was also continuing with my blog. The audience was growing, and I was delighted to discover how much I enjoyed writing. I also loved the continuing messages of encouragement that flooded in as a result and would take huge delight in checking my statistics for the site. It would tell me how many people had been on the site, how long for, and where they'd come from. It made me feel good to know that people were appreciating my writing.

But then one day I noticed that I was getting a huge amount of hits from Edinburgh. Not just one or two, no. In one day alone there had been over 70 hits, and by the next day that had gone up to nearly 160. This was not normal. By now I knew the typical patterns of readers and any one map-marker might hold a maximum of 15 up-to-date hits on it at any given time. So over 160? In two days? From Edinburgh? There was no doubt in my mind. Campbell had found my blog. So now it was personal.

THURSDAY, 15 APRIL 2010

I Know You're Out There . . .

'. . . *I can feel you now. And I know that you're afraid . . . afraid of us. You're afraid of change. I don't know the future. I didn't come here to tell you how this is going to end. I came here to tell how it's going to begin . . .*'

That is one of my favourite quotes from *The Matrix*, and we used it as part of a presentation to open a conference to teach some area managers the rudiments of coaching. And I am using it here because I know for sure that this blog is now being read by my estranged husband. So I thought I'd say hello in a style that would be sure to grab his attention.

Yes, it's true . . . once I found out he was watching me I considered shutting the blog down again. I worried that perhaps it might give him some kind of sick hold over me again. And then I decided to stand proud. I decided that I have nothing to hide. And there's nothing that he can do now to hurt me. I'm free. You see I am not afraid any more. This blog is MY voice, it's MY journey, and it's MY truth. And the truth will always out in the end.

I can't begin to guess his reasons for suddenly taking such an avid interest in what I'm doing. After all, he hasn't given me or Dylan a backward glance since the day I found out the truth about him. And, yes, I've been through hell and back in the days and months that followed. At times it has felt as though I have been trapped inside my own matrix, and insanity has felt never less than a heartbeat away. I had loved him with all my heart and with all my soul. I believed he loved me too, you see, and the shock at discovering the depth of his betrayal and deceit was just about enough to kill me.

I didn't know who I could trust. I worried that perhaps everyone else had known what was going on. I felt ashamed and stupid for not seeing what had been going on right under my nose – for years. How could I have been so blind? I couldn't sleep. Some days I could hardly breathe. The pain was indescribable, and my days were spent wading through treacle and trying to keep my head above the quicksand that was threatening to drag me down into the abyss. Dylan and I stuck together like glue, and together we worked our way through the mire. Together we made sense of a tortuous situation that forced us to realise that our family life had been nothing but a sham. A truth so inconceivably difficult to grasp that there are many people who simply cannot take it on board.

And I missed him. Terribly. Heart-wrenchingly. I missed his touch, his smell, his voice. The smile and the face I knew and loved so well. The way he would hold me. The way our bodies just seemed to fit together so well. The way he walked. Even the noise he made when he cleared his throat. I always said I could pick him out from a mile away just from that sound!

Yes, there would have been a time when I would never have

wanted him to know the pain and destruction his actions have caused. There would have been a time when I would have wanted to keep everything quiet. Damage limitation and all that malarkey.

And, yes, I've questioned whether there can be any threat from him now reading my stories. Perhaps smiling, sneering, thinking he's had such power over me. Perhaps he takes some kind of sick pleasure in reading my stories of soul-searching and making sense of my shattered life.

So, yes, the questions have been running around and around my head, and I have thought long and hard about what I was going to do. And I've decided through it all that I'm sticking exactly where I am. For I am now safe from harm and beginning to live the life of my dreams. I decided that that this blog, my story, my life, is just that. MY life. And I'm never going to shut up, bow down, hide or apologise ever again. I did that for far too long.

And you know what? Now I'm glad of it. Glad of the opportunity to clear out ALL the old shit. Not just the rubbish I'd accumulated over 11 years with my so-called 'soulmate', but also all the other emotional baggage I hadn't realised I had been carrying. I'm GLAD I was on my knees, and I'm proud of myself for finally letting myself surrender. For it was MY strength of character that allowed me to go there – not HIS perceived power over me. So, as I said in a previous post, thank you Cam. Thanks for leaving just enough of a trail for me to find you out. For had I not discovered the truth, I would be in a very different place right now.

Now I am free. Now I know for certain what it's like to feel secure. To feel loved. To feel inspired. To dream big and have the self-belief to follow those dreams. I've started now, and nothing, and no one can stop me.

I don't know how this is going to end. I'm here to tell you how it begins. For I have changed, and life will never be the same again.

29

The Mouse That Squeaked

That seemingly small bit of defiance did me the world of good! For the first time since I could remember, it felt that I was standing up for myself. Not only that, but standing up against the person who had so successfully held me down. OK, fair enough, I may not have actually said the words to him face to face, but that didn't matter. In actual fact, it was better. By that time, and with the understanding I had gathered about sociopathy, I realised that it wouldn't have mattered what I had said, how I had said it, or how loudly I might have shouted. It wouldn't have mattered because he wouldn't have cared. He wouldn't have baulked, and he'd have found some way to twist my words and once again make me feel small.

A sociopath, you see, has no conscience. Having no conscience, they cannot feel guilt for anything they're accused of doing. Because they cannot feel guilt, they will never respond in the way 'normal' people would expect. That is what makes them such expert manipulators and pathological liars. They do not flinch when they tell an untruth. They feel no guilt if they're caught out about something they've previously said or done, so they don't show even a glimmer of those tell-tale signs that lie-detectors are designed to pick up. Increased heart rate, perspiration on the skin, minor changes of skin temperature – none of these symptoms are displayed when a sociopath lies. That's what makes them so dangerous and confusing to be with. That's how people like me can begin to doubt what is in front of us. Slowly our sanity can be eroded as we become riddled with self-doubt, while all the time the sociopath stands by and gloats.

I often imagine what a great toy I must have been to Cam. Like one of those Weeble toys for kids – remember the ones I mean? Those smiling plastic 'people' that you could knock over and they'd bounce back up again because of weights in their rounded bottoms? Well, looking back, I picture myself jumping back up again after another psychological pummeling to the accompaniment of that annoyingly catchy jingle "Weebles wobble but they don't fall down!"

I'm pretty certain that I must also have kept a smile painted on my face at the same time. What fun he must have had, knocking me down and watching me come back, still smiling at him and offering him nothing but love and support.

But you know what? I don't regret a thing. Why not? Because the love I felt during our marriage was absolutely genuine. It was 100 per cent unconditional love, and I had never experienced it before. And you know what else? I adored every second of it. For the first time I'd felt alive, adored, loved. Special. And so very happy! At last I understood what it felt like to be head over heels in love, and not just for a short moment in time, for a prolonged period. I also knew, for the first time, that I was a person who could commit their heart and soul to another, and it felt good. Now, OK, it wasn't reciprocated. Only very cleverly mirrored. But it doesn't matter – nope, it really doesn't matter in the slightest, you see. Because, regardless of whether it was real or not, the experiences *I* had were absolutely real. And they are mine to keep forever.

Many of my friends warned me against becoming bitter or closed down as a result of what happened – 'It's going to be really difficult for you to trust anyone ever again', 'Do you think you'll be able to love somebody after this?', 'Please don't become resentful, Mel. Please stay the warm and open person we know you to be.'

All of these have been well-intentioned and spot-on pieces of advice. Yes, it's true, I am becoming much more selective about who I choose to trust. But I don't think that's because I'm closing down – far from it. I know for a fact it's because I'm finally opening up.

'How does that work then?' Gemma had asked when I'd tried to explain. 'How can you be less trusting and more open at the same time? I don't get it!'

Well, the point I'm making is this. As I now realise, I had been guilty of being a person who loves too much. I had been so focused on seeking approval, being accepted, loved, appreciated and all manner of other labels associated with feeling nurtured, that I'd given myself away too freely. I was always wanting to please. Always the one to go to the rescue. Always the one to put other people first, thoroughly believing that to be the right and proper thing to do. Also believing that it was right for me.

But I was wrong.

Yes, I still believe I was right in being so willing to help and support. But I think I was totally wrong in doing those things to the detriment of myself. And here's the rub. Until Cam caused me to feel so much pain, I didn't actually realise what I had been doing.

So, remember I said before that I learned pretty quickly to search for the gift in everything? Well, Cam's actions may have hurt me more deeply and over a more prolonged period of time than anything else I had ever experienced before. In actual fact, had I not experienced it for myself I would never have thought that a human soul could bear so much suffering. But the fact remains that through the agony I have found my true self. And I have found that the person I am, the real Mel, is actually no different from the person I've been all my life, it's just that now I don't have to hide away. And now I don't have to seek approval – not from anyone and not for anything. Because now I know for sure that I am already enough. I am already good enough. And I always was.

'Boo, you can do anything you want! Look at the world out there – it's waiting for you! All of it!' You may remember the words my Daddy said to me while I was on his shoulders? At that age, I absolutely knew that I was good enough, but I didn't know that I knew it, if that makes any sense! The thing was, though, when my Daddy died, my sense of safety died with him. From that moment I hid myself away, and, quite frankly, I now completely understand why.

That was why, over the torture and confusion of the months that followed my discovery of Cam's betrayal, I found I had to dig away at the layers of protection to once again find that little girl who already knew she was good enough. Because that, ultimately, was what saved me. And hiding myself away in the first place – an act of self-protection – ended up being the very thing that hurt me in the end. Because my protective layers made me so strong, I would put myself in danger without even realising, and as a result of the danger would create more defensive barriers. Catch 22? Yes. Absolutely.

I had to change.

It was June 2010 when I wrote this post.

SATURDAY, 19 JUNE 2010

The Mouse That Squeaked

. . . because I sure don't feel like roaring. I'm scared, you see. Don't get me wrong, I'm not scared of what's happened, nor of the battles I know are ahead of me, or the constant waves of challenges that face me on a daily basis.

No, I'm not afraid of those, because I've faced things like that before. You see, I know how to deal with them. I know how to be. I know how to act. I know what's expected. I know how to get through. So no, I'm not afraid of those.

But there is something else that is building. Something else that is gathering strength. Becoming real. Demanding attention. Developing an identity. Something I have ignored – or perhaps been all too acutely aware of – for longer than I care to remember.

And now this thing. This energy. This entity (is it any wonder I was so terrified at the film *Poltergeist*, for goodness' sake?) seems now to be demanding space. It's gathering form. Sound. Expression. And suddenly, those around me are echoing its very essence. Which frightens me. Because it tells me that this internal fear, this hidden doppelganger, this hideous nightmare that lives within me is about to be exposed and exorcised.

Bloody hell. I am about to be in the position where I HAVE to face my fears – whatever they might be. And you know what? I KNOW what they are. Perhaps we all do. I don't know. I DO know, however, that with each passing experience, each month, each year, each day, each living moment, I know I'm moving closer to the freedom I've craved for so long. And I also know that this particular fear is the one that's most debilitating.

Because I've discovered through this long journey that the one thing that I have allowed to hold me back, the one fear that I've so far failed to overcome, the one thing that I'm actually afraid of, is . . . me!

I've realised I've spent so many years protecting myself and gaining more skills and more strength with each additional body-blow, that I've forgotten who the real Melanie is. And over the past year or so, as each of my barriers have been falling down (hmm, annihilated would be a more accurate description in actual fact), well then the real me has been getting closer and closer to the surface. And I'm now at the point of no return, because the little vulnerable me that has been buried away for so long will no longer be ignored. It's her time now. She's gaining strength and is demanding to be noticed.

And I'm scared. Because I don't know who she is. I don't even know whether I'll like her. I don't know whether she'll like ME either. And I don't know how she's going to impact on my life and what new changes it will mean. Because surely this is indeed the herald of yet more change.

I had built her a castle, you see. A fortress. To keep her safe and protect her from harm. I trained the best soldiers to fight for her and dug the deepest, widest moat to keep harm away. And it worked very well. People admired the strength and beauty of the castle I'd built – it's served me well and I've been perfecting it for over 40 years. But now it's crumbling, and now the princess, my precious little girl who lives inside, wants to come out and live in the real world. I cannot stop her, and I'm scared.

I'm scared in case she's not ready. In case it's too soon. In case she gets hurt – or worse. How will she survive?

I'm scared because I think she might feel I've abandoned her. That I've betrayed her trust. I worry that, although I locked her away so long ago for her own safety, she might be very angry with me. She might be furious, in fact! Do you think she'll ever forgive me? I don't know . . .

And I don't know how to welcome her either. I don't know how to let her in or let her out. And I don't know where to turn. I just know that the increasing restlessness within my soul, the physical churning in my stomach and the constant electrical fizzing in my mind means that the time is near when I can no longer put off the inevitable.

My friends know what's happening. I can sense it in the way they're responding to me. The little nudges forward, the reassurances that I'm on the right track, together with the exploration of new connections – the deepening of existing friendships and the influx of new ones. They are all guiding me forwards, for they are now my army of soldiers.

So now I must give up my castle. I must walk forwards, move free from the rubble, and trust that this new world is ready for me.

I'm scared. But I'm doing it. Please catch me if I fall.

30
A Good Year!

The rest of 2010 was mainly focused on continuing to build on the good stuff. It was a time of discovery and exploration. There was no more real pain and less of the intense naval-gazing. Business continued to come in, and I was once again loving my work and noticing that, in actual fact, my skills had improved since the times I used to work with Cam.

Now I was gaining referrals and the most amazing feedback as a direct result of the work that I had created myself, and my confidence continued to grow. This meant that my money worries had all but disappeared, along with any lingering doubts of my ability to deal with my finances, far from it in fact! I had survived a financial famine worse than any I'd experienced before, and I had made it. No, I felt as rich as a queen living on far less money than Cam and I had been generating in the old days when we worked together. I had more time for myself and for Dylan, more energy, more focus, and I was happy.

In the autumn, I had registered myself in France as an Auto Entrepreneur. What did that mean? It meant that finally I could officially state that France was my home. Finally I could be included in the health system, and finallyI felt that life in general, along with explanations, were less complicated when it came to filling in forms or talking with Dylan's teachers. At last I felt like I belonged, and at last I felt that I had cleared away the vast majority of the crap that had been surrounding me for so long, both physically and emotionally.

I had a wonderful birthday at home, enjoying good home cooking (and a tad too many glasses of wine!) surrounded by lots of friends and lots of love. I finally felt I could relax. At last I believed that I could be me, for no other reason other than it was my choice. And I was starting to love my life, just because I could.

WEDNESDAY, 22 DECEMBER 2010

A Good Year

I've learned so much over the past 12 months that I know now, even against the odds, 2010 has actually been a very good year. Not one I care to repeat, thank you very much, but the good times and psychological shifts I've made surely mean that this year goes down in my memory, at least, as a good year. It's been a year of relentless challenges and frightening lows. There have been times when I've thought I wouldn't be able to come through. Times when I've even considered the worst – yes, I can say it now – and now, as I've just celebrated my 46th birthday, I can look back and appreciate just how far I've come.

This time last year, you may remember, I'd just been advised that the only option available to me was to sell my home in France, giving half the proceeds to my estranged husband, the rest to the Scottish debt agency who were advising me, and to take out a loan to repay the remainder of my creditors.

Boy have I moved on from there! It's been tough and the challenges have been uncompromising. Yet at every step of the way I have absolutely refused to take 'no' for an answer. I've learned that 'professionals' all have their own opinion, and that those opinions can vary tremendously. It would seem that there is no such thing as 'the' law, there is just 'a' law, which can be flexible in the extreme depending on who I'm talking to and how I phrase the question.

And let me tell you, some of the so-called 'professional' advice I've received this year has been risable – shameful, really, when I think that there must be many people in a similar situation to me who are not able to fight. Many times, as a child, I was chastised for being stubborn or pig-headed, but you know what? Those qualities have served me well through these times.

I'm glad that I'm stubborn, and I've also learned to love so many other aspects of my personality that I'm finally getting to know and understand. When I qualified as a Louise Hay trainer in 1997, we were taught to accept ourselves and others exactly as we are, and since that time, I've done my level best to do exactly that. And the thing is, whilst I've been good at spotting hidden treasures in others, I simply hadn't realised what else lay buried beneath my own shell. The soft, squishy parts of me, the 'little me', that had hidden away for so long.

Yes, this year has taught me to fight. I've learned how to make £10 last for two weeks. I've learned how to turn up at business meetings with a confident smile on my face, not knowing how I would even find the train fare back to my sister's place. I've learned to keep my head held high and my principles strong, fighting for justice against a stream of legal and financial obstacles. I've learned how to create a new business from scratch (with nothing to back me apart from my skills and my self-belief) and secure a wonderful range of clients doing the work I love. I've learned how to listen to other people's problems, even while feeling overcome by my own situation. I've learned humility and gratitude for the smallest acts of kindness that people have shown me – anonymous deliveries of vegetables, fruit and flowers from surrounding gardens, invitations to dinner, introductions to new friends and colleagues, shoulders to cry on, forgiveness for some of my more outrageous antics. I've learned that even though there were times when I might not have been able to buy a loaf of bread, that I'm always safe and rich beyond any 'outside' measure. For I am surrounded by a host of people I'm lucky enough to call my friends. People who care for me and who will never let me fall or fail.

So that, my friends, is why this year has been a good year. Perhaps the best. Because the lessons I've learned about myself and others are absolutely beyond measure. And I am grateful. And happy.

As this year draws to a close, I am excited and clear about my future. Next year is going to be an extraordinary year for me, I feel it in my bones. Will it be as extraordinary as the previous year? Yes, I'm confident that it will. This time, though, it will be much more joyful because I am already starting from a place of safety and happiness. Yes, finally I am content and secure, finally ready to accept all the good that life has to offer me, leaping into life with my arms and my heart wide open. If I achieved so much from a position of hopelessness and fear, well, who knows what endless possibilities are in store for me now.

Thank you, life. This has been a good year indeed!

Epilogue

It's now May 2012 and so much has happened since I finally decided I could relax and be happy with my lot.

I parted company with my solicitors at the beginning of 2011 as things weren't working out. Pretty soon afterwards I found exactly the right person to help me thanks to one of my business contacts. Funny, don't you think, that the right person had been there all the time? Laura proved to be a godsend. No nonsense, direct, straight talking and quoting specific costs and timescales to which she always delivered. Working with her was a breath of fresh air. She prepared every bit of paperwork I asked for – all of it legally binding, all of it making a final break between Cam and myself, all of it allowing me to secure a divorce. I was to keep my home in France together with the buy-to-let property I had saved from repossession. Cam was to keep the apartment in Edinburgh.

All that was left was to get the whole lot signed by Cam. That was likely to be the tricky bit, since he had steadfastly refused to respond to any correspondence sent by each one of my previous lawyers. That was how I came to find a company called MOL 4, a group of professionals who between them could provide legal and financial solutions, and the necessary know-how to get the job done. They are a great bunch of guys, and much like myself they don't like to see people mistreated. They agreed to take on my case and took the paperwork up to Scotland to be signed by Cam. Visiting him at his place of work seemed to be all that was needed to secure the signatures I required to make the paperwork legal and binding. I am very grateful to Steve Mungroo and his team for achieving what I had previously been told would be an almost impossible task. Thanks to them and to Laura, my divorce is now finalised.

Last summer I decided to part company with my literary agent. I have nothing against him as a person; in fact, I think he's a very warm and genuine human being. But for whatever reason, I felt that he didn't understand the way I wanted to proceed with my work, so we split on amicable terms. I am grateful for his early confidence in me, because without that I might not be where I am now – signed by an extremely well-known publishing house. A matter of days after finalising the split, I began to create a strategy around how to get my work more widely read. Remembering the site that had given me so much help in the early days, I went back onto Lovefraud and decided to make direct contact with the owner, Donna Andersen. It was a Friday evening and I sent her an email offering to add my voice to her crusade and including a link to my blog. She came back to me on the Monday, and we chatted over the next couple of days. The very next week I was introduced as a new author on Lovefraud, and I started contributing a weekly written column for the website. It is a great honour, and I am deeply touched and humbled by the messages I receive from people who are working their way out of life with a sociopath. It is not an easy journey, and I am delighted that in my small way I am able to help. It starts to make everything worthwhile.

In addition to my professional career taking on a whole new life of its own, I've been focused on getting myself into shape. Life with Cam took a toll on my body. I hadn't realised how much weight I'd gained, probably as some subconscious form of emotional protection. Since his departure, and my subsequent fight for survival, my weight continued to creep up, and it was a highly unflattering photograph taken by my friend's daughter that finally spurred me into action! That same photograph is still stuck on my fridge, but now I am more than 20 lb lighter than I've been for years. In addition to the change of diet, I have been introduced to yoga and have already attended two separate week-long yoga retreats run by a wonderfully gifted yoga teacher called James Jewell. The training he offers is amazing, and I recommend his programme to anybody – old or young, fit or broken, experienced or a complete yoga-virgin like myself.

On the emotional and spiritual side, I have also recently discovered another gifted teacher who has helped me shift another layer of old stuff – thank you Jennie, your kindness and strength have helped me feel prepared for whatever the future may hold.

In November 2011, I attended Dr Robert Hare's PCL-R checklist training programme and connected with the great man himself. As a result of that I also made contact with Misha Votruba, director of the movie "I Am <fishead(" and we are now exploring opportunities to work on creating educational and development programmes designed to wake people up to the dangers of psychopaths, including those who hide behind the corporate facade.

My beautiful sister Abigail continues to be successful in her chosen professional career. I am constantly amazed by her work and am incredibly proud of her achievements and what she has made of her life, despite her terrible experiences. It would have been all too easy for her to fall into any number of self-destructive patterns, but she has come out strong. She continues to inspire me, and I will be forever grateful that she is in my life both as a friend and a sister – thank you.

I continue to be blessed with wonderful friendships full of life, colour, noise and laughter. The incredibly warm bunch of amazing people who choose to share their life with me continue to teach me lessons on a daily basis. I am rich indeed, and am grateful to be surrounded by so much love.

Have I found any 'significant others' since Cam? Well, I have met a number of interesting and wonderful souls, but nobody to share my life with on a permanent basis. Anyway, for right now I'm focusing my attention on someone else. Someone who has been there all the time but who has been waiting in the wings. Or, put another way, perhaps someone I had refused to acknowledge. This person, though, is someone who will never leave me, someone who has never left me in actual fact. Someone who cannot let me down and who understands me completely. Someone who is absolutely with me, on my side, and will do everything within their power to make sure I live my life to the full, and fulfil or exceed all of my dreams.

So who is this person? Well, it may come as no surprise to learn that this person is... ME. Yes, me – Mel Carnegie. Here it is, and here I am. And I'm very happy to announce that yes, once again I'm in a committed and deeply loving relationship. But this time it's with myself. And that, as I have finally understood, is the most important relationship in the world. I'm confident that one day I will again experience the wondrous feelings of unconditional love and happiness. This time, though, it will be with a partner who loves me back in equal measure. So, therefore, it stands to reason that it can only be better than anything I've experienced before.

In the meantime, I am still living in France, and Dylan has been thriving at Lycee and is due to start university in the autumn. It's a huge personal achievement and I'm deeply proud of him.

I've learned that life and luck can turn on a sixpence. I also know now, though, that whatever happens, I am safe, I am loved and I am very, very blessed. All is well, and you know what? It always has been. I just didn't know it at the time.

Thank you for reading my story.

A final Message

As I write this note, Dylan is now the same age as I was myself when my mother died and I became an orphan. Thinking about my strong, wise and beautiful son, my heart bleeds even to imagine that he would ever have to endure the pain I went through. He is mature beyond his years, but underneath it all he is still a boy. He is still vulnerable and needs the support of a loving family and the safety of a secure environment. It brings home to me even more just how shocking it was for me to suddenly have to grow up so young. It was hard. Thank goodness I had no comprehension how much harder it was going to become.

Yes, at my son's age I lost the mother I loved and adored. But Dylan's immediate pathway, thank goodness, is very different from mine. Because at the same age I was when my life fell apart, Dylan's mother is not facing a death sentence. Far from it in fact. Dylan's mother is just starting to come alive, and the best is yet to come!

I love you.

"If you liked the book, come and join me online!"

Come and visit my website and join the many people who are now receiving tips, updates, and inside information about upcoming events! You'll also be able to find links to Facebook and Twitter, as well as the Life's Little Lettuces blog in full, which is where the roots of this book all began. Plus, when you sign up for my newsletter you'll be the first to know when anything new is happening…

On the site you will be able to find helpful resources, as well as learn more about the techniques I used – and still use to this day – to help me get through some of the toughest times in my life.

My experiences have taught me so much – yes it's been tough, but boy have I learned some amazing methods for survival… and ultimately how to achieve freedom and joy! I have often said that if through the lessons I learned in my life it means I am able to help other people deal with whatever difficulties they are facing, well then it makes everything worthwhile.

That's why my mission now is to share everything I have learned with as many people as possible.

Thank you for reading my story, and I look forward to connecting with you very soon!

See you online ☺

www.melcarnegie.com